149
JI

W9-BYB-630

MACROBIOTIC CUISINE

MACROBIOTIC CUISINE

by LIMA OHSAWA

Japan Publications, Inc.

This book was originally published under the title of *The Art of Just Cooking* by Autumn Press, Inc. in 1974. This Japan Publications Edition is completely revised, rewritten and expanded by arrangement with the author and Nippon C. I. Foundation.

©1984 by Nippon C. I. Foundation
Illustrations by Seiji Onishi

All rights reserved, including the right to reproduce this book or portions thereof in any form without the written permission of the publisher.

Published by JAPAN PUBLICATIONS, INC., Tokyo and New York

Distributors:
UNITED STATES: *Kodansha International/USA, Ltd., through Harper & Row, Publishers, Inc., 599 Lexington Avenue, Suite 2300, New York, N. Y. 10022.* SOUTH AMERICA: *Harper & Row, Publishers, Inc., International Department.* CANADA: *Fitzhenry & Whiteside Ltd., 195 Allstate Parkway, Markham, Ontario, L3R 4T8.* MEXICO AND CENTRAL AMERICA: *HARLA S. A. de C. V., Apartado 30–546, Mexico 4, D. F.* BRITISH ISLES: *Premier Book Marketing Ltd., 1 Gower Street, London WC1E 6HA.* EUROPEAN CONTINENT: *European Book Service PBD, Strijkviertel 63, 3454 PK De Meern, The Netherlands.* AUSTRALIA AND NEW ZEALAND: *Bookwise International, 54 Crittenden Road, Findon, South Australia 5007.* THE FAR EAST AND JAPAN: *Japan Publications Trading Co., Ltd., 1-2-1, Sarugaku-cho, Chiyoda-ku, Tokyo 101.*

First edition: November 1984
Fourth printing: November 1988

LCCC No. 84–080649
ISBN 0–87040–600–0

Printed in Japan

PREFACE

In Japan, as in other parts of the world, life has always been understood to draw its material and energy from food. Although often overlooked, the obvious fact that human existence depends foremost upon the foods provided by nature leaves no excuse for carelessness in our choice and preparation of foods, or in our manner of eating and drinking. Nevertheless, do not many of us take these activities for granted, treating them only as habits or sources for mere sensory satisfaction? We all too often forget that while food provides the vital energy capable of supporting life, it can, if improperly and excessively indulged in, put an end to life.

Practical macrobiotics begins with a studied appreciation of foods. Our philosophy first divides the available varieties into the two categories of animal (yang) and vegetable (yin). It is a law of ecology that all animal life depends for its existence upon the vegetable kingdom, for vegetal forms transmute nature's basic chemicals into digestible foods. A "food chain," a hierarchy of eater and eaten, dictates that large fish feed upon small ones, while the latter are nourished by sea or river plants. The carnivorous creatures of the world devour the herbivores. We humans, too, evolutionarily the most recent addition to the food chain, depend either directly or indirectly upon plant life for our nourishment. Macrobiotic philosophy, grounded in experience, teaches that although man continually proves himself capable (at a price) of eating whatever he wishes, his health and vitality improve the more completely and directly he draws his sustenance from the vegetable kingdom. For when we take our nourishment from animal sources, the basic life-giving elements we receive have been rearranged and unbalanced; some have been concentrated while others have been removed. In addition, we absorb toxic animal wastes as well as artificial chemicals introduced by industry.

The macrobiotic diet, however, is not a strict vegetarian regimen. We do not believe that if a man or woman eats vegetable foods exclusively he or she will, of necessity, achieve health or vitality, and live in harmony with the environment, or, for that matter, that every man *must* restrict himself to the vegetal realm if he wants to realize his nature. The natural order in our surroundings is both more precise and more flexible. The shape and relative number of our teeth, the gateway of food into the body, tell us more about the order in human nutrition. Of a total of thirty-two teeth, eight (one quarter of them) are incisors designed for cutting and slicing vegetables, four (one eighth) are canines designed for tearing flesh, and twenty (five eighths) are molars designed for grinding cereal grains. Guided by the structure of our digestive system, the macrobiotic diet centers around grains and vegetables and, like the teeth, emphasizes the importance of the former. George

Ohsawa devoted fifty years of his life to proving that, for man, cereals were first in order of nutritional importance. Room is left, however, on the plate as in the mouth, for proportionately small quantities of animal food if necessary or desirable. The animal foods we recommend are the lower forms of life, or those that have been least domesticated or processed by modern man. We do advise that as few animal foods as possible be part of one's daily fare. But what I cannot emphasize enough is that the random choice and improper preparation of even ideal foods can lessen their healthful and restorative effects. There is a proper order to be maintained in their selection, cutting, combining and cooking.

The macrobiotic diet is a very subtle regimen that makes use of the broadest possible range of available ingredients. It is the culinary expression of mankind's rich individuality, and believes in nurturing and cultivating that individuality. To follow the macrobiotic diet properly, each of us must come to know himself and understand the dynamics of food to discover how best to satisfy his own particular requirements. People's needs differ according to their physical constitution and nutritional background, their age and daily activities, their geographical location and the seasonal changes in their environment. A wife and mother must understand not only her own needs but also those of her family who entrust her with the responsibility of preparing their meals. The macrobiotic secrets to healthful living and eating are balance and moderation. You can be a vegetarian and derive all the vitamins, minerals, starches, oils and proteins needed for energy, growth and tissue repair from a well-balanced diet of grains, beans, fresh vegetables, fruits and nuts. But animal foods and dairy products can also find a place in a macrobiotic meal if prepared properly and combined harmoniously with the other elements included in our menu. We are free to eat whatever we wish. Nothing is forbidden but ignorance and carelessness.

The recipes presented here are for use in the average home. They are unlike those in an ordinary cookbook because they are based on the ancient philosophy of yin and yang. Indeed, macrobiotic cookery is not a new idea, but the oldest and most timeworn method of choosing and preparing food in harmony with nature. It expresses a philosophy of life that has been put into practice in a variety of ways throughout history, all over the world. If you observe the order of nature in your kitchen you can practice any style of traditional cooking, be it Japanese, French, Italian or Middle Eastern. You will find recipes in this book, therefore, from all over the world. George Ohsawa and I endeavored to revive this traditional practice by stressing the law of nature that underlies it, the law that binds man's health and happiness to the food he eats. For food provides the physical foundation out of which man's mind and spirit grow and develop. Today, with the pressing problems of environmental pollution, the widespread use of chemical fertilizer, and the addition of chemical colorings and preservatives to industrialized foods, I wish to offer the benefits of macrobiotic cooking and living to all my fellow human beings. I will attempt to outline our philosophy in the pages that follow, but I can offer here only a taste of its breadth and width. If this book contributes to your happiness, its purpose will have been achieved. I look forward to hearing from its readers.

In closing, I would like to thank Mr. and Mrs. Phillip Jannetta, Mr. Masanori Hashimoto, Ms. Himiko Sogabe and Ms. Fumi Sharon Johns for their help in preparing this volume, and Mr. Seiji Onishi for his skillfully executed illustrations. Many others have helped both materially and spiritually in the composition of this book, including the president of Japan Publications, Inc., Mr. Iwao Yoshizaki and Ms. Yotsuko Watanabe, editor. My deepest thanks to all who helped make this completely revised and expanded edition possible.

CONTENTS

2.   VEGETABLES FROM LAND AND SEA
75

INTRODUCTION

Cooking as Self-mastery

The next time you (man or woman) are making a meal for yourself, your family or your friends, stop and think a moment. Are you aware of the significance of what you are doing?

The primary purpose of cooking is to prepare foods that will sustain our physical and psychological well-being, nourish our humanity and improve the quality of our life. Macrobiotic methods are therefore designed to balance and enhance the life giving qualities of our daily food. We must never neglect or minimize the importance of flavor, aroma, texture or appearance in meal preparation. Good cooks however, are always aware that by their judgment and skill they are shaping the destiny of those they cook for.

The grand order of nature has its reflection in the small, delicate order of the ingredients we choose and the methods we use in cooking. Each natural taste —bitter, sweet, sour, salty, pungent and their innumerable variations—has a specific effect upon body, mind and spirit. Ingredients in combination accentuate, modify or moderate each other. In cooking we enhance or nullify these flavors and their effects in accordance with our needs and in harmony with our surroundings. This is our creative freedom as human beings, the first step in the mastery of our destiny. If we destroy our nourishment with artificial seasonings or improper cooking techniques, we invariably suffer for our discretion. To master the type of cooking that imparts health and inspires happiness we must study nature and use its principles both in food preparation and in our daily lives.

Cooking as Art

Daily food nourishes our body and determines the quality and the direction of our life. Preparing food that sustains and inspires ourselves and others is a creative act. Success in this art requires deep understanding, subtle delicacy and true dedication.

Cooking therefore is a vital skill—for men as well as women. It is especially important for those who cook each day with the welfare of others in mind. Macrobiotic cookery provides an opportunity for self-realization, and for a growing understanding of, and ability to use, the laws of nature.

Cooking challenges our judgment as we blend the colors, flavors, shapes, textures and fragrance of various foods into an integrated, harmonious whole. If music and painting are fine arts, the art of cooking stands at the pinnacle as the source of all human achievement. Life comes from food, and the quality of our life depends directly on the clarity of understanding that selects, prepares and serves our meals. From the macrobiotic perspective, cooking is the supreme art, and its devoted practitioners deserve the highest respect and gratitude.

Cooking with Harmony in Mind

Macrobiotic cooking involves the preparation of foods according to the laws of nature or the Order of the Universe. The practical application of this order is made possible by the principle of yin and yang. This principle expresses the harmonious interplay of opposites that governs the working of every plant and vegetable, as well as human affairs, and extends both inward and outward to every level of life from the preatomic to the cosmic. Thus it is called the Order of the Universe. If we understand this order and how to apply it in our daily lives, we can change the quality of our food to flexibly adjust ourselves to ever changing circumstances. This can be accomplished by using the simpliest ingredients from our environment to make meals that are attractive, delicious and healthful.

When planning your daily menu, keep this interplay of opposites in mind. For example, if you serve food that comes from the sea, combine it with appropriate food that grows on land. A serving of animal food (yang) should be balanced with vegetables and if desired fruit (yin). Foods rich in potassium (yin) are balanced with those rich in sodium (yang). Do not worry, you do not have to be a scientist. The macrobiotic principles are commonsense. Once intuition is recovered we realize that we have known and used these ideas all along, although in an unconscious, often haphazard way. With a little patience and practice macrobiotic cooking will become second nature, and you will marvel at its simplicity and practicality. Begin with the recipes offered in this volume and soon you will be creating your own dishes to suit the unique needs of your family and yourself.

The Harmony of Taste

To consistently make delicious and tempting meals, nurture a gentle touch and delicate sensibility. Never season with a heavy hand. There is a proper time in the cooking process when a seasoning should be introduced. Salt, for example, can be added fairly early to keep vegetables firm during cooking. *Miso* on the other hand, should be added toward the end. If it is overcooked *miso* loses much of its flavor and nutritional value. As you regain an appreciation and awareness of natural tastes, your skill in handling ingredients will grow. Creating a harmony of flavor with a variety of foods is an exciting challenge and one of the most important goals in macrobiotic cooking. If your palate has been dulled by chemicalized, processed or sugar rich foods, it will take time before your sensitivity returns. Be patient. Mastery of this most basic of skills frees us to create the type of life we truly desire.

The Harmony of Appearance

Serve foods with an eye toward the harmony of their colors, textures and shapes. Light foods should be served with heavy. The pungency of finely grated *daikon* radish, for example, enlivens fried *mochi* (sweet rice cakes), while the cool green stems of chopped scallion give a bowl of *soba* (buckwheat noodles) a bright lift.

The Unique Principle

The tool we use to understand nature and the art of preparing foods is the law of complementary opposites. Yin and yang represent the poles of contraction and expansion, positive and negative, winter and summer, activity and passivity. Foods can be classified into yin and yang according to the characteristics listed below.

	Yin	*Yang*
Biological	vegetable	animal
Agricultural	salad	cereal
Direction of Growth	up	down
Season of Growth	summer	fall, winter
Where Grown	tropical climate	temperate climate
Color	purple, green	red, orange
Water Content	high (juicy)	low (dry)
Weight	light	heavy
Taste	sweet, sour, spicy	salty, bitter
Element	potassium	sodium
Vitamin	C	A, D, K

Every food contains a unique balance of yin and yang elements, and both factors are present in everything. The ratio of yin to yang in whole brown rice (5:1) closely approximates the ideal balance in humans. This is the reason that brown rice is recommended as a daily food. All other foods are either more yin or more yang in relation to this balance. By applying the principles of yin and yang to food selection and preparation, we broaden our potential and our freedom to do whatever we choose. This is accomplished by yangizing foods that are more yin and yinnizing foods that are more yang to make balance with our particular environment and life-style. With techniques we learn from nature itself, we delicately alter the quality of our food to meet our needs and to maximize our freedom while staying within the bounds of biological and ecological order.

The yin or yang characteristics of a food are never good or bad in themselves. It is the balance we create that must be taken into consideration. That balance depends upon the quantity and quality of our ingredients and, most importantly, upon our skill in cooking. We must come to know our foods and discover the combinations and methods of preparation that best meet our individual requirements.

The use of salt, fire, pressure and time are the primary tools used in macrobiotic cooking to influence the quality of our food. We use our knowledge of the yin and yang factors of an ingredient to determine its preparation and seasoning, and to decide what other foods to combine with it. Yang vegetables (roots for example) require less salt and lower heat than do more yin vegetables. Overcooking can make our food too yang, undercooking can leave it too yin. Seasoning with sea salt, *miso* or soy sauce yangizes food, while reducing or eliminating salt and increasing the volume of water makes it more yin. Yang vegetables generally go best with yin ones. They complement each other. By applying these simple principles in our kitchens, we change the quality of foods, making yin ingredients more yang and yang ingredients more yin.

Eating foods in harmony with our environment, our personal condition and our way of life is the surest way to health and happiness. Wintry, cloudy or damp conditions are yin. We keep in dialectical (yin and yang) balance with them by becoming relatively more yang. This means choosing the appropriate ingredients, and cooking and seasoning them properly. Grains may compromise 50 to 70 percent of the diet in this case. A summerlike, bright and dry environment is yang. In this case we must adjust our balance toward the yin, eating moist, lightly cooked and sparingly salted dishes. Here, grain may account for only 40 to 50 percent of our daily menu. Vegetable quality side dishes and occasional fruits if desired may make up the rest. Observe the changes of season and the daily changes in both weather and your physical condition to select your ingredients and cooking methods correctly.

How to Begin

The change in diet from naturally grown, whole, seasonal vegetable quality foods to processed, chemicalized foods and large amounts of animal products has occurred gradually over the past two or three hundred years. Similarly, a return to more traditional patterns of eating centered around cereals and vegetables should also be gradual. A digestive system that is accustomed to the typical Western diet is often incapable of immediately deriving full nutritional benefit from grains, beans and land vegetables. Thus, make the change to the macrobiotic way of eating slowly.

Begin by eliminating red meat and substituting fish or fowl, reducing your intake as your needs and taste change. Attempt to cut out industrialized foods and drugs, refined sugar, coffee and artificially dyed teas from the outset. In their place enjoy fresh vegetables, grain coffee, and natural herb or grain teas. If you crave a sweetener, use a grain sweetener such as barley malt or rice syrup.

Excessively yang people—red-faced, husky, aggressive—are advised to adjust their daily menu toward the yin, reducing the amount of animal food in proportion to grains, beans, vegetables and occasional fruit. Very yin people—pale, frail, inactive and passive—can become more yang by increasing the percentage of grain and more yang vegetables and, if desired, can include occasional seafood in their diet. The amount of raw food and fruit should be reduced in this case. Create a new mental and physical balance for yourself by using a wide variety of natural foods selected and prepared properly according to the law of yin and yang. You will be well on your way to regaining health, vitality, and an ecstatic sense of harmony.

Drink enough to satisfy your thirst. The best measure of daily fluid intake is the frequency and color of urination. Generally the standard for males is three times and for females four times per day. The color should be pale gold. If urine is dark brown our condition is too yang. If it is clear like water, our condition is too yin. If you find yourself drinking too much reduce the amount of salt in your cooking and reflect upon any other yang ingredients you may be using to excess.

If you remember to chew each biteful of food from fifty to one hundred times, use a wide variety of foods, and do not overeat, you need not count calories in your menu. Macrobiotic foods, when properly prepared and enjoyed, will supply all the required nutritional factors in natural proportions.

Keep active. Daily physical exercise is indispensable for regaining bodily strength and stamina. Daily mental exercise is necessary for sharpening our judgment and achieving fuller spiritual awareness. The macrobiotic diet is an opportunity for you to achieve a deepened sensitivity to yourself and an enlivened awareness of your environment. For most people it is an invaluable and indispensable first step along the path to health, happiness and self-fulfillment. But these changes do not happen by themselves. Make a conscientious effort to harmonize your thoughts, feelings and actions with the natural flow of life's energy. Laziness, physical or mental, is taboo. Use your reinvigorated energy to greatest advantage. The macrobiotic approach to diet creates a healthy foundation upon which to build a happy and fulfilling life. How you use this potential is up to you.

As you begin the diet, and become more attuned to it, remember that all extremes change into their opposites and that flexibility is the key to success. Let us eat to regain and preserve our health, our happiness and, above all, our freedom to enjoy truly and deeply even the simplest pleasures afforded us by nature. Finally, please continue to study and to share your growing understanding with your family and friends. Read widely, attend classes and reflect on the philosophy behind the macrobiotic approach to diet. These activities will foster your continual development.

Where the Essentials Come from

A well-balanced diet of grains, beans, fresh vegetables, sea vegetables, nuts and seeds, and if desired, occasional seafood and fruits provides us with all the nutritional factors we need for health and vitality. Here are some of the best sources of vitamins, minerals, proteins, oils and starches found in our principal foods:

Vitamins

Vitamin A: Green leafy vegetables, dandelion greens, carrot, parsley, kale, lettuce, watercress, spinach

Vitamin B_1:   Almonds, kelp, soybeans, brown rice, beans, lentils

Vitamin B_2:   Sunflower seeds, rice bran, soybeans, peanuts, pinto beans, millet, wheat, rye, sesame seeds

Vitamin C: Parsley, watercress, cabbage, beets, carrot tops

Vitamin D: Dried fish, some vegetables (sunlight is the best source of this vitamin)

Vitamin E: Rice and all whole cereals, nuts, beans, green leafy vegetables

Vitamin F: Vegetable oils, olive and sesame oils

Vitamin K: Green leafy vegetables (cabbage, parsley, spinach), brown rice (also produced by the intestinal flora)

Minerals

Calcium: Sesame seeds, sea vegetables, green vegetables (watercress, dandelion), nuts, sunflower seeds

Magnesium: Sea vegetables, soybeans, lentils, green leafy vegetables

Phosphorus: Cereals, sea vegetables, nuts, beans

Potassium: Sea vegetables, soybeans, dried fruits, nuts, vegetables

Iron: Sea vegetables, sesame seeds, green vegetables, beans, brown rice, millet, oats, buckwheat and buckwheat noodles

Iodine: Sea vegetables, green vegetables

Sodium: Sea vegetables, green leafy vegetables, dried fruits

Proteins

Cereals, beans, nuts, seeds, assorted vegetables and seafood if desired contain all the essential amino acids we need. *Miso* and soy sauce, and other soybean products (*tofu, natto* and *tempeh* for example), are particularly rich in these essential nutrients.

Fats and Oils

In the macrobiotic diet our principal oils and fats are the unsaturated type. We derive most of our oils from the whole foods we eat. Among the cereal grains, oats have the highest amount of fat. Beans are also rich in oil, while small amounts are found in almost all vegetables. Oil in cooking is generally used for flavor and to cook foods quickly. (Oil being very yin attracts heat, yang, quickly.)

Starches (Carbohydrates)

Natural sugars are found in abundance in cereals and vegetables, fruits and nuts.

Living Ecology

Translated literally from the Greek, from which the word was taken, "Macrobiotics" means great life. *Macro* refers to the macrocosmic universe, the infinite source of the *Bios*, or biological evolution. *Macro-bios* implies the order that knits the entire universe into oneness. Living according to this law—expressed as yin and yang—is the way to achieve health, happiness and fulfillment. Practical macrobiotics is the attempt to grasp this elusive order in nature and to enable every man and woman to apply it in everyday life. By so doing we strive to create a civilization of free and happy people in harmony with the environment around us. Human life is nourished by sunlight, air, water and earth either directly or taken indirectly as food from the mineral, vegetable and animal worlds. We stress the importance of choosing and eating foods that are native to our terrain and climate, those that grow within a radius of about 500 miles of our homes. Below are seven simple guidlines that summarize the macrobiotic approach to cooking and eating. They are all based on the basic principle of ecology traditionally expressed in the Oriental phrase, *Man and Earth are not Two.*

(1) Primary Food
Grains have been the central food of all great civilizations until very recently. Short-grain brown rice is ideally balanced, particularly for people living in temperate climates and at sea level. In mountainous regions, increase the proportions of wheat or buckwheat in your diet. Use a rich variety of staples—rice, buckwheat, wheat, millet, barley, rye, oats and corn—selecting what grows locally and has been traditionally enjoyed in your part of the world. The grains you eat should be organically grown, free of chemical fertilizer and poisonous spray.

Whatever grain you choose should be used in its whole form. The rich deposits of vitamins and minerals in a grain's outer layer play an essential role in digesting the carbohydrate that makes up its bulk. Milling or otherwise processing a grain results in an incomplete food, one robbed of its full nutrition. This strains the body's delicate adjustive mechanisms and is ecologically wasteful. In addition to vitamins and minerals, we lose the unanalyzable essence of wholeness. Plant a whole kernel in the earth and a stalk will grow yielding many more. Bury a milled kernel and, cultivate it as you will, it will never sprout. It has lost its life.

(2) Secondary Food
Our second staple consists of fresh, locally grown vegetables. They are secondary in that their quantity will vary in proportion to the amount of primary food, grain, in our meal. Use all the parts of a vegetable and whenever possible see that it, too, has been naturally fertilized and tended. Choose what is native to your locale from among both cultivated produce and wild grasses. Sea vegetables are rich in iodine and other essential minerals and can be included in your diet even if you live far from the sea. We each carry an ocean within us in the form of our bloodstream

and body fluid. It may take a little time, but once you have accustomed yourself
to the unique tastes of the various sea vegetables they will become an important
part of your diet. Learn to use them every day.

When we enter our kitchens, cooked grains and vegetables are uppermost in
our mind and our daily menu revolves around them. But in a given meal we may
wish to include a soup, salad, some animal food, or a fruit. Soups are a fine way of
taking liquid and adding nutrition to our diet. *Miso* soup, for example, is an excellent source of protein and energy. Beans, too, are a rich source of valuable
proteins that complement those present in grains. Fresh or pressed salads are
delightfully refreshing in summer and can help, during any season, to balance a
side dish of fish or fowl.

Remember that no foods are forbidden except when your body tells you so.
Learn to recognize the signals of your daily condition. If you choose to prepare
animal food, remember that its proportion to the rest of your meal should be
secondary. Most important, using yin and yang, prepare it properly and serve it
together with the appropriate complementary food. Because fish and other seafood
are yin compared to land-roving animals, they are easier to balance and are therefore preferable to meats. Such animal food, when served in small portions, is often
invigorating. When using eggs, buy ones that come from hens raised on organic
feed. Fowl may be enjoyed occasionally but, being very yang, it requires careful
balancing. Meats, like eggs should be as free as possible from the contamination of
artificial chemicals. Dairy products, particularly goat's cheese and goat's milk
—yang entries in this generally yin food category—can also find an occasional
place in a macrobiotic meal, if balanced properly.

Enjoy local fruits when fresh and in season. Apples and strawberries are ideal,
while berries and melons can be wonderfully refreshing on a hot summer day.

(3) Seasonings
The main macrobiotic seasonings are natural sea salt, *miso* (soybean paste), soy
sauce and unrefined vegetable oils.

Our use of seasonings should reflect the weather, our geographical location and
our individual activities and needs. We season with a pinch more salt and oil in
cold, northerly regions than in warm, southerly climates. We need more of both oil
and salt if doing hard, physical labor. Adults whose bodies contain too much
potassium and a deficiency of sodium require more salt, while those with too much
sodium and not enough potassium require less or, in extreme cases, even none
at all. Never underestimate the importance of salt in your diet, especially natural
sea salt which is much stronger than ordinary table salt. A deficiency may lead to
fatigue; an excess to a rigid, nervous feeling and inability to sleep.

(4) Preparing Vegetables and Fruits
Naturally fertilized, unsprayed vegetables and fruits require only a light rinsing
under running cold water. Scrub them with a natural bristle brush (*tawashi*) as you

rinse. Peel them only if they have been waxed to preserve their shelf life in the supermarket. Use all their parts, wasting nothing. Cut and cook them with a balance of their yin and yang factors in mind.

(5) The Order of Eating

Chew your food well—each mouthful from fifty to one hundred times. Proper mastication is indispensable to good digestion because the enzymes in saliva begin the digestive process. This is especially true of grains because their major constituent, carbohydrate, is digested by an enzyme that flows in the mouth (ptyalin). For better digestion, proceed from yang to yin in your order of eating. Begin your meal with soup and/or a few bitefuls of grain, then alternate grain with the most yang food before you. When this dish is finished, go on to the next, always returning to grain as your central focus. Follow the meal with a beverage and dessert if desired. Never eat to full capacity. Always leave the table with room left for just a little more.

(6) Following the Path of Nature

Modern methods of cultivating, processing, preserving and distributing foods have diluted our awareness of the importance of seasonality and of our ties to the earth and its cycles. *Refining* a food has come to mean removing essential nutrients. When food is packaged, chemicals are often added to preserve its shelf life and coloring to make it more appealing. We can now serve tomatoes and cucumbers at parties celebrating the New Year despite the fact that in temperate climates these are summer foods. They have either been brought from far away or grown in artificial environments. Is it not obvious that this violates the ecological order of life? I never cease to wonder at the many people who try so hard to "return to nature" in mountains and forests, only to draw heavily refined foods, meats and chocolate candies out of their rucksacks.

To preserve your health and happiness, and to live in true harmony with the natural environment, avoid industrialized foods, refined flour products and refined sugar. These denatured foods strain and deplete the body's resources in its efforts to maintain an alkaline balance in the blood and to adjust them to its real needs. As a rule, abstain from the extremes of yin and yang: refined sugar, artificial chemicals and drugs on the one hand, and meat, eggs, salty cheese, and excess salt on the other. It is true that taken together they constitute a very wide balance, but not an ideal or healthful one. To gain a more thorough understanding of why these foods can be harmful, refer to the works listed in the bibliography.

Whether you live in city or country, you will be amazed at how quickly and spontaneously your mind and body will be reattuned to the cycles of nature simply by eating locally grown, whole foods macrobiotically chosen and prepared.

(7) Enjoying Your Food

The law of nature is change. Macrobiotic living, eating and cooking must flow with the movement of these changes. Our body and each of its cells change from season to season, day to day and even moment to moment. Our nutritional requirements change with them. Vary your diet from meal to meal according to your needs. Do not be rigid in your cooking or eating; enjoy life and be creative. I invite you to begin with the recipes in this book but caution you that they are meant only as a general guide to your own creative self-expression. After trying them once or twice, adjust them to fit your personal taste and the requirements of your family. Be free to be yourself in harmony with nature's order.

Practical Hints

(1) Outfitting Your Kitchen

A well outfitted kitchen invites success. After carefully choosing your ingredients, have the tools on hand to prepare them properly. You will need: a fine mesh strainer for washing grains, beans or seeds; a natural bristle brush (*tawashi*) for scrubbing vegetables; a 1-inch-thick (at least) unvarnished cutting board, and a heavy all-purpose Japanese knife (*hocho*) for cutting vegetables neatly, quickly and easily; a *suribachi*, or serrated earthenware mortar, for grinding seeds and making purées; and a stainless-steel or porcelain grater with a fine section for grating *daikon* radish or ginger root.

Cookware made of yang materials (earthenware, cast iron, stainless steel, baked enamel) give the best results. A stainless-steel or porcelain-enamel pressure cooker is indispensable in a macrobiotic kitchen. One or two cast-iron skillets and heavy saucepans are best for sautéing and dry-roasting. A large soup pot or Dutch oven with a tight-fitting lid serves well for soups and noodles, or for steaming vegetables. A *wok* or Chinese cooking pot is good for deep-frying and fast cooking, while an oil strainer aids in removing pieces of vegetable or fish *tempura* from the cooking oil. A bamboo or metal colander is handy for draining noodles or lightly boiled greens. Casserole dishes, bread pans, a cookie sheet and pastry brush will be essential for baking.

Wooden implements are best for stirring foods while they cook because they do not scratch or otherwise harm the surface of pots and pans. They can also be used for serving. Have several pairs of long chopsticks, a bamboo rice paddle, and wooden spoons of various sizes near at hand.

(2) Stocking up on the Basics

Keep your kitchen well stocked with the basic ingredients. Needless to say, it is inconvenient to reach for something that is not there.

Brown Rice and Other Grains. Short-grain brown rice is recommended in a temperate climate, because it is more yang than the long-grain variety. Have other grains—buckwheat, millet, rolled oats, etc.—on hand as well to add variety to your meals.

Flour. You will need flour for breads, crepes and sauces. Whole-wheat flour is indispensable, while a few pounds of corn, rice and buckwheat flour will add color, flavor and aroma to your baked goods.

Noodles. Several packages of whole-wheat and buckwheat noodles made without eggs will make for quick and easy meals to please the hungriest of unexpected visitors.

Beans. Beans are high in proteins that complement those present in grains. Tiny, red *azuki* beans are the most yang, and have a unique, delicious flavor. Keep well stocked with your favorites.

Sea Vegetables. Sea vegetables are usually dried before packaging and therefore store easily. *Hijiki* is said by many Westerners to be the most enjoyable to those first getting accustomed to sea vegetables. Purple *nori* comes in sheets that need only be lightly toasted. *Wakame* is delicious in soups and salads, while *kombu* is essential for soup stock.

Dried Fruits, Nuts and Seeds. These delicacies are handy for desserts or snacks. Make sure that the fruits are sun-dried, and free of sulfur dioxide.

Bancha Tea. This is a green Japanese tea. Undyed, it is the most important and widely used beverage in macrobiotics.

Kuzu. Kuzu is a white thickening agent used in sauces, soups and desserts. Arrowroot starch may be substituted, but it is more yin.

Kanten. Kanten, or agar is a sea vegetable gelatin used as a jelling agent in desserts.

Chirimen iriko. These are tiny dried fish used as a flavoring agent in soup stocks. They may also be ground up in a *suribachi* and eaten as a condiment with rice and vegetables.

Condiments and Seasonings

Sea Salt. Use unrefined, white sea salt, best because it contains a wide variety of trace minerals and has not been treated with sugar, iodine, or chemicals. Store in an airtight container.

Miso. Miso paste is a mixture of cooked soybeans, grain and salt, fermented by an enzyme and then aged for at least one and a half years (except *kome-miso* which is aged less). *Hatcho-miso* is the strongest: it is dark brown and very salty, and is best used during winter. *Mugi-miso*, made with barley, is lighter than *Hatcho-miso* and is ideal for year-round use. *Kome-miso* is made with rice and much less salt. It is ideal for summer use and good for children and older adults.

Soy Sauce. This is traditionally made with natural ingredients—soybeans, fermented parched wheat, salt and water. Soy sauce is aged naturally for at least eighteen months. Salty and rich tasting, it is used as a seasoning and table condiment.

Umeboshi. These are small plums pickled in salt brine for two years or more. The plums themselves and their juice are used as seasoning agents in place of salt.

Oil.   Use unrefined, natural sesame, corn, soy or sunflower oil. Deep-bodied and aromatic, these cold-pressed high-quality oils give the best results in cooking and baking.

Gomashio.   Gomashio is a mixture of toasted sesame seeds and salt, ground together in a *suribachi*. It is perfect with rice or other grains, and goes well with almost anything.

Spices and Herbs.   Because spices are rather yin, they are used only sparingly in the macrobiotic diet. They are not completely excluded however, and a touch of cinnamon or saffron can give a wonderful accent to a meal. Herbs such as basil and thyme can also find a place in a macrobiotic dish.

(3)   Economizing

Macrobiotic meals should, in principle, cost as little as possible. Use whole foods to avoid waste. Learn to prepare leftovers in new and attractive ways. Shop wisely and buy the nonperishables you intend to store when they are in season and inexpensive. Never allow a flame to burn idly, and be efficient with your time.

(4)   Preparing Ahead Wisely

Before starting to cook have a fully formed menu and step-by-step plan of preparation in mind. Place the ingredients in order of use and keep your cooking utensils in easy reach. Do not light your fire until your ingredients are ready, and do not allow water to boil unnecessarily.

See to it that pots and pans are cleaned thoroughly after each use, dried well, and made as bright as new. Taking good care of utensils increases their life-span. Besides, you cannot be a successful cook if you use a scorched pot or one with burned food stuck to its bottom.

Keep your kitchen neat and clean. Storage areas should express your personal sense of order. Be able to reach into a cupboard and find a pot or pan, knife or condiment immediately. Keep your vegetable knife clean and sharp if you want to do your best work. When a knife is dull, its chopping block soon wears out. A good cook creates an environment of gentle orderliness and care in which to work.

Healthful Living

My husband devised seven guides to evaluate a person's health and the progress made in mastering macrobiotics. If your practice of macrobiotics is correct they should describe you.

1.   No Fatigue—Having worked through the day you can eagerly begin again the next morning.
2.   Good Appetite—You can thoroughly enjoy the simplest food and take deep pleasure in natural flavors.
3.   Good Sleep—Your sleep is deep and you fall asleep within minutes after put-

ting your head on the pillow. You neither thrash about nor dream, and you can awake spontaneously at a predetermined hour without the help of an alarm clock. You awake fully refreshed after four or five hours sleep.

4. Good Humor—From morning until night living is a joy for which you feel deep gratitude. You fear nothing and are grateful for everything. Out of misfortune you create joyful promise and opportunity.

5. Good Memory—You never forget and, as you age, your ability to remember the names of an ever-increasing number of friends improves.

6. Good Judgment and Smart Action—You make all decisions confidently and quickly. Your movements are swift and graceful.

7. A Striving for Justice—You keep your promises and are always faithful. You neither lie nor deceive, and you value deeds above words. You live an unselfish life in pursuit of beauty, truth and justice. Living this way you are happy.

The first three measures are physiological; the second three are psychological. If you realize only these, however, you have yet to really succeed in mastering the macrobiotic way of life. But if you are truthful to yourself, admitting and reflecting on your shortcomings, there is a good possibility that you will eventually succeed at them all. Mastery of macrobiotics is not limited to physical and psychological characteristics. True health is gauged by the seventh, unlimited measure. It is a spiritual state reflected in an unselfish attitude toward our fellowman and in the quality and direction of our life. Achieving this state depends upon the level of our judgment which, in turn, depends upon our physical condition. The food we eat creates and sustains both. While we emphasize the importance of our daily meals, always remember that our goal is wisdom, humanity, harmony and joy. If you devotedly pursue the law of nature, cultivate gratitude for both hardship and ease, and desire to realize your finest potential as a human being, you can succeed in macrobiotics. It is never too late.

A Table of Daily Foods

▽▽▽=Very yin
▽▽=More yin
▽=Yin
Very yang=△△△
More yang=△△
Yang=△

CEREALS
corn ▽
rye
barley
oats
wheat
rice △
millet
buckwheat △△

VEGETABLES
eggplant ▽▽▽
tomato
sweet potato
potato
Japanese mushroom (shiitake)
beans (except azuki)
cucumber
spinach
asparagus
artichoke
bamboo sprouts
mushroom
snow peas ▽▽

celery
cauliflower
broccoli
purple cabbage
beet
green cabbage
dandelion leaves △
lettuce
endive
kale
turnip
radish
coltsfoot
onion
garlic
parsley
pumpkin △△
carrot
burdock
watercress
dandelion root
jinenjo △△△

FISH
oyster ▽
clam
octopus
carp
mussels
halibut
lobster

trout
sole
salmon △
shrimp
herring
sardine
red snapper
caviar △△

ANIMAL FOODS
snail △△
frog
pork
beef
horsemeat
hare
chicken ▽
pigeon △
duck
turkey
eggs △△
pheasant △△△

DAIRY PRODUCTS
yogurt ▽▽▽
sour cream
sweet cream
cream cheese
butter
cow's milk ▽▽
Camembert

Gruyère
Roquefort △
Edam
goat's milk △△

FRUITS
pineapple ▽▽▽
mango
grapefruit
banana
fig
orange
pear
peach ▽▽
lime
melon
almond
peanut
cashew
hazelnut
olive ▽
cherry
strawberry △
chestnut
apple △△

BEVERAGES
synthetically dyed tea ▽▽▽
coffee
artificially sweetened drinks

fruit juice
champagne
wine
beer ▽▽
mineral water
carbonated water
water
thyme tea
mugwort ▽
bancha
chicory
grain coffee
dandelion coffee
burdock tea
Mu tea △△
ginseng △△△

MISCELLANEOUS
sugar ▽▽▽
honey
molasses
margarine
coconut oil ▽▽
peanut oil
olive oil
soy oil
sunflower oil ▽
corn oil
sesame oil
safflower oil

Vegetable Cutting Techniques

The Harmony of Form

Food should always be presented in a way that appeals to the eye. As in every aspect of meal preparation, cutting should be done in an attractive, orderly fashion, according to the principles of nature. Here are several ways to slice and shape natural ingredients so that each piece maintains an integral harmony of yin and yang:

Hasugiri, **or slicing on the diagonal.** Cut into diagonal slices.

Sengiri, **or slivering.** Cut into *hasugiri* then cut each diagonal slice into matchstick-size pieces.

Koguchigiri, **or cutting into bite-size pieces.** Cut into thin rounds.

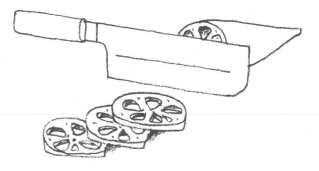

Koguchigiri Hanagata, **or cutting into bite-size flowered pieces.** Cut into thin rounds; then cut small wedges from each round.

Rangiri, **or cutting into irregular wedges.** Cut into large diagonal wedges.

Wagiri, **or cutting into thick rounds.** Cut into rounds, thicker than *koguchigiri.*

Hangetsu, **or cutting into half-moons.** Cut lengthwise into halves. Then cut *koguchigiri.*

Ichogiri, **or cutting into gingko leaves.** Cut lengthwise into halves. Cut each half full-length again, then cut *koguchigiri.*

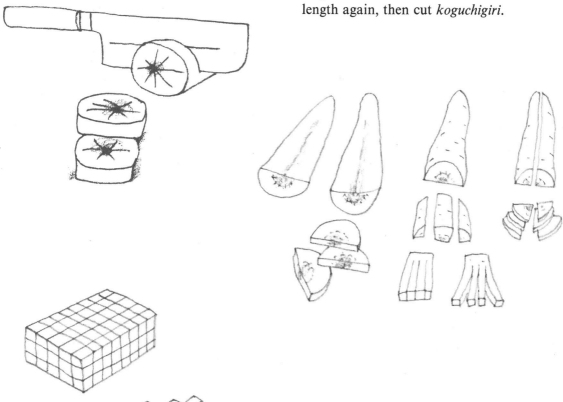

Sainome, **or dicing.** Cut vegetables into ⅓-inch cubes.

Tanzaku, **or cutting into rectangles.** Cut into 1½-inch rounds; cut each round on the diagonal into 4 or 5 pieces; then cut each piece into thin rectangular slices.

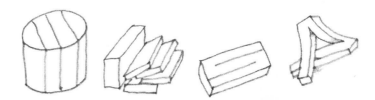

Kikukagiri, or cutting chrysanthemum style. Cut into even pieces across vegetable, keeping pieces attached at base. Cut across opposite pole to same depth and thickness. Soak in ice-cold water to open the vegetables like a flower.

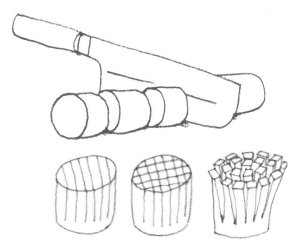

Mawashigiri, or cutting into half-moons/ crescents. Cut vegetable lengthwise into halves. Turn on axis and cut vertically into thin moon-shaped slices.

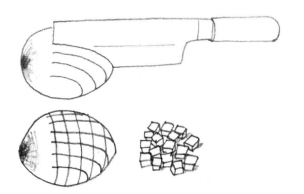

Mijingiri, or onion-dicing. Cut into halves about $\frac{1}{8}$ inch from root end. Cut each half into thin sections; then slice in the opposite direction, keeping same distance from root end. Next dice into small pieces.

Cutting leaves into strips. Separate full leaves, stack together, and cut into thin strips.

Sasagaki, **or shaving.** Pencil shave beginning at the bottom of vegetable, rotating vegetable slightly with each cut of the knife. Shave thick or thin.

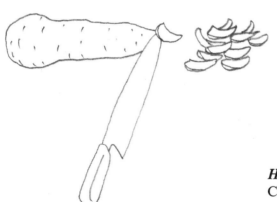

Hanagata, **or cutting into flower shapes.** Cut 4 or 5 small thin wedges full-length along the vegetable. Then cut into rounds.

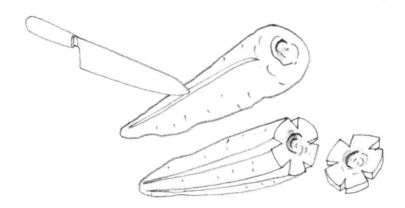

1. WHOLE GRAINS AND FLOUR

Brown Rice

Brown Rice (Pressure-Cooked)   *Serves 4*

2 cups brown rice, washed
3 cups water
pinch of sea salt per cup of rice

1)   Combine ingredients in a pressure cooker, cover, and bring rapidly to full pressure over a high flame.
2)   Reduce flame to low, and simmer 40–45 minutes.
3)   Remove from heat and allow pressure to return to normal.
4)   Uncover and mix rice gently with a wooden spatula or rice paddle that has been moistened in cold water to prevent sticking.
5)   Place rice in a wooden bowl and cover with a damp cotton cloth.

   Rice at the bottom of the pressure cooker should be a deeper brown than rice toward the top. However, if some rice sticks to the bottom, add a little cold water and soak 2–3 minutes. This will loosen the rice and make it easy to remove.

Boiled Brown Rice   *Serves 4*

2 cups brown rice, washed
4 cups water
pinch of sea salt per cup of rice

1)   Combine ingredients in a heavy saucepan. Cover pan with a thick cotton cloth, and put a tight-fitting lid on top. A stone or other weight can be placed on the lid to help keep in moisture.
2)   Bring quickly to a boil over a high flame, lower flame to medium-low, and simmer 50–60 minutes, or until all the water has been absorbed.
3)   Reduce flame to very low, cook for 1 minute more, then turn off heat.
4)   Remove rice with a wooden spatula and place in a wooden bowl.

   This is a more yin style of cooking, and will produce lighter, fluffier rice.

Baked Brown Rice   *Serves 4*

2 cups brown rice, washed
3 cups cold or boiling water
2 pinches sea salt

1)   Preheat oven to 350°F.
2)   Place rice in a heavy skillet and roast over a medium flame. Stir constantly and gently, until rice is dry and a deep brown color.
3)   Transfer rice to a casserole dish. Add water and salt.
4)   Cover and bake 50 minutes.
5)   Mix gently and let stand 5 minutes before serving.

Roasted Rice   *Serves 5 or 6*

3 cups brown rice, washed
3 cups water
3 pinches sea salt

1)   Dry-roast rice in a pressure cooker until golden brown. Stir constantly and gently to prevent scorching.
2)   Add water and salt, and cover.

3)   Bring rapidly to full pressure over a high flame.

4)   Reduce flame to low and cook 40–45 minutes.

5)   Remove from heat and allow pressure to return to normal.

6)   Uncover and mix gently.

7)   Place rice in a wooden bowl and cover with a damp cloth until ready to serve.

This is a more yang style of preparing rice.

Brown Rice Cream (Boiled)   *Serves 5*

   1 cup brown rice, washed
   10 cups water
   2 pinches sea salt
   1 muslin sack (Fold a 1½-yard square of
      unbleached muslin cloth into a triangle and
      sew one side with a double seam.)

1)   Dry-roast rice in a heavy saucepan until golden brown. Stir constantly to assure even heating.

2)   Add water and salt, and bring rapidly to a boil over a high flame.

3)   Reduce flame to medium-low, and cover with a tight-fitting lid.

4)   Simmer 3 hours.

5)   Remove from heat and allow to cool until lukewarm.

6)   Spoon the lukewarm rice into the muslin sack and twist the opening close.

7)   Hold the sack over a saucepan and squeeze all the liquid out.

8)   When the sack is squeezed dry, remove the grains and set aside for use in fried rice balls (p. 36).

■ *To serve the rice cream:*

1)   Stir in 4–5 cups water and bring just to a boil.

2)   Season with salt to taste, and serve topped with croutons and garnished with a sprig of parsley.

This is a very good dish for sick people or for those with digestive problems. Do not add croutons if serving to someone who is sick.

To make a thin cream or tea, add 10 cups water and bring just to a boil.

This dish can be made more yang by preroasting the rice in 1 tablespoon sesame oil. It can be made more yin by not roasting the rice at all.

Variations

A prepackaged rice cream powder is available at most natural food stores and macrobiotic outlets.

1)   Combine 1 cup of the powder with 4 cups water. Stir constantly to prevent lumping. Then add a pinch of sea salt.

2)   Bring to a boil over a high flame, reduce flame to low, and cover with a tight-fitting lid.

3)   Simmer for about 1 hour.

Brown Rice Cream   *Serves 5*
(Pressure-Cooked)

   1 cup brown rice, washed
   2 pinches sea salt
   10 cups water

1)   Place rice, salt and 5 cups water in a pressure cooker.

2)   Cover and bring rapidly to pressure over a high flame.

3)   Reduce flame to low, and simmer 45–60 minutes.

4)   Turn off heat and remove regulator to release pressure rapidly.

5)   Uncover, and stir in 5 more cups of water.

6)   Without covering, bring just to a boil.

7)   Remove from stove and allow to cool until lukewarm.

8)   Proceed from step 6 of the boiled rice cream recipe above.

Brown Rice with Chestnuts   *Serves 6*

3 cups brown rice, washed
½ cup shelled chestnuts, fresh or dried
4½ cups water
3 pinches sea salt

If using dried chestnuts, soak overnight.
1)   Combine all ingredients in a pressure cooker, cover, and bring rapidly to full pressure over a high flame.
2)   Reduce flame to low, and simmer 40–45 minutes.
3)   Remove from heat and allow pressure to return to normal.
4)   Uncover and mix gently with a lightly moistened rice paddle.
5)   Place rice in a wooden bowl and cover with a damp cotton cloth until ready to serve.

Brown Rice with Barley   *Serves 5*

1¾ cups brown rice, washed
¼ cup barley, washed
2⅔ cups water
2 pinches sea salt

1)   Combine all ingredients in a pressure cooker, cover, and bring rapidly to full pressure over a high flame.
2)   Reduce flame to low and simmer 40–45 minutes.

3)   Remove from heat and allow pressure to return to normal.
4)   Uncover and mix gently with a lightly moistened rice paddle.
5)   Place rice in a wooden bowl and cover with a damp cloth until ready to serve.

Rice Balls (*Musubi*)   *Serves 7*

5 cups cooked brown rice
several *umeboshi* plums
4 sheets *nori*, toasted
3–4 Tbsp roasted sesame seeds

1)   Cook rice according to the directions on page 33.
2)   When rice is done, remove from heat. Then remove pressure regulator to allow steam to escape.
3)   Mix rice gently with a moistened rice paddle. Then replace cover and let cool to room temperature.
■ *To assemble:*
1)   Moisten your hands in cold water to prevent sticking. Then shape a portion of the rice into 14 triangular wedges, approximately ½ inch thick.
2)   Form remaining rice into balls.
3)   Cut each sheet of toasted *nori* into 4

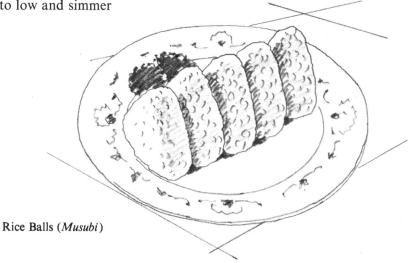

Rice Balls (*Musubi*)

strips. Then wrap 1 strip around the center of each of 7 of the wedges.

4) Press a piece of *umeboshi* at the center of the remaining 7 wedges. Then wrap a piece of *nori* around the center of each.

5) Roll the balls in the roasted sesame seeds, coating thoroughly.

6) Arrange the *musubi* on a large platter, decorate with sprigs of parsley and serve.

Wonderful for parties, picnics or box lunches.

Variations

A. Add a pinch of salt to 2 tablespoons soy flour. Then roll the rice balls in the flour, coating thoroughly.

B. Fried Musubi:

1) Heat a heavy skillet and coat with 1 tablespoon sesame oil.

2) When oil is hot, cook triangular *musubi* uncovered, over a medium flame.

Brown Rice with *Azuki* Beans *Serves 10*

5 cups brown rice, washed
½ cup *azuki* beans, washed
7 cups water
pinch of sea salt per cup of rice

1) Combine all ingredients in a pressure cooker, cover, and bring rapidly to full pressure over a high flame.

2) Reduce flame to low and simmer 40–45 minutes.

3) Remove from heat and allow pressure to return to normal. For drier rice, remove pressure regulator and allow steam to escape.

4) Uncover and mix gently with a lightly moistened rice paddle.

■ *To prepare in a saucepan:*

1) Simmer beans in 1½ cups water until their skins wrinkle, about 20 minutes.

2) Drain the beans and combine with rice. (Save the cooking water for use as a soup base.)

3) Add 10 cups water and a pinch of salt per cup of rice.

4) Bring rapidly to a boil over a high flame, then reduce flame to low.

5) Cover with a tight-fitting lid and simmer 50–60 minutes.

6) Reduce flame to very low and cook 1 minute more.

7) Remove from heat, and place *azuki* rice in a wooden bowl.

8) Cover with a moist cotton cloth until ready to serve.

Japanese people used to eat *azuki* bean rice on the first and 15 of each month.

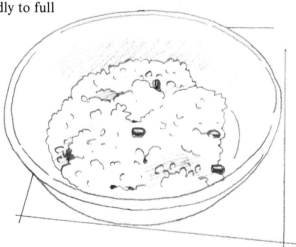

Brown Rice with *Azuki* Beans

Brown Rice with Hokkaido
Pumpkin

Brown Rice with Pinto Beans *Serves 6*

3 cups brown rice, washed
½ cup pinto beans, washed
pinch of sea salt per cup of rice
4 cups water, approximately

1)   Simmer beans in 2 cups water for about
30 minutes, or until slightly tender and
wrinkled.
2)   Drain and save cooking water.
3)   Combine rice, beans and salt in a
pressure cooker.
4)   Add liquid left over from boiling the
beans, plus enough freshwater to equal
4 cups.
5)   Bring rapidly to full pressure over a
high flame, reduce flame to low, and simmer
40–45 minutes.
6)   Remove from heat and allow pressure
to return to normal.
7)   Mix gently with a lightly moistened
rice paddle, then place rice in a wooden
bowl. Cover with a moist cotton cloth until
ready to serve.

Variation
Substitute ½ cup chick-peas for the pinto
beans. Soak chick-peas overnight or
pressure-cook in 3 parts water to 1 part
beans for 40 minutes.
   Then proceed from step 2 above.

Brown Rice with Soybeans *Serves 10*

5 cups brown rice, washed
½ cup soybeans, washed and soaked overnight
6½ cups water
pinch of sea salt per cup of rice

1)   Combine all ingredients in a pressure
cooker, cover, and bring rapidly to full
pressure over a high flame.
2)   Reduce flame to low and simmer
40–45 minutes.
3)   Remove from heat and allow pressure
to return to normal. For a drier rice remove
pressure regulator and allow steam to escape.
4)   Mix gently with a moistened rice paddle.
5)   Place rice in a wooden bowl and cover
with a damp cotton cloth until ready to
serve.

Brown Rice with Hokkaido Pumpkin *Serves 6*

3 cups brown rice, washed
4 oz Hokkaido pumpkin or acorn squash, peeled
   and cut into 1-in cubes
3½ cups water
pinch of sea salt per cup of rice
minced parsley, for garnish

1)   Combine the first four ingredients in a
pressure cooker, and bring rapidly to full
pressure over a high flame.

2) Reduce flame to low and simmer 40–45 minutes.

3) Remove from heat and allow pressure to return to normal. For a drier rice, remove pressure regulator and allow steam to escape.

4) Mix gently with a moistened rice paddle, then place rice in a wooden bowl.

5) Cover with a damp cotton cloth until ready to serve.

6) Serve with a sprinkling of minced parsley.

As a variation, serve topped with mock Béchamel sauce (p. 133) and garnish with minced parsley.

Brown Rice with Vegetables   *Serves 10*

5 cups brown rice, washed
6½ cups water
¼ tsp and 2 pinches sea salt
2 tsp sesame oil
3 cups carrots, slivered thin
1 cup lotus root, sliced into thin quarters
1 Tbsp soy sauce
greens from 1 carrot
1 sheet *nori*

1) Combine rice, water and ¼ teaspoon salt in a pressure cooker.

2) Cover and bring rapidly to full pressure over a high flame.

3) Reduce flame to low and simmer 40–45 minutes.

4) Remove from heat and allow pressure to return to normal.

■ *While rice is cooking:*

1) Heat a heavy skillet and coat with 1 teaspoon sesame oil.

2) When oil is hot, sauté carrot slivers over a medium flame. Stir constantly to coat evenly with oil and prevent scorching.

3) After 2–3 minutes, add a pinch of salt and ⅓ cup water.

4) Cover pan and cook another 4–5 minutes. If any liquid remains, remove lid and simmer until dry.

■ *Heat another skillet and:*

1) Coat with 1 teaspoon oil.

2) When oil is hot, reduce flame to low and add lotus root.

3) Sauté 1–2 minutes, stirring lightly.

4) Add 1 tablespoon soy sauce and 2 tablespoons water.

5) Cover skillet and simmer 15 minutes, or until lotus root is tender and liquid has evaporated or been absorbed.

■ *Bring a small pan of water to a boil over a high flame and:*

1) Add a pinch of salt, then drop in carrot greens.

2) Return water to a boil and cook 1–2 minutes, or until stems are tender.

3) Drain, cool, then chop the greens fine.

■ *Place the rice in a wooden bowl and:*

1) With long wooden chopsticks, gently mix in the carrot slivers and lotus root quarters.

2) Then fold in the carrot greens.

3) A moment before serving, toast 1 side of the *nori* by waving it over a low flame for several seconds, until just crisp.

4) Crumble *nori* and serve as a garnish, sprinkled over individual portions of the vegetable-rice.

Brown Rice with Mushrooms   *Serves 4*

2 cups brown rice, washed
3¼ cups water
pinch of sea salt per cup of rice
4 medium *shiitake* mushrooms*
1 tsp sesame oil
½ Tbsp soy sauce

1) Combine rice, 3 cups water and salt in a pressure cooker.

2) Cover, and bring rapidly to full pressure over a high flame.

3) Reduce flame to low, and simmer 40–45 minutes.

Brown Rice with Mushrooms

4)   Remove from heat, and allow pressure to return to normal.

Soak *shiitake* mushrooms in cold water about 20 minutes, or until soft. Then remove the hard stems, and slice the broad caps fine.

■ *After removing pressure cooker from stove:*

1)   Heat a heavy skillet, and coat with the oil.

2)   When oil is hot, sauté the mushrooms over a medium flame until tender, stirring lightly.

3)   Add ¼ cup water and ½ tablespoon soy sauce. Then cover pan, and reduce flame to low.

4)   Simmer 5 minutes, then uncover and simmer until all liquid has evaporated.

5)   Uncover rice and mix gently. Then, using a pair of long wooden chopsticks, mix in the sautéed *shiitake* mushrooms.

6)   Serve while still warm and fragrant.

*Available at macrobiotic outlets and Oriental food stores.

Sushi Stuffed *Agé* (*Inari-Zushi*)   *Serves 10*

>   3 cups brown rice, washed
>   4½ cups water
>   6 pinches sea salt
>   10 pieces *agé*
>   1-in long piece *kombu*
>   3 Tbsp soy sauce, approximately
>   10 green beans, rinsed and trimmed
>   1 tsp sesame oil
>   3 cups carrot, slivered

1)   Combine rice, water and 3 pinches salt in a pressure cooker.

2)   Cover and bring to full pressure over a high flame.

3)   Reduce flame to low and simmer 40–45 minutes.

4)   Remove from heat and allow pressure to return to normal.

Sushi Stuffed *Agé* (*Inari-Zushi*)

■ *To prepare agé*:
1)   Cut each *agé* piece into halves and pull open the center of each half to make a pouch.
2)   Place *agé* in a strainer and pour hot water over them to drain away excess oil.
3)   Place the *kombu* in the bottom of a sauce pan and arrange the *agé* on top.
4)   Add enough water to cover, and stir in 1–2 tablespoons of soy sauce for each cup of water used.
5)   Cover with a tight-fitting lid, or insert a smaller lid so that it fits directly over the *agé* pouches and keeps them in place.
6)   Bring to a boil and cook until all the liquid has evaporated and the pouches are well flavored.
7)   Drain and allow to cool.
■ *To prepare the green beans*:
1)   Bring a small pan of water to a boil and add a pinch of salt.
2)   Drop in the green beans and quickly return to a boil.
3)   Cook 4–5 minutes, or until beans are bright green and tender, but still crisp.
4)   Arrange on a plate and sprinkle with a pinch of salt.
5)   When cool, slice the beans fine on a diagonal.
■ *To prepare carrot slivers*:
1)   Heat a heavy skillet and coat with the oil.
2)   When oil is hot, sauté the carrot slivers over a medium flame for 2–3 minutes, stirring constantly.
3)   Sprinkle with a pinch of salt, add just enough water to cover, and bring to a boil.
4)   Cover pan, reduce heat, and simmer about 5 minutes, or until tender.
5)   If any liquid remains after carrot is done, remove lid and simmer until evaporated.
■ *To stuff the agé*:
1)   Uncover the rice and stir lightly. Then

place rice in a wooden bowl.
2)   Using wooden chopsticks, gently mix the vegetables into the rice.
3)   Fill the *agé* pouches to about ¾ full with the vegetable-rice mixture.
4)   Fold the lip of each pouch to form a flap. Serve hot.

Nori-Rolled Sushi (*Nori-Maki*) Serves 5

    3½ cups brown rice, washed
    5 cups water
    7 pinches sea salt
    2 Tbsp brown rice or *umeboshi* vinegar
    1 medium carrot
    1 medium lotus root
    1–2 Tbsp soy sauce
    20 green beans, rinsed and trimmed
    4 sheets *nori*, toasted on 1 side

1)   Combine rice, water and 4 pinches salt in a pressure cooker.
2)   Cover and bring to pressure over a high flame.
3)   Reduce flame to low and simmer 40–45 minutes.
4)   Remove from heat and allow pressure to return to normal. Then mix gently.
5)   Immediately pour over the rice a mixture of 1 tablespoon vinegar and 1 tablespoon water.
6)   Fan rice to cool it quickly to room temperature.
■ *While rice is cooking*:
1)   Quarter the carrot and lotus root lengthwise, then cut each quarter into logs about ⅓ inch thick.
2)   Add a pinch of salt to the carrots, and mix well in a heavy skillet.
3)   Heat the carrots over a medium flame for 1–2 minutes, stirring gently.
4)   Add 2 tablespoons water, reduce flame to low, and cover pan.
5)   Simmer for 15 minutes. If any liquid remains, uncover and cook until it evaporates.
6)   Remove from heat and set aside.

Nori-Rolled Sushi
(*Nori-Maki*)

■ *The lotus root:*
1) Soak the lotus root for 10 minutes in a mixture of 1 tablespoon vinegar and 1 tablespoon water.
2) Place lotus root and soaking mixture in a heavy skillet.
3) Add the soy sauce, and simmer until all liquid has evaporated.
4) Remove from heat and set aside.

■ *The green beans:*
1) Bring a small pan of water (just enough to cover the beans) to a boil, then add a pinch of salt.
2) Drop in the beans, and return quickly to a boil.
3) Cook 4–5 minutes, until beans are bright green and tender, but still crisp.
4) Drain beans, then sprinkle with a pinch of salt.

■ *To assemble ingredients:*
1) Place 1 sheet of toasted *nori* on a bamboo mat, or *sudare*.
2) Divide the rice into 4 portions, and spread 1 portion over most of the *nori*, leaving a ¼–½ inch edge at one end.
3) Place a double row of carrot sticks across the center of the rice. Then lay 5 green beans and a double row of lotus sticks on top of the carrot.

4) Lightly moisten both the exposed edges of the *nori* and the vegetables. Then roll up the mixture in the mat, pressing the ingredients together into a firm cylinder approximately 1½ inches in diameter.
5) Remove mat and repeat with remaining ingredients.
6) Use a sharp knife to slice each *nori* roll (*nori-maki*) into ½-inch rounds. For neat slices, wipe the knife clean after each cut with a damp cloth.

   Serve in place of plain rice, or as a side dish.

Festive Porridge (*Azuki* Bean Rice Porridge)
Serves 4

   2 cups brown rice, washed
   ½ cup *azuki* beans
   12 cups water
   2 pinches sea salt

1) Dry-roast rice in a pressure cooker until deep brown. Stir constantly to prevent scorching.
2) Add the beans, 6 cups water and salt.
3) Bring rapidly to pressure over a high flame. Then reduce flame to low and simmer 40–45 minutes.
4) Remove from heat and allow pressure

to return to normal.

5) Remove lid and add 6 cups boiling water to the pressure cooker. Then recover with a lid from a regular pot or skillet.

6) Cook over a very low flame for 20 minutes more.

7) Season with salt to taste before serving.

If your pressure cooker is large enough to hold 12 cups of water safely, combine all ingredients in the pressure cooker and cook 40–45 minutes.

Brown Rice Porridge   *Serves 4*

1 cup brown rice, washed
4 cups water
pinch of sea salt

1) Combine ingredients in a pressure cooker, cover, and bring to full pressure over a high flame.

2) Reduce flame to low and simmer 40–45 minutes.

3) Remove from heat and allow pressure to return to normal.

4) After the pot has cooled, remove the lid. If you open the pressure cooker too soon, the contents may boil over.

5) After uncovering, stir the thin layer of water resting on the surface, back into the rice.

6) Serve hot.

Brown Rice Porridge   *Serves 5 or 6*
with Corn

2 cups brown rice, washed
¼ cup fresh corn kernels
12 cups water
2 pinches sea salt

1) Combine all ingredients in a pressure cooker and bring to full pressure over a high flame.

2) Reduce flame to low, and simmer 40–45 minutes.

3) Remove from heat and allow pressure to return to normal.

4) When pot has cooled, carefully uncover and stir gently.

5) Reheat, if necessary, to serve.

Golden Porridge   *Serves 5 or 6*

2 cups brown rice, washed
1½ medium Hokkaido pumpkin or acorn squash, cut into ½-in cubes
12 cups water
¼ tsp sea salt

1) Combine all ingredients in a heavy saucepan and bring to a boil over a high flame.

2) Reduce flame to low and cover with a tight-fitting lid.

3) Simmer 4 hours, stirring occasionally.

If rice is still not tender after all water has been absorbed or evaporated, add more water and simmer longer.

■ *To prepare porridge more quickly:*

1) Simmer under pressure for 1½ hours.

2) Remove from heat and allow pressure to return to normal. Be sure pot is cool before carefully uncovering.

3) Stir gently before serving.

This porridge is a wonderful remedy for fatigue.

Brown Rice Porridge with   *Serves 5*
Vegetables and *Miso*

2 cups brown rice, washed
2 pinches sea salt
10 cups water
1 Tbsp sesame oil
2 medium scallions, cut into ¼-in rounds
5 medium taro potatoes, diced into ½-in cubes
2 cups carrots, cut into ¼-in cubes
2 Tbsp *miso*

1) Combine rice, salt and water in a pressure cooker and bring to full pressure over a high flame.

2)   Reduce flame to low and simmer 40–45 minutes.

3)   Remove from heat and allow pressure to return to normal and the pot to cool.

■ *Begin preparing vegetables after removing rice from heat:*

1)   Heat a heavy skillet and coat with the oil.

2)   When oil is hot, sauté scallion over a medium flame, stirring gently, until the strong aroma is no longer released.

3)   Add taro potatoes and carrots and sauté 2–3 minutes.

4)   Dilute 2 tablespoons *miso* in 1 cup water.

5)   Pour *miso* mixture over the vegetables, cover, and cook about 5 minutes.

■ *Carefully uncover the porridge and:*

1)   Blend in the vegetable-*miso* sauce.

2)   Recover and simmer 2–3 minutes.

3)   Serve individual portions topped with minced watercress and crumbled toasted *nori*, or sprinkle with *gomashio*.

This porridge will keep you warm on the coldest days.

Fried Rice with Carrots and Sesame Seeds   *Serves 5*

4 cups cooked brown rice
2 Tbsp sesame oil
1 heaping Tbsp sesame seeds
1 small carrot, slivered
pinch of sea salt
1–2 Tbsp minced parsley

1)   Heat a heavy skillet and coat with 1 tablespoon oil.

2)   When oil is hot, roast the sesame seeds over a medium-high flame for several minutes. Stir constantly and occasionally shake the pan to heat evenly.

3)   When seeds turn light brown and fragrant, add the carrots and sauté well.

4)   Add the salt and 1 tablespoon water

and cover pan immediately.

5)   Let the water cook away over a medium-low flame. Then set aside.

6)   Heat another skillet and coat with 1 tablespoon oil.

7)   When oil is hot, add the rice and sauté over a medium flame until all the grains are separated and well coated with oil.

8)   Mix in the carrot-sesame mixture and sauté until it is evenly distributed throughout the rice.

9)   Serve garnished with minced parsley.

This is a good dish for people who are sick or for those with weak digestion.

Brown Rice and Onion Fritters   *Serves 5*

3 cups cooked brown rice
$\frac{1}{2}$ tsp sesame oil
1 cup minced onions
pinch of sea salt
oil for deep-frying
$\frac{1}{2}$ cup whole-wheat pastry flour
$\frac{1}{3}$ cup water, approximately

1)   Heat a heavy skillet, then coat with the oil.

2)   When oil is hot, sauté onions until translucent.

3)   Combine rice, onion and salt in a large bowl, and mix thoroughly.

4)   With moistened hands, form each cup of the mixture into 2 ovals or balls.

5)   To assure thorough cooking, flatten each oval so that it is no more than $\frac{2}{3}$ inch thick.

6)   Fill a heavy skillet or deep-fryer with 3 inches oil, and heat to 360°F.

7)   While oil is heating, combine flour and water to form a thin batter.

8)   Dip ovals into batter, coating them completely. Then drop into hot oil and deep-fry until crisp and golden.

9)   Drain on a wire rack or absorbent paper before serving.

Chinese Fried Rice (*Chao Fan*) *Serves 5*

4 cups cooked brown rice
1 tsp sesame oil
⅓ cup minced onion
¼ cup minced carrot
⅓ cup snow peas
sea salt

1) Heat a heavy skillet and coat with the oil.
2) When oil is hot, sauté onion over a medium flame for 2–3 minutes, or until translucent. Stir gently and constantly.
3) Add carrots and snow peas, in that order, and sauté together 1–2 minutes.
4) Season with salt, and add 2–3 tablespoons water to almost cover the carrots and peas.
5) Cover immediately and simmer over a medium-low flame until the liquid has completely evaporated.
6) Add rice. Break up any lumps by slicing the rice in a checkerboard pattern with a rice paddle or wooden spoon.
7) Cook until ingredients are mixed thoroughly and the rice is heated all the way through.

Brown Rice Croquettes *Makes 15*

5 cups cooked brown rice
1 tsp sesame oil
1 cup onion, minced
1 cup carrot, minced
pinch of sea salt
1 cup whole-wheat pastry flour
2 cups bread crumbs
oil for deep-frying
Batter:
1½ cups whole-wheat pastry flour
¾ cups water
pinch of sea salt

1) Heat a heavy skillet, then coat with the oil.
2) When oil is hot, sauté onions until translucent.
3) Add carrots and salt, and sauté

another 2–3 minutes. Then set aside.
4) Place rice in a large bowl, and separate the grains with a lightly moistened rice paddle.
5) Fold the onions and carrots into the rice.
6) Add about 1 cup flour, or just enough to hold the mixture together.
7) Form each cup of the mixture into 3 oval croquettes, then set aside.
8) Make a batter by combining the ingredients listed above, and mix well.
9) Place the bread crumbs in a separate bowl.
10) Dip each croquette into the batter first, then cover with bread crumbs.
11) Fill a heavy skillet or deep-fryer with 3 inches oil, and heat to 350°F.
12) Drop the croquettes into the hot oil and deep-fry 3–5 minutes, or until crisp and golden and cooked through.
13) Drain on a wire rack or absorbent paper before serving.

Brown Rice Pie *Serves 4*

3 cups cooked brown rice
3 cups whole-wheat flour
¼ tsp and 2 pinches sea salt
8 Tbsp sesame oil
1½ cups water
1 Tbsp sesame seeds

■ *The pie crust:*
1) Combine the flour and ¼ teaspoon salt in a large bowl. Mix thoroughly.
2) Add 7 tablespoons oil, rubbing the mixture through your palms to blend evenly.
3) Gradually add enough water to form a dough, and knead lightly for 8–10 minutes.
4) Separate dough into 2 portions, one slightly larger than the other.
5) On a floured board, roll the larger piece into a circle slightly larger than an 8-inch pie pan.

6) Lightly oil the pan and gently fit the pastry into it.

7) Roll out the rest of the pastry, and cut into narrow strips to make a lattice top.

■ *The pie filling:*

1) Roast the sesame seeds in a heavy skillet over a moderately high flame. Stir constantly until light brown and fragrant.

2) Remove from heat and chop fine with a heavy knife.

3) Put the chopped seeds into a small bowl and add 2 pinches salt. Mix well.

4) Heat another skillet and coat with 1 tablespoon oil.

5) Add the rice and sauté 3 minutes, stirring to coat the grains evenly with oil.

6) Turn off heat and sprinkle rice with sesame seed-salt mixture. Stir to blend evenly.

■ *Baking the pie:*

1) Preheat oven to 350°F.

2) Fill pie shell with rice.

3) Arrange pastry strips on top to form a lattice.

4) Pinch the edges of the lattice to seal it to the lower pastry.

5) Brush pastry lightly with oil and bake pie 30 minutes, or until nicely browned.

6) Remove pie from pan and allow to cool slightly before serving.

Sweet Rice with *Azuki* Beans   *Serves 4*

    3 cups sweet brown rice, washed
    ¼ cup *azuki* beans, washed
    3 cups water
    3 pinches sea salt

1) Place *azuki* beans and 3 parts water in a saucepan. Simmer for 10 minutes.

2) Combine rice, cooked beans and the salt in a pressure cooker. Add any water left over from cooking the beans, plus 3 cups freshwater.

3) Cover and bring to pressure over a high flame. Then reduce flame to low and simmer 40–45 minutes.

4) Remove from heat and allow pressure to come down naturally.

Mochi   *Makes 2 pounds*
(Sweet Rice Cakes)

    6 cups sweet brown rice, washed
    5½ cups water
    pinch of sea salt per cup of rice

1) Combine ingredients in a pressure cooker and bring to full pressure over a high flame.

2) Reduce flame to low and simmer 45–50 minutes.

3) Remove from heat and allow pressure to return to normal.

4) Place rice in a large wooden bowl.

5) Using a large wooden pestle (*surikogi*) pound the rice vigorously until the outer skin breaks and a paste forms.

Occasionally sprinkle the rice with a few drops of cold water and wet the pestle to prevent sticking. From time to time, grind the rice in a heavy circular motion.

6) When individual grains can no longer be distinguished, the dough is ready.

7) With moistened hands, form each cup of sweet rice dough into 2 cakes $3 \times 2 \times \frac{1}{4}$ inch thick. Or form each cup of dough into 4 balls.

If dough is too moist, add just enough sweet brown rice flour to hold it together.

8) Serve fresh or pan-toasted, seasoned with soy sauce to taste. Or add to soups about 5 minutes before the soups are done.

9) Refrigerate to store.

A festive food, *mochi* fits in perfectly at parties and get-togethers. It also makes a quick lunch as well.

Mochi with Roasted Soy Bean
Flour (*Abekawa*)

Sweet Rice Cakes with Topping (*Ohagi*)

Follow the recipe for making *mochi* (p. 45), but pound the rice only until approximately half has been turned to paste. Then:
1) Using a moistened paddle, mix whole grains and paste together.
2) With moistened hands, form each cup of the sweet rice dough into 4 balls.
3) Roll the balls in a mixture of soy bean flour and salt, toasted sesame seeds or *azuki* bean paste. They are also delicious covered with pumpkin or squash purée.

For parties, serve some of each kind, arranged attractively on a large platter.

Mochi with Roasted Soy Bean Flour (*Abekawa*)   Serves 5

10 pieces *mochi*, $3 \times 2 \times \frac{1}{4}$ in
3 Tbsp roasted soybean flour
pinch of sea salt

1) Place *mochi* in a dry skillet, cover, and roast over a low flame.
2) When the bottom begins to brown, turn *mochi* over and roast until it softens and begins to puff up.

3) Combine the flour and salt, mixing thoroughly.
4) Dip the toasted *mochi* into hot water, then roll in the flour to coat thoroughly.
5) Serve 2 per person.

Daikon Mochi   Serves 4

8 pieces *mochi*, $3 \times 2 \times \frac{1}{4}$ in
5 Tbsp *daikon* radish, finely grated
2½ Tbsp soy sauce

1) Bake the *mochi* in an oven; or place in a dry skillet, cover, and roast over a low flame until the pieces soften and begin to puff up. Turn the *mochi* once to prevent burning.
2) Serve the *mochi* dipped in grated *daikon* that has been covered with soy sauce to taste.

Walnut *Mochi*   Serves 4

8 pieces *mochi*, $3 \times 2 \times \frac{1}{4}$ in
10 walnuts, shelled
2–3 Tbsp water
soy sauce to taste

1) Roast the walnuts in a heavy skillet over a medium flame. Stir constantly until

lightly toasted and fragrant.

2)   Place roasted walnuts in a *suribachi* and grind to a paste. Then add water and soy sauce to make a cream.

3)   Bake the *mochi* in an oven; or place in a dry skillet, cover, and roast over a low flame until the pieces soften and begin to puff up. Turn the *mochi* once to prevent burning.

4)   Cover each piece of *mochi* with the walnut cream, and serve.

Walnut *Mochi*

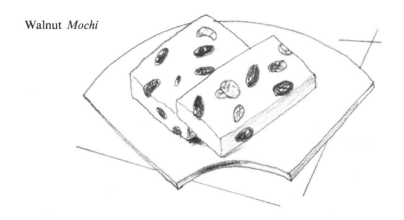

Black Sesame *Mochi*   *Serves 5*

8 pieces *mochi*, 3 × 2 × ¼ in
3 Tbsp black sesame seeds, washed
2 Tbsp water
2 Tsp soy sauce
1 sheet *nori*

1)   Roast the sesame seeds in a heavy skillet over a moderately high flame for several minutes, or until lightly toasted and fragrant. Stir constantly to prevent burning.

2)   Place the seeds in a *suribachi* and grind lightly so as to break the seeds but not express their oil.

3)   Add water and soy sauce to taste, and blend into a thin paste.

4)   Toast 1 side of the *nori* by waving it over a low flame for several seconds, until crisp.

5)   Using scissors, cut the sheet into halves, place the halves together, and cut crosswise into 3 strips.

6)   Bake the *mochi* in an oven; or place in a dry skillet, cover, and roast over a low flame until the pieces soften and begin to puff up. Turn the *mochi* once to prevent burning.

7)   Cover the *mochi* with the sesame seed-soy sauce mixture.

8)   Wrap 1 strip of *nori* around the center of each piece of *mochi*, and serve 2 pieces per person.

Quick *Mochi* Soup (*Zoni*)   *Serves 4*

8 pieces *mochi*, 3 × 2 × ¼ in
4 cups *kombu dashi* (p. 113)
soy sauce to taste
2 Tbsp *chirimen iriko*
1 medium scallion, sliced into thin rounds
nori as garnish

1)   Place *mochi* in a dry skillet, cover, and roast until they soften and begin to puff up. Turn the *mochi* once to prevent burning.

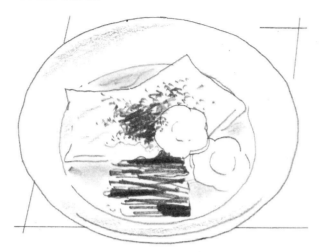

Quick *Mochi* Soup (*Zoni*)

2) Bring the *dashi* to a boil and season with soy sauce. Return just to a boil and turn off heat.

3) Place 2 toasted rice cakes in each of 5 serving bowls. Divide the *chirimen* among the bowls and pour in the hot broth.

4) Serve topped with scallion rounds and crumbled *nori*.

Sea Vegetable *Mochi*   *Serves 4*

8 pieces *mochi*, $3 \times 2 \times \frac{1}{4}$ in
soy sauce
2 sheets *nori*

1) Place *mochi* in a dry skillet, cover, and roast over a low flame until they soften and begin to puff up. Turn *mochi* once to prevent burning. Then brush both sides lightly with soy sauce.

2) Toast 1 side of each *nori* sheet by wav-ing it over a low flame for several seconds, until crisp.

3) Using scissors, cut the sheets in half, place the halves together, and cut crosswise into 3 strips.

4) Wrap 1 strip of *nori* around the center of each toasted *mochi* cake, and serve.

Toasted *mochi* makes an excellent addition to box lunches on outings. Retoasted over a picnic fire, it tastes fresh and delicious.

Variation

Blend 3 tablespoons sesame butter (*tahini*), 2 tablespoons water and 1 teaspoon soy sauce to a paste. Spread over the toasted *mochi* before wrapping in the toasted *nori* strips.

Sea Vegetable *Mochi*

Other Grains

Barley
Serves 5

1 cup barley, washed
3 cups water
pinch of sea salt

1) Combine all ingredients in a heavy saucepan, and bring to a boil over a high flame.
2) Reduce flame to low, and cover with a tight-fitting lid.
3) Simmer 30–40 minutes.
4) Remove from heat and place in a wooden bowl.
5) Toss gently, and cover with a damp cotton cloth until ready to serve.

Variations
A. Dry-roast barley in a saucepan over a medium flame, stirring constantly, until deep brown. Combine with remaining ingredients and proceed as above.
B. *Barley Porridge:*
Combine 1 cup barley, 4–5 cups water and a pinch of sea salt in a heavy saucepan, and simmer 1½ hours. Stir gently before serving.

Buckwheat Groats (Kasha)
Serves 5

2 cups buckwheat groats
1 Tbsp sesame oil
3 cups boiling water
pinch of sea salt

1) Heat a heavy saucepan or deep skillet and coat with the oil.
2) When oil is hot, sauté the groats over a medium flame for 5 minutes if they are preroasted, or for 10 minutes if not. Stir constantly to heat evenly.
3) Add boiling water and a pinch of salt.
4) Cover, reduce flame to low, and simmer 15–20 minutes.
5) Turn off heat and toss lightly with a wooden fork. Then let stand for several minutes more.
6) Serve with *gomashio* and lightly boiled greens.

Variation
To make buckwheat porridge:
1) Combine 1 cup sautéed buckwheat groats with 3 cups boiling water and a pinch of salt.
2) Simmer in a covered pan for 20 minutes.
3) Mix gently before serving.

Buckwheat Dumplings (*Soba Gaki*)
Serves 5

1 cup buckwheat flour
1½ cups boiling water
soy sauce

1) Pour the boiling water into the flour while stirring vigorously with 4 long wooden chopsticks to reduce sticking.
2) When the mixture is thick, shape into 10 small balls about 1 inch in diameter.
3) Serve as a side dish, seasoned with soy sauce to taste.

Variation
To prepare a clear soup:
1) Bring 4 cups of *kombu dashi* (p. 113) to a boil and season with 2 tablespoons soy sauce.
2) Place 2 dumplings in each of 5 serving bowls, and pour in the soup.
3) Serve garnished with chopped scallion rounds and bits of toasted *nori*.

Kasha Croquettes   *Makes 6–8 Croquettes*

3 cups buckwheat groats, cooked
3 small *shiitake* mushrooms, or 6 fresh mushrooms
5 green beans, rinsed and trimmed
4 pinches sea salt
1 Tbsp sesame oil
1 medium onion, minced
$\frac{1}{2}$ cup whole-wheat pastry flour
oil for deep-frying
$\frac{1}{2}$ cup water, approximately
2 cups bread crumbs or corn meal

1)   Soak the *shiitake* in cold water for 20–30 minutes. Then remove the hard stems and slice the caps fine. If using fresh mushrooms, rinse them in lightly salted water, then slice fine.
2)   Bring a small pan of water (just enough to cover the green beans) to a boil and add a pinch of salt.
3)   Drop in the beans, return to a boil, and cook 3–5 minutes, or until beans are bright green and tender, but still crisp.
4)   Drain beans in a colander and allow to cool. Then slice fine on a diagonal.
5)   Heat a heavy skillet over a low flame and add 1 tablespoon oil.
6)   When oil is hot, add minced onions and sauté until translucent.
7)   Add *shiitake* and green beans and sauté 1 minute more.
8)   Add 2 pinches salt, mix and turn off flame.
9)   Place kasha in a bowl, then add the vegetables and enough flour to hold the mixture together.
10)   Form the mixture into 8 croquettes and set aside.
■ *Deep-frying:*
1)   Fill a heavy skillet or deep-fryer with 3 inches oil, and heat to 350°F.
2)   Combine remaining flour with enough water to form a thin batter. Then add a pinch of salt.
3)   Dip croquettes into the batter, then roll in the bread crumbs, coating thoroughly.
4)   Drop immediately into the hot oil and deep-fry 3–5 minutes, or until cooked through, crisp and golden.
5)   Drain on a wire rack or absorbent paper before serving.

Sacks of Gold   *Serves 6*
(Stuffed *Agé* Sacks)

2 cups buckwheat groats, cooked
6 pieces *agé*
12 strips (2-in long) *kampyo*
1 Tbsp sesame oil
$\frac{1}{3}$ cup onion, minced
$\frac{1}{3}$ cup lotus root, minced
pinch of sea salt
5 cups *kombu dashi* (p. 113)
soy sauce
6 thin strips lemon peel

1)   Pour boiling water over the *agé* to remove excess oil.
2)   Drain, cut pieces in half, and pull open the center of each piece to make a pouch. Then set aside.
3)   Rinse the gourd strips in lightly salted water, squeeze them dry, and set aside.
4)   Heat a heavy skillet and coat with the oil.

Sacks of Gold
(Stuffed *Agé* Sacks)

5) When oil is hot, sauté the onion over a medium flame, stirring constantly, until translucent.

6) Add the lotus root and sauté together for 1 minute.

7) Season with a pinch of salt, and stir in the kasha. Mix thoroughly.

8) Add enough water to just cover, and put on a lid.

9) Simmer until all the water is gone.

10) Half fill each *agé* sack with the kasha and vegetable mixture.

11) Draw the pouch edges together and tie with a gourd strip to form a sack.

12) Bring the *kombu dashi* to a boil and season with soy sauce.

13) Place the pouches carefully into the *dashi* and simmer 20 minutes.

14) Remove pouches and place 2 in each of 6 serving bowls.

15) Place a strip of lemon in each bowl, then gently pour in the stock. Serve immediately.

Buckwheat Cream   *Serves 2*

$\frac{1}{2}$ cup buckwheat flour
1 tsp sesame oil
2 cups water
pinch of sea salt
1 Tbsp scallion, chopped finely into rounds

1) Heat a heavy skillet and coat with the oil.

2) When oil is hot, sauté the flour over a medium flame for 1–2 minutes, until fragrant. Stir constantly.

3) Remove from heat and allow to cool.

4) Return pan to stove and gradually stir in the water while bringing to a boil.

5) Stir constantly as the cream thickens, and simmer 10 minutes.

6) Season with salt and serve topped with scallion rounds.

Variation

For added sweetness, stir $\frac{1}{4}$ cup sautéed onion into the cream while it simmers.

Bulgur (Steamed Wheat)   *Serves 5*

2 cups bulgur
2 Tbsp sesame oil
4 cups boiling water
2 pinches sea salt

1) Heat a heavy saucepan and coat with the oil.

2) When oil is hot, sauté the bulgur over a medium flame, stirring constantly, for 3–5 minutes.

3) Stir in boiling water, season with the salt, and cover with a tight-fitting lid.

4) Turn flame to low, and simmer 15 minutes.

5) Remove from heat, toss lightly with 2 wooden forks, and let stand for several minutes.

Delicious served with a *kuzu* sauce of carrot and onion, seasoned with a dash of curry powder.

Quick and easy to make, this delicious dish is perfect for those hungry but unexpected guests.

Bulgur with Vegetables   *Serves 5*

2 cups bulgur, washed
2 cups water
3 pinches sea salt
pinch of thyme (optional)
1 tsp sesame oil
1 small onion, cut into thin half-moons
$\frac{1}{2}$ small carrot, finely cubed
$\frac{1}{2}$ medium red turnip, finely cubed
2 Tbsp parsley, chopped

1) Put bulgur in a heavy saucepan. Add water, a pinch of salt and thyme if using.

2) Bring to a boil over a medium flame. Then reduce flame to low and cook 20 minutes.

3)   Remove from heat and let sit 1–2 minutes.

■ *While bulgur is simmering:*

1)   Heat a skillet and coat with the oil.

2)   When oil is hot, sauté the onion over a medium flame, stirring lightly, until its strong aroma is gone.

3)   Add the carrot and sauté together 1–2 minutes.

4)   Add water to cover and a pinch of salt. Then cover pan and reduce flame.

5)   Simmer 20 minutes, or until vegetables are tender and cooking water has evaporated. If any liquid remains when vegetables are done, uncover and simmer until dry.

6)   Bring a small pan of water to a boil and add a pinch of salt.

7)   Drop in the turnip cubes, return to a boil, and cook 10 minutes, or until tender.

8)   Drain turnip cubes in a colander.

■ *When bulgur is ready:*

1)   Uncover and toss lightly with a fork.

2)   Blend in sautéed vegetables and turnip.

3)   Serve sprinkled with chopped parsley.

Bulgur Croquettes
Makes 10–12 Croquettes

   3 cups cooked bulgur
   ½ tsp sesame oil
   ¼ cup onion, minced
   ½ cup carrot, minced
   2 pinches sea salt
   ½ cup whole-wheat flour
   oil for deep-frying
   1 cup whole-wheat pastry flour
   ⅔ cup water, approximately
   2 cups bread crumbs or corn meal

1)   Heat the oil and sauté onions and carrots until translucent and tender.

2)   Combine bulgur, onion and carrot, mixing thoroughly.

3)   Add a pinch of salt and enough whole-wheat flour (if necessary) to hold mixture together.

4)   Form each cupful of the mixture into 3–4 croquettes and set aside.

■ *Deep-frying:*

1)   Fill a heavy skillet or deep-fryer with 3 inches oil and heat to 350°F.

2)   Combine pastry flour with enough water to form a thin batter. Add a pinch of salt.

3)   Dip croquettes into the batter, then roll in the bread crumbs, coating thoroughly.

4)   Drop immediately into the hot oil and deep-fry 3–5 minutes, or until cooked through, crisp and golden.

5)   Drain on a wire rack or absorbent paper before serving.

Bulgur Gratin
Serves 2–3

   1 cup bulgur, washed
   2 Tbsp sesame oil
   2 cups boiling water
   4 pinches sea salt
   10 green beans, washed and trimmed
   1 medium onion, minced
Mock Béchamel Sauce:
   1 Tbsp sesame oil
   ½ cup white pastry flour
   1 cup water
   pinch of sea salt

■ *The bulgur:*

1)   Heat a heavy saucepan, then coat with 1 tablespoon oil.

2)   When oil is hot, sauté the bulgur over a medium flame, stirring constantly, for 3–4 minutes.

3)   Stir in the boiling water, and season with 2 pinches salt.

4)   Bring to a boil over a high flame, then reduce flame to low.

5)   Cover and simmer 20 minutes, then turn off heat.

■ *The vegetebles:*

1)   Bring a small pan of water (just enough to cover the beans) to a boil over a high flame. Then add a pinch of salt.

2) Drop in the beans, return to a boil, and cook 5 minutes, or until beans are bright green and just tender.

3) Scoop out the beans with a slotted spoon, and drain in a colander.

4) When cool, slice thin on a diagonal, then set aside.

5) Heat a heavy skillet and coat with 1 tablespoon oil.

6) When oil is hot, sauté the onion over a medium flame, stirring gently, for 4–5 minutes, or until translucent.

7) Add the cooked green beans and sauté 1 minute more.

8) Sprinkle with a pinch of salt and turn off heat.

9) Fold the vegetables into the bulgur and mix well.

■ *Mock Béchamel sauce:*

1) Heat a heavy skillet over a low flame and coat with 1 tablespoon oil.

2) When oil is hot, add the flour and cook about 30 seconds, stirring constantly.

3) Remove from heat, cool, then return to stove.

4) Add ¼ cup cold water and stir until smooth.

5) Bring to a boil over a medium flame, adding enough water to make a creamy consistency.

6) Reduce flame and simmer 5 minutes, stirring constantly.

7) When done, season with a pinch of salt, or to taste.

■ *The gratin:*

1) Preheat oven to 350°F.

2) Place the bulgur-vegetable mixture into a lightly oiled gratin dish.

3) Pour Béchamel sauce on top and then lightly brush with oil.

4) Bake 20 minutes, or until nicely browned.

Corn on the Cob   *Serves 5*

5 medium ears of fresh corn, husks and silks removed
water
pinch of sea salt

1) Cover the bottom of a pot with 2–3 inches water and bring to a boil.

2) Add the corn, return to a boil, and season with a pinch of salt.

3) Cover and simmer 10 minutes, or until tender.

4) Turn off heat and allow to stand several minutes before serving.

Save the cooking water to use in soups.

Variations

■ *To pressure cook:*

1) Pour a little less than 1-inch water in the bottom of the pot.

2) Add a pinch of salt and the ears of corn, then cover.

3) Bring rapidly to full pressure, then reduce flame to low.

4) Simmer 3 minutes, turn off heat, and allow pressure to return to normal.

■ *To bake:*

1) Preheat oven to 450°F.

2) Replace corn in husks after removing silk, or wrap in aluminum foil.

3) Bake 10–15 minutes.

Morning Cereal   *Serves 4*

1 cup cornmeal
1 tsp corn oil (optional)
4 cups boiling water
pinch of sea salt

If not using oil proceed to step 2 and dry-roast instead of sautéing.

1) Heat a heavy skillet, then coat with 1 teaspoon oil.

2) When oil is hot, sauté the cornmeal over a medium flame for 5 minutes, or

until golden and fragrant. Stir constantly
to heat evenly.
3)   Bring 4 cups water to a boil, and add
cornmeal.
4)   Season with the salt, and cover with
a tight-fitting lid.
5)   Reduce flame to low, and simmer
25–30 minutes.
6)   Remove from heat, stir gently, and
allow to stand about 5 minutes before
serving.

Cornmeal Mold
Serves 6–8

2 cups cornmeal
1 tsp corn oil
8 cups *kombu dashi* (p. 113)
$\frac{1}{4}$ tsp sea salt

1)   Heat a heavy saucepan and coat with
the oil.
2)   When oil is hot, stir in the cornmeal,
and sauté 5 minutes, or until golden and
fragrant. Stir constantly to heat evenly.
3)   Remove from heat and allow to cool.
4)   Return to stove and gradually add
kombu dashi, stirring until smooth.
5)   Bring to a boil over moderately high
flame, season with the salt, and cover with a
tight-fitting lid.
6)   Reduce flame to low, and simmer
40–60 minutes, stirring occasionally.
     If the mixture thickens early stir in more
dashi or water.
7)   Pour mixture into a rinsed mold and
allow to cool and harden.
8)   When firm, tap out carefully and cut
into slices.
     Delicious when served with sesame butter.
I discovered this simple delicacy in the
Italian countryside.

Country-Style Cornmeal
Serves 5–7

2 cups cornmeal

5 cups *kombu dashi* (p. 113)
$\frac{1}{4}$ tsp sea salt
2 Tbsp soy sauce
1 medium scallion, sliced into thin rounds

1)   Dry-roast cornmeal in a heavy saucepan,
stirring constantly, for 5–10 minutes.
2)   Allow to cool, then gradually pour in
the *dashi*, stirring until smooth.
3)   Stir and bring to a boil over a moderately high flame.
4)   Season with the salt and soy sauce, and
cover with a tight-fitting lid.
5)   Reduce flame to low, and simmer 40–
45 minutes, stirring occasionally. If the
cornmeal thickens early stir in a little water.
6)   After 40 minutes the cornmeal should
be thick enough to spoon out.
7)   Turn off heat and serve as a side dish,
topped with scallion rounds.

Couscous with Chick-Peas
Serves 5

2 cups couscous
1 cup dried chick-peas, soaked overnight
6 cups water
$\frac{1}{4}$ tsp and 4 pinches sea salt
4 Tbsp olive oil
2 small onions, cut into thick half-moons
1 small carrot, cut into $\frac{1}{2}$-in cubes
2-in square of *kombu*, wiped clean with a dry
     cloth
2 bay leaves (optional)
8 medium Brussels sprouts
$\frac{1}{2}$ small cauliflower, separated into flowerets
parsley sprigs

■ *The chick-peas:*
1)   Combine chick-peas and 3 cups water
in a pressure cooker and bring rapidly to
full pressure over a high flame.
2)   Reduce flame to low, and simmer
60 minutes.
3)   Remove from heat and allow pressure
to return to normal.
■ *The couscous:*
1)   Bring remaining 3 cups water to a boil
in a heavy saucepan, add a pinch of salt,

Couscous with Chick-Peas

then gradually stir in the couscous.

2) Simmer 4–5 minutes, cover, then turn off heat.

3) Allow pan to remain on stove for 10 minutes, gently steaming.

4) Uncover, toss grains lightly with 2 wooden forks, and set aside.

■ *To cook couscous with a pressure cooker:*

1) Combine equal parts couscous and water in a pressure cooker and add a pinch of salt.

2) Bring rapidly to full pressure, and then reduce flame to low.

3) Simmer 5 minutes, remove from heat, and allow pressure to return to normal.

4) Toss lightly, recover, and set aside.

■ *Next, heat a heavy skillet and:*

1) Coat with the oil. When oil is hot, sauté the onions over a medium flame until translucent.

2) Add the carrot cubes and cooked chick-peas, mix the ingredients together, and sauté 1–2 minutes more.

3) Place *kombu* on the bottom of the pan, add slightly more than enough water to cover, and bring to a boil.

4) Season with ¼ teaspoon sea salt, reduce flame to low, and, if using, drop in the bay leaves.

5) Cover pan and simmer about 30 minutes, or until vegetables and chick-peas are tender.

■ *Next:*

1) Bring a small pan of water to a boil over a high flame and add a pinch of salt.

2) Drop in the Brussels sprouts, return to a boil, and cook 3–5 minutes, or until the vegetable is bright green and just tender.

3) With a slotted spoon, remove Brussels sprouts and drain in a colander.

4) Bring another small pan of water to a boil, add a pinch of salt, and drop in the cauliflowerets.

5) Return to a boil, and cook 3 minutes, or until tender, but still crisp.

6) Remove flowerets, and drain in a colander.

■ *When the chick-peas and vegetables are ready:*

1) Mix in the Brussels sprouts and cauli-flowerets.

2) Season with salt to taste, bring just to a boil, then turn off heat.

To serve, spread the couscous on a large platter and cover with the vegetables and broth. Garnish with sprigs of parsley.

Grain Milk (*Kokoh*)   *Serves 4*

1 cup *kokoh**
1 tsp sesame oil
5 cups water
sea salt
3 tsp croutons
parsley sprigs

1)   Heat a heavy saucepan and coat with the oil.

2)   When oil is hot, sauté the *kokoh* over a medium flame until fragrant. Stir constantly to heat evenly.

3)   Remove pan from stove and allow to cool.

4)   Return pan to stove, and gradually stir in the water.

5)   Bring rapidly to a boil over a medium-high flame, stirring constantly.

6)   Cover with a tight-fitting lid, reduce flame to low, and simmer 30–40 minutes, stirring occasionally.

7)   Season with salt to taste, and serve topped with croutons and garnished with sprigs of parsley.

*Kokoh is a nutritious mixture of roasted and finely ground rice, sweet rice, oatmeal, soybeans and sesame seeds. It is available prepackaged at macrobiotic outlets and natural food shops. *Kokoh* can be served as a morning cereal or thick tea, and used as a base for desserts and in baking.

Millet   *Serves 5*

1 cup millet, washed
4 cups water
sea salt

1)   Heat a heavy saucepan and dry-roast the millet over a medium flame until lightly browned and fragrant. Stir constantly.

2)   Remove pan from stove and allow to cool, then gradually stir in water.

3)   Return pan to stove, season with salt to taste, and bring rapidly to a boil.

4)   Cover, reduce flame to low, and simmer 30 minutes.

5)   Stir gently and let stand 5 minutes before serving.

Millet is a very yang grain and is best served in winter.

Variation
For added sweetness, stir ¼ cup sautéed onion into the millet and simmer together.

Beignets de Millet   *Serves 4–5*

½ cup millet flour
½ cup whole-wheat flour
½ cup onion, minced
2 Tbsp and ½ tsp sesame oil
pinch of sea salt
½ cup water, approximately
oil for deep-frying

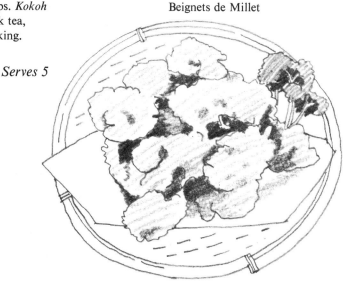

Beignets de Millet

parsley sprigs
4–5 Tbsp grated *daikon* radish
soy sauce

1) Sauté the minced onion in ½ teaspoon oil until soft and translucent. Then set aside.
2) Combine the two flours and the salt in a large bowl, mixing thoroughly.
3) Add 2 tablespoons oil and blend evenly by rubbing the mixture through your palms.
4) Mix in the onions and add enough water to form a thick batter.
5) Fill a heavy skillet or deep-fryer with 3 inches oil, and heat to 360°F.
6) Drop the batter into the hot oil by the tablespoon and deep-fry until crisp and light gold in color.
7) Drain on a wire rack or absorbent paper.
8) Garnish with parsley and serve 2–3 pieces per person. Accompany each serving with a tablespoon of finely grated *daikon* lightly seasoned with soy sauce for dipping.

This simple dish can provide great stamina and vitality. For people with a weak condition, it can be served twice a week.

Millet Burgers with *Kuzu* Sauce *Serves 5*

    3 cups cooked millet
    ½ tsp sesame oil
    ½ cup minced onion
    ½ carrot, minced
    pinch of sea salt
    ½ cup whole-wheat pastry flour
    ½ tsp sesame oil
    oil for frying
Kuzu Sauce:
    1 Tbsp *kuzu*
    ½ cup water
    1 cup *kombu dashi* (p. 113)

1) Heat the oil in a heavy skillet. Then sauté the onions and carrots until tender.
2) Add the vegetables to the cooked millet and mix thoroughly.
3) Add the salt and enough flour to hold

the mixture together.
4) Form the mixture into 10 burgers.
5) Cover the bottom of a heavy skillet with approximately ⅓-inch oil. When oil is hot, pan-fry the burgers over a medium flame. Do not cover pan.
■ *The kuzu sauce:*
1) Dissolve the *kuzu* in the water. Then combine with the *dashi* in a small saucepan.
2) Simmer 3–4 minutes, until thick. Stir constantly.
3) Serve over the burgers.

Oat Flakes *Serves 4*

    1 cup oat flakes (or flakes of millet, rye, wheat or rice)
    ½ Tbsp sesame oil
    1 small onion, minced
    3 cups boiling water
    2 pinches sea salt

1) Dry-roast the flakes in a heavy saucepan over a medium flame, for 5 minutes, or until lightly browned. Stir the flakes and shake the pan to heat evenly and to prevent scorching. If desired, use 1 tablespoon oil to sauté the flakes instead of dry-roasting.
2) Remove pan from stove and allow to cool.
3) Heat a heavy skillet and coat with the oil.
4) When oil is hot, sauté the onion, stirring gently, for 3–4 minutes.
5) Add the onion to flakes, pour in the boiling water, and season with the salt.
6) Bring to a boil over a moderately high flame, stirring constantly.
7) Cover with a tight-fitting lid, and reduce flame to low.
8) Simmer 30 minutes.
9) Serve with *gomashio*.

Whole-Wheat Cream

Serves 4

1 cup whole-wheat flour
1 Tbsp sesame oil
4 cups water
sea salt
Garnish:
deep-fried croutons, parsley or deep-fried *mochi*
    cut into small cubes

1) Heat a heavy saucepan, and coat with the oil.
2) When oil is hot, sauté the flour over a medium flame, stirring constantly, until fragrant and light brown. Stir constantly to avoid burning.
3) Remove from heat, and allow to cool.
4) Return pot to stove, and gradually stir in the water.
5) Season with salt, and bring to a boil over a medium-high flame.
6) Reduce flame to low, and simmer 30 minutes, stirring occasionally.
7) Garnish with one of the toppings listed above.

In this and many other recipes, use the liquid left over from boiling vegetables, in place of water.

Variation

1) Drop 5–6 kale leaves into a pan of boiling water.
2) Return to a boil and cook until tender.
3) Purée in a *suribachi*, then add to the cream during the last 10 minutes of cooking.

Noodles

Homemade Buckwheat Noodles (*Soba*)

Serves 4–5

4 cups buckwheat flour
½ tsp sea salt
1 small piece (5 in-long) *jinenjo*, peeled and grated
1–1½ cups water
1 scallion, sliced finely into rounds
1 sheet toasted *nori*, cut into thin slices
Dipping Sauce:
2 cups *kombu dashi* (p. 113)
2 Tbsp soy sauce
pinch of sea salt

■ *The dough:*
1) Combine buckwheat flour and salt in a large bowl, and mix well.
2) Add grated *jinenjo* and enough water to form a semidry dough.
3) Knead at least 20 minutes, until dough is stiff and smooth.

Homemade Buckwheat Noodles
(*Soba*)

Soba Gratin

4) On a floured board, roll dough out into a rectangular sheet 1/10 inch thick. Dust thoroughly.

5) Fold dough into quarters, and slice crosswise into thin strands.

■ *The noodles:*

1) Bring 2 quarts unsalted water to a rolling boil and drop in noodles.

2) Return to a boil over a high flame, and immediately add 1 cup cold water.

3) Repeating this procedure, return to a boil twice more, adding 1 cup cold water each time. (By adding cold water, the inner core of the noodle is cooked before the surface is overcooked.)

4) When noodles reach their third boil (after first addition of cold water), turn off heat and drain in a colander, reserving cooking water.

5) Rinse noodles immediately under running cold water, separating the strands and cooling thoroughly. Then set aside to drain. They can be patted dry with a clean cloth if desired.

   Use the liquid left over from cooking the noodles for baking or making sauces.

■ *Dipping sauce:*

1) Combine sauce ingredients listed above in a saucepan, and bring to a boil. Allow to cool before serving.

2) Serve noodles with the dipping sauce. Garnish with the scallion rounds and *nori* strips.

Soba Gratin   *Serves 5*

   1 package soba (buckwheat) noodles
   6 cups water
   3 pinches sea salt
   2 Tbsp sesame oil
   1 small onion, cut into crescents
   ½ small carrot, cut into quarter-rounds
   5 Tbsp *seitan* (p. 71)
   2 heaping Tbsp whole-wheat pastry flour
   parsley sprigs, finely chopped

■ *The noodles:*

1) Bring 4 cups water to a rolling boil and drop in noodles.

2) Return to a boil over a high flame and add 1 cup cold water.

3) Bring to a boil again, reduce flame to medium-low, and cook until done.

4) Turn off heat, and rinse under running cold water until thoroughly cooled.

5) Sprinkle a pinch of salt over the noodles, and set aside to drain.

■ *The gratin:*

1) Heat a heavy skillet and coat with 1

tablespoon oil.

2)   When oil is hot, sauté the onion crescents over a medium flame, stirring gently, until translucent.

3)   Add carrots and *seitan*, mix ingredients together, and sauté 2–3 minutes more.

4)   Sprinkle lightly with a pinch of salt, and turn off heat.

■ *Heat another skillet and:*

1)   Coat with 1 tablespoon oil.

2)   When oil is hot, add the flour and cook over medium flame for 3–4 minutes, or until flour is lightly browned, stirring constantly.

3)   Remove from heat and allow to cool, or dip the bottom of pan into cold water.

4)   Stir in remaining 1 cup water, and return pan to heat.

5)   Add a pinch of salt, and cook 1–2 minutes, or until edges of sauce bubble. Stir constantly.

■ *Baking:*

1)   Preheat oven to 425°F.

2)   Place noodles in a lightly oiled gratin dish, then cover with the vegetables.

3)   Pour in sauce to cover the *soba*, then brush the top with sesame oil.

4)   Bake 20 minutes, or until browned.

5)   Serve garnished with chopped parsley.

Cold *Soba* with Vegetables (*Mori Soba*)   Serves 4

1 package *soba* noodles*
2 pinches sea salt
20 green beans, rinsed and trimmed
1 small carrot, cut into thin diagonal slices
½ block *tofu* or *seitan* (p. 71),
      enough for 4 servings
3 medium scallions, cut into thin rounds
dipping sauce (pp. 58 and 59)

■ *The noodles:*

1)   Bring 2 quarts unsalted water to a rolling boil and drop in the noodles.

2)   Return to a boil over a high flame, and immediately add 1 cup cold water.

3)   Repeating this procedure, return to a boil twice more, adding 1 cup cold water each time.

4)   When noodles reach their third boil (after first adding cold water), turn off heat and drain noodles in a colander.

5)   Rinse noodles immediately under running cold water, separating the strands and cooling noodles thoroughly.

6)   Set noodles in a colander, and set aside to drain.

■ *The vegetables:*

1)   Bring a small pan of water to a boil over a high flame, and add a pinch of salt.

2)   Drop in the beans, return to a boil, and cook 3–4 minutes, or until beans are bright green and tender, but still crisp.

3)   Drain, then slice the beans crosswise into halves.

4)   Place beans in a colander and set aside.

■ *Bring another small pan of water to a boil and:*

1)   Add a pinch of salt, then drop in carrot slices.

2)   Return to a boil, and cook 2–3 minutes, or until tender.

3)   Drain in a colander.

■ *Serving:*

1)   Douse noodles with a kettle of hot water to reheat.

2)   Place individual portions of noodles in serving bowls, and top with vegetables and either *tofu* or *seitan*.

3)   Garnish with scallion slices and serve with dipping sauce.

■ *If using tofu:*

1)   Cut into ½-inch cubes, and drop into a pan of boiling water.

2)   Boil several minutes, then remove from water, drain and set aside.

■ *If using seitan:*

1)   Cut into thin strips or bite size cubes.

2) Using *kofu* (unflavored *seitan*), cook in *dashi* seasoned with soy sauce. For each cup of *dashi*, add 1 tablespoon soy sauce.
3) Use just enough *dashi* to cover and cook until all the liquid is absorbed.

*Prepackaged Japanese noodles are quite salty and need not be boiled in salt water.

Fried *Soba* (*Yaki Soba*)   Serves 4

    2 packages *soba* noodles, cooked (p. 60)
    oil for deep-frying
    4 portions *tofu* or *seitan* (p. 71)
    1 Tbsp sesame oil
    2 medium onions, cut into thin crescents
    1 small carrot, slivered
    pinch of sea salt
    2 Tbsp chopped parsley
Kuzu Sauce:
    2 Tbsp *kuzu*
    ¼ cup water
    soy sauce

■ *Deep-frying:*
1) Fill a heavy skillet or deep-fryer with 3 inches oil, and heat to 360°F.
2) Drop in the *tofu* or *seitan* and deep-fry until swollen and crisp.
3) Drain on absorbent paper.
4) Deep-fry the noodles by the handful, until golden and crisp.
5) Drain on absorbent paper, then set aside in a warm oven (120°F).
■ *The vegetables:*
1) Heat a heavy skillet and coat with the oil.
2) When oil is hot, sauté the onion over medium heat for 2–3 minutes, stirring gently.
3) Add the carrot and either *tofu* or *seitan*, and sauté mixture 3 minutes more.
4) Add a pinch of salt, and enough water to cover, then bring to a boil.
5) Cover pan, reduce flame to low, and simmer 10–15 minutes, or until vegetables are tender.
■ *Kuzu sauce:*
1) Dissolve the *kuzu* in ¼ cup water,

stirring until smooth.
2) Two or three minutes before turning off the heat under the simmering vegetables, stir in the *kuzu*, and season with soy sauce to taste.
3) Simmer several minutes more, stirring as the *kuzu* thickens.
4) Turn off heat.
■ *Serving:*
1) Place 1 serving of noodles in each of 4 dishes, then cover with the *kuzu* sauce.
2) Serve sprinkled with chopped parsley.

Tempura Soba   Serves 5

    2 packages *soba* noodles, cooked (p. 60)
    3–4 kale leaves
    pinch of sea salt
    oil for deep-frying
    1 small carrot, slivered
    ¾ cup lotus root, cut into quarter-rounds
    8 pieces scallion, sliced diagonally into 1-in
        lengths
Tempura Batter:
    1 cup whole-wheat pastry flour
    pinch of sea salt
    1–1¼ cups cold water
Tsuke-Jiru (Dipping Sauce):
    1 piece (2-in square) *kombu*
    5 cups water
    pinch of sea salt
    soy sauce

■ *The kale:*
1) Bring a small pan of water to a boil, then add a pinch of salt.
2) Drop in the kale, return to a boil, and cook 2–3 minutes, or until stems are tender.
3) When cool, squeeze the leaves between your palms, then chop fine.
■ *Deep-frying:*
1) Fill a heavy skillet or deep-fryer with 3 inches oil, and heat to 360°F.
2) Combine the flour, salt, and enough water to form a thick batter.
3) Mix carrot, lotus root and scallions into the batter.
4) Scoop out 1–2 tablespoons of batter

Tempura Soba

and place on a spatula. Batter should be thick enough to stick to the spatula's surface.

5) Shape the batter into a round patty and, using chopsticks, scrape it off the spatula into the hot oil.

6) Deep-fry until crisp and golden, then drain on a wire rack or absorbent paper.

■ *Dipping sauce:*

1) Place the *kombu* in a saucepan and cover with 5 cups water.

2) Bring to a boil, and add a pinch of salt and soy sauce to taste.

3) Return to a boil, then turn off heat.

■ *Serving:*

1) Reheat the noodles by dousing them with a kettle of hot water, or place them in a strainer and dip strainer into a pot of boiling water.

2) Divide the noodles among 5 serving bowls, and top each portion with 1–2 pieces of vegetable *tempura* and chopped kale.

3) Pour in hot broth, and garnish with scallions.

Summer *Soba* with *Daikon*   Serves 3

    1 package *soba* noodles, cooked (p. 60)
    2 pieces (1½-in long) *daikon* radish
    1 sheet *nori*
    grated *daikon* radish
    1 scallion, julienne cut
    2 cups *tsuke-jiru* (p. 135)

1) Pare each piece of *daikon* to half its thickness in a long continuous strip.

2) Cut the *daikon* sheets lengthwise into thin, noodle-length strips.

3) Soak the strips in cold water for 20 minutes.

■ *Serving:*

1) Toss noodles and *daikon* strips together, and divide the mixture among individual serving bowls.

2) Lightly toast 1 side of the *nori* by waving it over a low flame for several seconds, until just crisp.

3) Using scissors, cut the sheet into halves, put the halves together, and cut crosswise into thin strips.

4) Top each portion of noodles with the toasted *nori*, grated *daikon*, and chopped scallion.

5) Serve with *tsuke-jiru* dipping sauce.

Homemade *Udon*   Serves 5
(Wheat Noodles)

    2 cups whole-wheat pastry flour
    1 cup unbleached white flour
    ½ tsp sea salt
    ⅔ cup water, approximately
    4 cups *tsuke-jiru* (p. 135)

■ *The dough:*

1) Combine the 2 flours and the salt in a large bowl, and mix thoroughly.

2) Gradually add enough water to form a soft dough.

3) Knead at least 20 minutes, until dough is stiff and smooth.

4) On a floured board, roll out dough into a rectangular sheet 1/10 inch thick. Then dust thoroughly.

5) Fold dough in quarters, and slice crosswise into strands.

■ *Cooking the noodles:*

1) Bring 2 quarts unsalted water to a rolling boil, then drop in the noodle strips.

2) Return to a boil over a high flame, then reduce flame and cook 10 minutes, or until noodles are tender, but still slightly firm at the core.

3) Drain noodles in a colander, saving the cooking water.

4) Rinse noodles immediately under cold running water, separating the strands and cooling thoroughly.

5) Keeping the noodles in the colander, set aside to drain.

■ *Serving:*

1) Divide 4 cups *tsuku-jiru* dipping sauce among 5 bowls.

2) Top with scallion rounds, toasted *nori*, or grated *daikon* radish.

Variations

A. Daikon Udon:

1) Lightly toast 1 side of a sheet of *nori* by waving it over a low flame for several seconds, until just crisp.

2) Using scissors, cut the sheet in half, put the halves together, and cut crosswise into thin strips.

3) Grate 5 tablespoons of *daikon*, and cut 2 tablespoons of scallion rounds.

4) Divide the noodles among 5 serving

bowls, and add 1 tablespoon grated *daikon* to each bowl.

5) Divide 4 cups *tsuke-jiru* dipping sauce among the 5 bowls.

6) Top with scallion rounds and toasted *nori*.

B. Tempura Udon:

1) Place 1–2 pieces of vegetable *tempura* (p. 101) over individual servings of boiled *udon*.

2) Serve in bowls of *tsuke-jiru* broth, and garnish with grated *daikon* and scallion rounds.

C. Udon with Agé:

1) Douse 1 piece of *agé* with boiling water to remove excess oil. Drain.

2) Place 1 piece *kombu* in the bottom of a saucepan, and the *agé* on top.

3) Add just enough water to cover, bring to a boil, and season with soy sauce.

4) Cover, and cook until all the water is gone and the *agé* is well flavored.

5) Drain, then slice the *agé* lengthwise into thin strips.

6) Place cooked *udon* noodles into individual serving bowls, cover with *agé* strips then pour in a hot broth.

7) Serve garnished with grated *daikon* and chopped scallion rounds.

D. Curry Udon:

1) Prepare a *kuzu* sauce (p. 61) with your favorite vegetables and a pinch of curry powder.

2) While still hot, pour over individual servings of *udon*, and serve.

E. Table Top Udon:

1) Keep a large pot of water simmering over a gas or alcohol burner at the center of the table.

2) Serve a large platter of cooked *udon* noodles together with several small bowls of chopped scallions and toasted *nori* strips.

3) Provide each person with a bowl of

tsuke-jiru dipping sauce topped with toasted and finely chopped sesame seeds, and garnished with the scallion and *nori*.

4)   Each guest can heat bitefuls of noodles in the simmering pot, then dip the noodles in the sauce.

Steamed *Udon*   *Serves 4*

3 cups *udon* noodles, cooked (p. 63)
4 cups *kombu dashi* (p. 113)
pinch of sea salt
soy sauce to taste
2 eggs
4 small cubes (½-in) *seitan* (p. 71), deep-fried
10 pieces carrot, cut into flowers and lightly boiled

1 medium scallion, sliced diagonally into ½-in lengths

1)   Bring *kombu dashi* to a boil, add a pinch of salt and soy sauce to taste. Allow to cool.
2)   Beat eggs well an add to the *dashi*. Then set aside.
3)   Divide noodles among 5 custard cups, and attractively arrange the *seitan*, carrot slices and scallion pieces around the *udon*.
4)   Carefully pour in enough *dashi* to cover the ingredients.
5)   Cover the cups and steam over a high flame for 20 minutes.

Breads, Snacks and Other Good Things from Flour

Unleavened Bread (Ohsawa Loaf)   *Makes 1 Loaf*

This is a batter bread that requires no kneading.

3 cups whole-wheat flour
2 cups millet flour
1 cup brown rice flour
½ tsp sea salt
3 Tbsp sesame oil
3 cups water, approximately

1)   Preheat oven to 325°F.
2)   Combine the flours and salt in a large bowl, mixing thoroughly.
3)   Add the oil, and gently rub the mixture through your palms to blend evenly.
4)   Stir in the water, making sure that it is absorbed evenly.
5)   Lightly oil a 9×5×3-inch loaf pan and preheat.
6)   Turn batter into the pan, aerating it.
7)   With a moistened spatula, gently smooth the top of the batter and pull it away from the sides of the pan.

8)   Bake 1 hour, or until nicely browned, then remove bread from pan and cool on a rack before slicing.

Variations
A.   Add 1–2 cups leftover cooked grain, freshly sautéed vegetables or a purée of sweet potato, squash or apples to the batter.
B.   Add 1 teaspoon ground cinnamon to the batter and sprinkle top with sesame seeds.
C.   Add peanuts, almonds, cashews, raisins, currants, etc., to the batter.

Chapati   *Makes 15*

5 cups whole-wheat pastry flour
½ tsp sea salt
1¼ cup water
sesame oil
1 onion, cut into crescents
3 leaves cabbage, cut into fine diagonal slices
1 carrot, cut into fine diagonal slices
sea salt
curry powder

WHOLE GRAINS AND FLOUR • 65

■ *The dough:*

1) Combine flour and salt in a large bowl, mixing well.

2) Gradually stir in water to form a soft dough.

3) Knead 10–15 minutes, until smooth.

4) Divide dough into 15 parts. Then, on a floured board, roll out each part into a 3-inch round. These rounds should be as thin as possible.

■ *Cooking the chapati:*

1) Preheat both a heavy skillet and a metal grille over a medium-low flame.

2) Coat the skillet with oil and brown the *chapati* 1–2 minutes, or until the edges curl.

3) Turn over quickly, and brown again for 1 minute.

4) Remove *chapati* from pan, place on the metal grille, and cook until it puffs up.

5) Remove from grille and lightly brush one side with sesame oil.

6) Repeat with remaining ingredients until all are cooked.

■ *The topping:*

1) Heat a heavy skillet and coat with oil.

2) When oil is hot, sauté onions until translucent.

3) Add the cabbage and stir gently for a few minutes.

4) Add the carrots and sauté until tender. Then add salt and curry powder to taste.

5) Serve as a side dish with the *chapati*.

Variation

1) To make *puri* (a very light, fried wheat cake of India), knead dough 20–30 minutes.

2) Roll out on a floured board into a rectangular sheet 1/10 inch thick. Then cut dough into 2-inch rounds with a jar top or cookie cutter.

3) Pour 3 inches oil into a heavy skillet or deep-fryer and heat to 360°F.

4) Drop the *puri* into the hot oil and deep-fry, holding the *puri* under the surface with a pair of long chopsticks.

5) When puffed, turn *puri* over carefully (do not puncture the surface) and deep-fry again.

6) Drain on absorbent paper before serving.

Chick-Pea Muffins   *Makes 15*

   4 cups cooked chick-peas, mashed
   3 cups whole-wheat pastry flour
   2 tsp sea salt
   4½ cups water, approximately
   sesame oil

1) Combine the flour and salt, and stir in the water until well mixed.

2) Lightly oil muffin tins and half fill with batter.

3) Add a layer of mashed chick-peas, then add more batter until mold is four-fifths full.

4) Bake 40–50 minutes, or until muffins are puffed and nicely browned.

Variations

A. Substitute cornmeal or buckwheat flour for whole-wheat pastry flour.

B. Instead of chick-peas, use 1 cup squash, sweet potato or chestnut purée, or apple butter, raisins or nuts (whole or as butters).

Buckwheat Crepes with   *Makes 15*
Azuki-Chestnut Jam

Jam:
   ½ cup *azuki* beans, washed
   3 cups water
   2 pinches sea salt
   ½ cup shelled chestnuts, fresh or dried
Batter:
   pinch of sea salt
   2 cups buckwheat flour
   1 beaten egg (optional)
   2 cups water, approximately
   sesame oil for frying

■ *The jam:*

1) Boil *azuki* beans in 1½ cups water for 1 hour or until wrinkled. Then add a pinch of salt.

2) If using dried chestnuts, cook them in 1½ cups water until tender.

3) Mix cooked beans and chestnuts together. Then add a pinch of salt to bring out their sweetness.

■ *The batter:*

1) Add a pinch of salt to the buckwheat flour. Then, if using, stir in the beaten egg.

2) Add enough water to form a thick, smooth batter.

3) Heat a heavy skillet, brush lightly with oil, then reduce flame to medium-low.

4) Ladle in just enough batter to cover surface of pan.

5) Fry until set. Then, using a thin spatula, carefully turn the crepe and fry the other side.

6) Spread 1 heaping tablespoon of *azuki*-chestnut jam over the crepe, then fold in half.

7) Place on a platter and serve as a main dish.

Buckwheat Crepes with *Azuki*-Chestnut

Deep-Fried Crackers (*Karinto*)

Makes 12–16

1 cup whole-wheat pastry flour
¼ tsp sea salt
1 Tbsp sesame oil
6–8 Tbsp water
flour for dusting
oil for deep-frying

■ *The dough:*

1) Combine flour and salt, mixing well.

2) Add the oil, then rub the mixture through your palms to blend evenly.

3) Gradually add water to form a dough.

4) Dust with flour, and knead lightly 2–3 minutes, until smooth and elastic.

5) Roll out on a floured board as thin as possible.

6) Cut into strips $\frac{2}{3} \times 2$ inches, and cut a short slit in the middle of each strip. Then thread one end of the strip through the slit.

■ *Deep-frying:*

1) Fill a heavy skillet or deep-fryer with 2–3 inches oil. Heat to 360°F.

2) Drop dough into the hot oil and deep-fry until puffed, crisp and light gold in color, about 3–4 minutes.

3) Drain on absorbent paper before serving.

Deep-Fried Crackers (*Karinto*)

Variations

A. Use one of the following combinations and proceed as above:

½ cup whole-wheat flour
½ cup buckwheat flour
¼ tsp sea salt
1 Tbsp sesame oil
⅓–½ cup water

½ cup whole-wheat flour
½ cup rice flour
¼ tsp sea salt
1 Tbsp sesame oil
6–8 Tbsp water

½ cup oat flour
½ cup whole-wheat pastry flour
¼ tsp sea salt
1 Tbsp sesame oil
⅓–½ cup water

B. Knead the following combinations 8–10 minutes, until stiff. If desired, add unroasted sesame seeds while kneading. Then proceed as above.

1 cup buckwheat flour
¼ tsp sea salt
1 Tbsp sesame oil
½ cup water
1 Tbsp sesame seeds

½ cup millet flour
½ cup whole-wheat pastry flour
½ tsp sea salt
1 Tbsp sesame oil
½ cup water, approximately

Sprial Crackers   *Makes 12*

oil for deep-frying
Dough A:
1 cup whole-wheat pastry flour
¼ tsp sea salt
1 Tbsp sesame oil
6–8 Tbsp water
Dough B:
⅔ cup whole-wheat pastry flour
⅓ cup *yannoh* (grain coffee)
¼ tsp sea salt
1 Tbsp sesame oil
6–8 Tbsp water

Spiral Crackers

■ *The dough:*

1) Combine dry ingredients in A, mixing well.

2) Add oil, rubbing mixture through your palms to blend evenly.

3) Gradually add water to form a dough.

4) Knead lightly about 3 minutes, until smooth and elastic.

5) Roll out on a floured board.

6) Repeat these steps with ingredients in B.

■ *Deep-frying:*

1) Fill a heavy skillet or deep-fryer with 2–3 inches oil. Then slowly heat oil to 360°F.

2) Place B dough on top of A dough, matching edges.

3) Roll into a tight cylinder and cut into 12 slices.

4) Drop each slice into the hot oil and deep fry until crisp and golden, about 3–4 minutes.

5) Drain on absorbent paper before serving.

Millet Cookies   *Makes 1 Dozen*

   1 cup millet flour
   1 cup whole-wheat pastry flour
   ½ tsp sea salt
   ½ tsp ground cinnamon
   2 Tbsp sesame oil
   ½ cup chopped peanuts
   ½ cup water, approximately
   flour for dusting

1) Combine flours, salt, and cinnamon, mixing well.

2) Add oil, rubbing mixture through your palms to blend evenly.

3) Add peanuts and enough water to form a dough.

4) Knead lightly 3–4 minutes, until smooth and elastic.

5) Cover with a damp cotton cloth and let stand 1 hour.

6) On a floured board, roll out dough into

a 1/5-inch-thick sheet, then dust with flour.

7) Place on a lightly oiled cookie sheet, and cut into squares with a heavy knife.

8) Preheat oven to 350°F.

9) Brush squares lightly with oil, and bake 25 minutes, or until nicely browned.

Soba Cookies   *Makes 10*

   1 cup buckwheat flour
   pinch of sea salt
   ⅓ tsp ground cinnamon
   1 Tbsp sesame oil
   ½ cup water, approximately
   10 almonds

1) Preheat oven to 350°F.

2) Combine flour, salt, and cinnamon, mixing thoroughly.

3) Add oil, rubbing mixture through palms to blend evenly.

4) Gradually add water to form a smooth, thick batter.

5) Drop onto a lightly oiled cookie sheet by the spoonful, and top each piece with an almond.

6) Bake 25 minutes, or until nicely browned.

Deep-Fried Cookies   *Makes 18*

   1 cup whole-wheat flour
   ¼ tsp sea salt
   ⅓ tsp ground cinnamon
   1 Tbsp sesame oil
   6–8 Tbsp water
   flour for dusting
   oil for deep-frying

■ *The dough:*

1) Combine the flours, salt and cinnamon, mixing well.

2) Add oil, and rub mixture through your palms to blend evenly.

3) Gradually add water to form a dough.

4) Knead lightly about 3 minutes, until smooth and elastic.

5) Roll out on a floured board into a rectangular sheet approximately 1/10 inch thick.

6) Dust with flour, then cut into strips ⅔ × 2 inches.

■ *Deep-frying:*

1) Fill a heavy skillet or deep-fryer with 2–3 inches oil. Slowly heat to 360°F.

2) Hold both ends of each strip of dough, twist, then drop into the hot oil.

3) Deep-fry until puffed, crisp and golden, about 3–4 minutes.

4) Drain on absorbent paper before serving.

Rice Cookies   *Makes 10*

    2 cups brown rice flour
    ½ tsp sea salt
    1 Tbsp sesame oil
    ½ cup water, approximately

1) Combine flour and salt, mixing well.

2) Add oil, rubbing mixture through palms to blend evenly.

3) Gradually add water to form a dough.

4) Knead lightly 1–2 minutes, until smooth and very elastic.

5) Pinch off and roll into balls.

6) Press balls between palms to flatten, then use a chopstick to draw a floral design on each.

7) Brown in a lightly oiled skillet over a medium flame, or bake in a preheated 350°F oven 20–25 minutes.

Buckwheat Cookies (Sarasen *Yaki*)   *Makes 10–20*

    2 cups buckwheat flour
    ¼ tsp sea salt
    2 Tbsp sesame oil
    2 cups boiling water

1) Preheat oven to 350°F.

2) Combine flour and salt and mix well.

3) Add oil and rub mixture through palms to blend evenly.

4) Add boiling water while stirring vigorously with 4 long chopsticks. This will keep sticking to a minimum.

5) When well mixed, form dough into flattened rounds approximately 1 inch in diameter.

6) Decorate in one of the following ways:
   - Shape into floral, leaf or fan designs.
   - Indent and top with an almond, peanut or cashew.
   - Sprinkle with sesame seeds. This variation is good for sick people.

7) Place on a lightly oiled cookie sheet and bake about 25 minutes, until nicely browned. Instead of baking, you can lightly oil a heavy skillet and brown on both sides.

Buckwheat Cookies
(Sarasen *Yaki*)

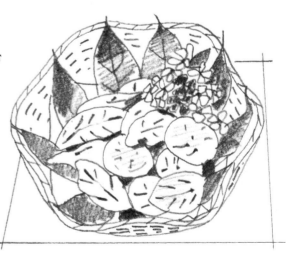

Vegetable Pancakes   *Makes 15*
(*Okonomi Yaki*)

    oil for frying
Filling:
    1 tsp sesame oil
    1 cup onion, cut into crescents
    ¾ cup cabbage, cut into thin strips
    ¾ cup slivered carrot
    pinch of sea salt
Batter:
    ½ cup buckwheat flour
    ½ cup whole-wheat pastry flour
    2 pinches sea salt
    4 cups water (approximately 5 times the amount
        of flour)
    sesame oil

■ *The filling:*
1)   Heat a heavy skillet and coat with 1
teaspoon oil.
2)   When oil is hot, sauté onion over
medium heat for 2–3 minutes, stirring gently,
until the strong aroma is gone.
3)   Add cabbage, then the carrot, and sauté
together 2–3 minutes more.
4)   Mix ingredients together, sprinkle with
a pinch of salt, and turn off heat.
■ *The batter:*
1)   Combine buckwheat and whole-wheat
pastry flours and 2 pinches salt, mixing
well.
2)   Add water to form a batter, stirring
until smooth.
3)   Heat a heavy skillet and brush lightly
with oil.
■ *Cooking:*
1)   Ladle in enough batter to cover surface
of pan, then immediately sprinkle sautéed
vegetables over surface of batter.
2)   Fry until set, then turn carefully with a
thin spatula and brown other side.
3)   Fold in half like an omlette, and serve
with a clear *kuzu* vegetable sauce (p. 135)
or brush lightly with soy sauce.

Wheat Gluten (*Kofu*)

Kofu is a valuable source of protein that
may be eaten in any season. It has always
been popular among vegetarian people
throughout the world. First introduced to
Japan from China by Buddhist monks, *kofu*
became a popular food in Zen Temples. It
is delicious in soups and stews and mixed
with sautéed vegetables.

Homemade Wheat Gluten *Makes 5 Cups*
(*Kofu*)

    10 cups whole-wheat flour
    4 cups whole-wheat pastry flour
    2 tsp sea salt dissolved in 5 cups cold water

1)   Combine the flours in a large bowl,
mixing well. Then add the salted water to
form a dough.
2)   Knead vigorously 20–30 minutes, until
dough is smooth and soft.
3)   Place dough in a large dry bowl, and
let stand uncovered for 40 minutes.
4)   Cover dough with 2½ quarts cold water.
Then knead vigorously. When water clouds
with a cream-colored sediment (starch), drain
and save the liquid for use in baking.
5)   Add 10 cups more water, knead until
cloudy, and drain. Repeat this procedure
5 more times, or until water is only slightly
sedimented.
6)   After final draining, knead dough until
stiff.
7)   Wrap gluten dough in a damp cloth
and steam 30 minutes over a high flame.
Or pinch off small pieces, about 1-inch

Seitan Cutlet

square, and drop them into 2½ quarts boiling water. Remove when they rise to the surface.

8)   Drain, then cool the gluten thoroughly under running water. Refrigerate to store.

The gluten may be eaten as is, seasoned with soy sauce. Or it may be prepared in the following way.

■ *Seitan*

Seitan is *kofu* that has been seasoned.

> **1 Tbsp sesame oil**
> **1 Tbsp minced ginger root**
> **1–2 cups soy sauce**
> **5 cups wheat gluten (*kofu*) separated into small pieces**

1)   Heat a heavy saucepan and coat with the oil.

2)   When oil is hot, sauté the ginger root over a medium flame for 3–4 minutes. Stir constantly.

3)   Pour in the soy sauce and bring to a boil.

4)   Drop in wheat gluten pieces and reduce the flame. Then simmer, covered, for 2–3 hours. Stir frequently.

5)   Uncover and continue to simmer until liquid has evaporated. Refrigerate if keeping longer than a day.

Seitan Cutlet   *Serves 5*

> **½ lb *kofu***
> **1 piece *kombu*, 1 in long**
> **soy sauce**
> **2 pinches sea salt**
> **1–1½ cups whole-wheat pastry flour**
> **⅔–1 cup water**
> **2 cups bread crumbs**
> **oil for deep-frying**
> **½ Tbsp sesame oil**
> **4 cabbage leaves, fine slivered**
> **¾ cup carrot, fine slivered**
> **parsley sprigs**
> **5 red radishes, cut into flowers**

■ *The cutlets: To season kofu (wheat meat):*

1)   Slice into 2½ × 2 × ½-inch strips.

2)   Place *kombu* on the bottom of a saucepan, and the *kofu* strips on top.

3)   Add water to just cover, and season with soy sauce and a pinch of salt. (For each cup of water, add about 1 tablespoon soy sauce.)

4)   Simmer over a medium-low flame until water is completely absorbed.

5)   Set aside to cool before continuing as follows.

If using seitan (seasoned kofu):

Slice the *seitan* into 2½ × 2 × ½ inch strips.

■ *The batter:*

1)   Make a batter with 1–1½ cups pastry

flour and 2/3–1 cup water. Use just enough water to make a thick, sauce-like consistency.

2) Dip *seitan* pieces into the batter, then coat them thoroughly with bread crumbs.

■ *Deep-frying:*

1) Fill a heavy skillet or deep-fryer with 3 inches oil, and heat to 360°F.

2) Deep-fry the *seitan* pieces until brown and crisp.

■ *The vegetables:*

1) Heat a heavy skillet and coat with the sesame oil.

2) When oil is hot, sauté the cabbage and carrots over a high flame, stirring constantly, for 5 minutes. Then season with a pinch of salt.

3) Arrange vegetables on serving dishes as a bed for the cutlets.

4) Place a cutlet on each dish, and serve garnished with sprigs of parsley and red radish flowers.

Seitan Shish Kebab   *Serves 4*

8 pieces *seitan*
1 cup *kombu dashi* (p. 113)
1 Tbsp soy sauce
8 green beans, rinsed and trimmed

4 Tbsp *mugi* (barley) *miso*
4 Tbsp fresh orange juice
1 Tbsp minced orange peel

1) Bring the *dashi* to a boil and add the soy sauce.

2) Drop in the *seitan* and return to a boil. Cook until the liquid is gone and the *seitan* is well flavored.

3) Bring a small pan of lightly salted water to a boil. Drop in the green beans and cook until bright green. Drain and cut the green beans into thirds.

4) Place the *miso* in a *suribachi* and add the orange juice. Mix well. Place in small dishes and garnish with the minced orange peel.

5) Skewer 1 piece of *seitan*, 3 pieces of green beans, then another piece of *seitan*.

6) Serve individual portions with side dishes of the *miso* dip.

Seitan with Mixed Vegetables   *Serves 4*

8 small pieces *seitan*
4 *shiitake* mushrooms

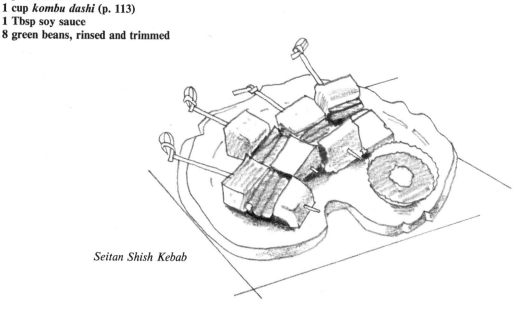

Seitan Shish Kebab

Seitan with Mixed Vegetables

2 cups *kombu dashi* (p. 113)
½ Tbsp *saké*
1½ Tbsp soy sauce
1 carrot
2 pinches sea salt
4 Tbsp fresh-squeezed orange juice
5¼ oz lotus root, cut into ¼-in rounds
4 taro potatoes, peeled
16 snow peas, washed and trimmed

1) Soak the *shiitake* in lightly salted cold water until tender, about 20 minutes.
2) Remove the hard stems, and score the caps with a shallow cross.
3) Combine 1 cup *dashi*, ½ tablespoon *saké* and 1 tablespoon soy sauce in a saucepan. Bring to a boil and add the *shiitake*.
4) Cook for 10 minutes. Then remove the mushrooms and allow to cool.
5) In the same liquid, cook the *seitan* over a low flame. Simmer until dry.
6) Cut the carrot into ½-inch lengths. Then cut each in half lengthwise. Then cut each piece in half crosswise.
7) Boil the carrot pieces in lightly salted water until tender.
8) Add a pinch of salt to the orange juice. Then add the lotus root rounds and soak 10 minutes.

9) Place the lotus root and soaking liquid in a saucepan. Bring to a boil, turn down the flame and simmer 5 minutes.
10) Combine 1 cup *dashi*, ½ tablespoon soy sauce and a pinch of salt in a saucepan. Bring to a boil.
11) Add the taro potatoes and cook until tender. Then drain and cut in half.
12) Boil the snow peas in lightly salted water until bright green.
13) Divide the ingredients among 4 individual serving bowls. Arrange attractively.

Seitan with Orange *Miso* Sauce

Serves 4

8 pieces *seitan*
1 Tbsp sesame oil
4 Tbsp *mugi* (barley) *miso*
4 Tbsp fresh-squeezed orange juice
2 tsp minced orange peel

1) Heat a heavy skillet and coat with the oil.
2) When oil is hot, add the *seitan* and sauté 1–2 minutes.
3) Place the *miso* in a *suribachi* and grind well. Then add the orange juice and 1 teaspoon orange peel and mix well.

4)   Place 2 pieces of *seitan* in each of 4 serving dishes. Spread the *miso* sauce on top and garnish with the remaining orange peel.

Seitan with Orange *Miso* Sauce

2. VEGETABLES FROM LAND AND SEA

Daily Vegetable Dishes

Broccoli in Béchamel Sauce   *Serves 5*

½ small broccoli, separated into flowerets
2 pinches sea salt
mock Béchamel sauce (p. 113)
parsley sprigs

1)   Bring a small pan of water to a boil,
then add the salt.
2)   Drop in the broccoli flowerets, return
to a boil, and cook 5 minutes, or until
bright green and just tender.
3)   Drain in a colander, and cool to room
temperature.
4)   About 5 minutes before the Béchamel
sauce is done, add the broccoli and simmer
together.
5)   Serve garnished with parsley.

Kimpira (Burdock, Carrot   *Serves 5*
and Lotus Root)

1 cup burdock root*, thin slivered
½ cup lotus root, thin half-moons
¼ cup carrot, thin slivered
1½ Tbsp sesame oil
2 Tbsp soy sauce, approximately

1)   Heat a heavy skillet and coat with oil.
2)   When oil is hot, add the burdock slivers
(they should sizzle softly when they touch
the surface of the pan), and sauté over a
medium flame until they no longer release
their strong aroma. Stir gently and constantly to coat evenly with oil and to prevent burning.

Kimpira (Burdock, Carrot and Lotus Root)

3)   Add lotus slices, then carrot slivers,
and mix vegetables well.
4)   Sauté 1–2 minutes longer, then add
enough water to cover bottom of pan.
5)   Cover pan, bring to a boil, then reduce
flame to low.
6)   Simmer 25–30 minutes, or until vegetables are tender. Add water occasionally
if necessary.
7)   Uncover, season with soy sauce to taste,
and simmer until dry, while gently stirring.
8)   Serve 2–3 tablespoons per person.

Variations
For a dish used traditionally in the Orient
for respiratory ailments, make lotus root

the major ingredient. Use 1½ cups lotus root, ½ cup carrots and ½ cup burdock. The burdock may be shaved as well as slivered.

*The nutritious burdock root plays an important role in the macrobiotic diet.

Burdock with Sesame   *Serves 5*

    1 burdock root, about 15–20 inches long
    1 Tbsp sesame oil
    4–5 Tbsp soy sauce
    3 Tbsp toasted sesame seeds

1)   Scrub burdock with a natural fiber brush (*tawashi*), then cut into logs that will fit into your skillet.

2)   Heat the oil in a heavy skillet, then sauté the burdock until its strong aroma is no longer released.

3)   Add slightly more than enough water to cover, and bring to a boil.

4)   Reduce flame and cover the pan.

5)   Cook until burdock is tender and no longer resistant to the insertion of a food pick or skewer. Add water during cooking if necessary.

6)   Season with soy sauce to taste, and simmer until dry.

7)   Cut the logs into ⅔-inch lengths and serve upright, topped with a sprinkling of toasted sesame seeds.

Burdock with *Miso*   *Serves 5*

    2½ cups burdock root, cut into thin rounds
    2 Tbsp sesame oil
    1–2 Tbsp *miso*
    3–6 Tbsp water
    3 Tbsp sesame seeds, toasted

1)   Heat a heavy skillet and coat with the oil.

2)   When oil is hot, sauté the burdock rounds until their strong aroma is no longer released.

3)   Add water to cover, then bring to a boil.

4)   Reduce flame, cover pan, and cook until tender. Add water during cooking if necessary.

5)   Thin *miso* in 3 parts water and add to the pan when burdock is tender.

6)   Stir and simmer over very low flame until all liquid has evaporated.

7)   Add sesame seeds and sauté together 1–2 minutes more.

  For balance, serve with lightly boiled green beans, kale, or watercress.

Burdock with Sesame

Burdock *Nori* Roll (Burdock Wrapped in *Nori*)

Serves 5

2 cups burdock root, grated
oil for deep-frying
1 tsp ginger root juice, from grated ginger
¼ cup whole-wheat pastry flour
1 sheet *nori*
water
1 Tbsp *miso*
2 Tbsp sesame butter (*tahini*)

1)   Pour 3 inches oil into a heavy skillet or deep-fryer and heat to 330°F.
2)   When oil is hot, combine the grated burdock, ginger root juice, and enough flour to hold the mixture together.
3)   Form into a log and place at one edge of the *nori*.
4)   Combine 1 tablespoon flour with 1 tablespoon water to form a thin paste.
5)   Roll the *nori* into a cylinder and seal the edge with the flour paste.
6)   Drop into the hot oil, and deep-fry until crisp. Then drain on absorbent paper.
7)   When cool, cut into 1-inch pieces.
8)   Grind equal amounts of *miso* and *tahini* together in a *suribachi*. Then thin with water to the desired consistency and serve over the *nori*-roll slices.

Cabbage and Carrots

Serves 5

4–5 cabbage leaves, slivered
½ small carrot, slivered
1 tsp sesame oil
sea salt

1)   Heat the oil in a heavy skillet.
2)   Add the cabbage and sauté briskly over a high flame, stirring constantly.
3)   When cabbage is tender, add carrot slivers and sauté together 4–5 minutes more.
4)   Cover pan, reduce flame to very low, and simmer 10–15 minutes. Then season with salt to taste.

Cabbage in Sesame Sauce

Serves 5

4–5 cabbage leaves, slivered
2 pinches sea salt
1 tsp sesame oil
½ small carrot, slivered
1 Tbsp soy sauce
1½ Tbsp water, approximately
1 Tbsp sesame butter

1)   Bring a pan of water (just enough to cover the cabbage leaves) to a boil, then add a pinch of salt.
2)   Using long chopsticks, hold the stems of the cabbage leaves under the water, and cook until tender.
3)   Submerge the upper part of the leaves for an instant, then drain and cool to room temperature.
4)   Heat the oil in a heavy skillet, then sauté the carrot slivers 4–5 minutes, or until they begin to soften. Stir constantly.
5)   Season with a pinch of salt, then remove from heat.
6)   Add the soy sauce and enough water to the sesame butter to make a creamy sauce.
7)   Add the cabbage and carrot slivers to the sesame sauce, and toss well.

Cabbage Rolls

Makes 10 Rolls

10 cabbage leaves
3 *shiitake* mushrooms
1 Tbsp sesame oil
1 small onion, cut into thin crescents
1 small carrot, slivered
pinch of sea salt
1 piece of *kombu*, 2-in square
4–6 Tbsp soy sauce
1 cup mock Béchamel sauce (p. 133)
1–2 tsp minced parley

■ *The vegetables:*
1)   Put the cabbage leaves in a colander and douse with boiling water until they start to wilt.
2)   Drain, then trim the cores smooth, and set aside.

Cabbage Rolls

3)   Soak the *shiitake* 20–30 minutes, or until tender, then remove the tough stems and slice the mushrooms fine.
4)   Heat a heavy skillet and coat with the oil.
5)   When oil is hot, sauté the onion over a medium flame for 5 minutes, or until lightly browned.
6)   Add carrot slivers, then mushroom slices, and mix ingredients together.
7)   Season with a pinch of salt, then turn off heat.
■ *The rolls:*
1)   Place 2–3 tablespoons of the sautéed vegetables at the bottom end of a cabbage leaf, then roll the leaf to cover filling.
2)   Tuck in edges of the leaf, roll again, then secure with a food pick.
3)   Repeat with remaining ingredients until all are used.
4)   Put the *kombu* in a saucepan and arrange the cabbage rolls on top.
5)   Add just enough water to cover, bring rapidly to a boil, and simmer 15 minutes.
6)   Season with 1 tablespoon soy sauce for each cup water used to cover. Then simmer 10 minutes more.
7)   Turn off heat and drain cabbage rolls.

8)   Serve topped with mock Béchamel sauce and a sprinkling of minced parsley.

Carrot with *Tofu* Dressing   *Serves 5*

1 small carrot, finely slivered
1 oz *shirataki*
1 Tbsp sesame oil
2 pinches sea salt
1 Tbsp sesame seeds, toasted
½ cake *tofu*, boiled, drained and mashed
soy sauce

1)   Drop the *shirataki* into a pan of boiling water, and cook 2–3 minutes.
2)   Drain and set aside.
3)   Heat a heavy skillet, then coat with the oil.
4)   When oil is hot, sauté the carrot slivers over a medium flame for 3–4 minutes, or until they begin to soften.
5)   Add the *shirataki* and sauté together several minutes more.
6)   Season with the salt, remove from heat, and allow to cool.
7)   Add carrot-*shirataki* mixture and the toasted sesame seeds to the mashed *tofu*, and toss together.
8)   Season with soy sauce to taste.

Carrots with Sesame (*Ninjin Soboro*)

Serves 5

1 cup carrot, grated
2 tsp sesame oil
2 Tbsp sesame seeds, toasted
2 pinches sea salt

1) Heat a heavy skillet, then add 1 teaspoon oil.
2) When oil is hot, add the sesame seeds, and stir until they can be easily crushed between your fingers.
3) Heat another skillet, then add 1 teaspoon oil.
4) When oil is hot, sauté the grated carrots over a medium flame for 3 minutes.
5) Add sautéed sesame seeds and mix well.
6) Season with salt to taste, and serve.

Carrot *Agé* Roll (*Ninjin Shinoda*)

Serves 6

3 pieces of *agé*
2–3 medium carrots
12 strips (3 in long) of *kampyo*, washed
6 cups *kombu dashi* (p. 113), approximately
½–¾ cup soy sauce
parsley sprigs

1) Pour boiling water over the *agé* to remove excess oil.
2) Using scissors, open the *agé* pieces by cutting 1 long and 2 short sides.
3) Soak the *kampyo* until it softens, then squeeze dry.
4) Quarter the carrots lenghtwise, then trim each piece to the length of the *agé*.
■ *The roll:*
1) Put a piece of *agé* on a bamboo mat or *sudare*, and pile 3 carrot sticks on the edge of the *agé*.
2) Roll into a tight cylinder, then tie with gourd strips at 4 equidistant points.
3) Repeat until all ingredients are used.
■ *Cooking the rolls:*
1) Place enough *kombu dashi* in a saucepan to cover the rolls, then bring to a boil.
2) Season with 2 tablespoons soy sauce for each cup of *dashi* used.
3) Add the rolls, and cover pan with a tight-fitting lid. Or use a smaller lid that will rest directly over the rolls and keep them in place.
4) Cook until half the liquid is gone. Then turn rolls over, and cook until dry.
5) Drain rolls thoroughly, then slice each into 4 pieces.
6) Serve garnished with parsley sprigs.

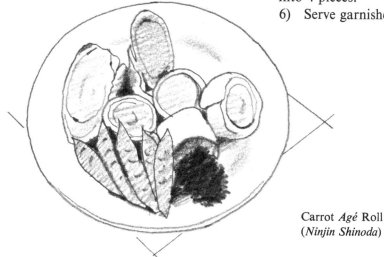

Carrot *Agé* Roll
(*Ninjin Shinoda*)

Sautéed Celery
Serves 5

1–2 celery stalks
1 tsp sesame oil
soy sauce

1)   Slice celery diagonally into bite-size pieces.
2)   Heat the oil in a heavy skillet.
3)   Add the celery and sauté briskly over a high flame for several minutes.
4)   Cover the bottom of the pan with a mixture of equal parts soy sauce and water.
5)   Reduce flame and simmer to the desired degree of tenderness, or until the liquid has cooked off.

Celery in Sesame Sauce
Serves 5

1 celery stalk, shaved into thin pieces
2 pinches sea salt
3 Tbsp sesame seeds, washed
2 Tbsp water
1–2 Tbsp soy sauce

1)   Bring a small pan of water to a boil, and add salt.
2)   Drop in the celery pieces and cook for 30 seconds.
3)   Drain thoroughly and allow to cool.
4)   Toast the sesame seeds in a heavy skillet over a moderately-high flame for 5 minutes, or until brown and fragrant.
5)   Grind the seeds to a paste in a *suribachi*, adding water and soy sauce for the right consistency and taste.
6)   Add the celery to the *suribachi* and toss the ingredients together.
   This is a delicious side dish that goes well with fish.

Chinese Cabbage Rolls
Serves 5

9 Chinese cabbage leaves
2 pinches sea salt
1 bunch watercress
Sesame soy sauce:
1 Tbsp *tahini*
2 Tbsp soy sauce
2 Tbsp water
lemon juice

■ *The Chinese cabbage:*
1)   Bring 6 cups water to a boil, then add a pinch of salt.
2)   Using long chopsticks, hold the stems of the Chinese cabbage under the water, and cook until just tender.
3)   Submerge the upper portion of the leaves for an instant, then remove from heat and drain.
4)   Trim away the protruding portion of the lower stems, so that they are almost even with the leaves.
■ *The watercress:*
1)   Bring a small pan of water (just enough to cover the watercress) to a boil, then add a pinch of salt.
2)   Drop in the watercress, return to a boil, and cook until the stems are tender.
3)   Drain in a colander, then cool to room temperature.
■ *The rolls:*
1)   Place 3 cabbage leaves, edges overlapping, on a bamboo mat or *sudare*. (Arrange leaves so that they point in alternating directions.)
2)   Lay the watercress in a neat double row. (Alternate stem and leaf in the same direction as the cabbage.)
3)   Roll up from the wide edge of the mat into a tight cylinder.
4)   Squeeze roll to remove excess water. Then remove mat, and slice roll into 1-inch-thick sections.
5)   Repeat with remaining ingredients until all are used.
6)   Combine the first 3 ingredients for the sesame soy sauce, then add lemon juice to taste.
7)   Serve rolls topped with sesame soy sauce.

Variations

A. For added color, place a row of boiled carrot slivers alongside the watercress before boiling.

B. Include 3 pieces of *agé* to the ingredients listed above. To prepare:

1) Douse the *agé* with boiling water to remove excess water, then drain.

2) Using scissors, open the pieces by cutting 1 long and 2 short sides.

3) Place in a saucepan, and add enough water to cover.

4) Bring to a boil, then add 2 tablespoons soy sauce for each cup water used.

5) Cover pan with a tight-fitting lid, then cook until all liquid is gone and the *agé* is well flavored.

6) Drain and allow to cool. Then place 1 piece of *agé* on a bamboo mat.

7) Place 3 cabbage leaves on top of the *agé*, then proceed as above.

Cucumber and *Wakame* with Walnut *Miso*   *Serves 5*

1 cup *wakame*
1 medium cucumber, washed
pinch of sea salt
walnut *miso* (p. 135)

1) Soak the *wakame* in water for 10–15 minutes, or until soft.

2) Separate the leaves from the tough stem, then chop the leaves into small pieces.

3) Sprinkle the cucumber generously with salt, then roll it back and forth several times on a cutting board.

4) Wash off salt, and slice the cucumber fine on the diagonal.

5) Sprinkle the slices with a pinch of salt, and mix well.

6) Set aside for 10 minutes. Then squeeze the slices to remove excess liquid and salt.

7) Toss *wakame* and cucumber together.

8) Serve with walnut *miso* for dipping.

Cucumbers in *Miso* Sauce   *Serves 5*

2 small cucumbers
sea salt
2 tsp *kuzu*
2 cups water
1 Tbsp *miso*
1 Tbsp sesame oil

1) Trim the tips from the cucumber, then rub them against the exposed ends until a white foam is no longer released. Rinse off the foam.

2) Sprinkle salt on a cutting board. Then, using both palms, roll the cucumbers back and forth over the salt.

3) Slice cucumbers lengthwise into halves, then into quarters. Finally, slice the quarters into 1-inch lengths.

■ *The miso sauce:*

1) Prepare a mixture of 2 teaspoons *kuzu* and 2 cups water. Make sure the *kuzu* is completely dissolved.

2) Add 1 tablespoon *miso*, mix well, then set aside.

3) Heat a skillet and cover lightly with oil.

4) When oil is hot, sauté the cucumber slices 4–5 minutes over a low flame.

5) Pour the *kuzu-miso* sauce over the cooking cucumbers and mix gently until a thick transparent sauce is formed.

6) Remove from heat and serve.

Sautéed *Daikon*   *Serves 5*

1 cup *daikon* radish, cut into thick half-moons
2 Tbsp sesame oil
1½ cups onion, cut into ½-in quarter rounds
¾ cup carrot, cut into quarter rounds
3 pieces *agé*, cut in six pieces each
soy sauce

1) Heat a heavy skillet and coat with the oil.

2) When oil is hot, sauté the onions over a medium flame, stirring gently, for 2–3 minutes, or until translucent.

3) Add *daikon*, carrot and *agé*, in that

order, sautéing each lightly as you add it.
4) Half cover the vegetables with water, cover, and simmer 15–20 minutes. Add a little water only if necessary to prevent burning.
5) Season with soy sauce to taste.

Simmered *Daikon* (*Furofuki Daikon*)

Serves 5

> 10 rounds (¾ in thick) of *daikon* radish
> 5–6 cups *kombu dashi* (p. 113)
> 5–6 Tbsp soy sauce
> 3 Tbsp sesame seeds, washed
> 1 Tbsp *miso*

■ *The daikon:*
1) Bring 5–6 cups *kombu dashi* (enough to more than cover the *daikon*) to a boil.
2) Add 1–2 tablespoons soy sauce for each cup of *dashi* used.
3) Drop in the *daikon* and cook 30 minutes, or until tender.
■ *The sauce:*
1) Dry-roast the sesame seeds in a heavy

skillet over a moderately high flame until lightly toasted and fragrant. Stir constantly.
2) Place toasted seeds in a *suribachi* and grind to a paste.
3) Blend in *miso* and thin the mixture with 2–3 tablespoons of the *kombu dashi* used to cook the *daikon*.
■ *Serving:*
1) Divide the *daikon* among 5 individual serving dishes.
2) Serve topped with the sesame-*miso* sauce.

Variation

1) Fill the bottom of a steamer with 2–3 inches of *kombu dashi*.
2) Arrange *daikon* in a steamer above the *dashi* and steam 20–30 minutes, or until tender.

Sautéed *Daikon* Leaves

Serves 5

> leaves from 1 *daikon* radish, chopped fine
> 1 Tbsp sesame oil
> 2 pieces *agé*, slivered
> soy sauce

1) Heat the oil in a heavy skillet.
2) Add the leaves and sauté over a medium flame for 5 minutes, or until leaves have wilted.
3) Add the *agé* slivers and sauté together 1–2 minutes.
4) Season with soy sauce, then simmer until dry.
  Delicious served with brown rice.

Simmered *Daikon*
(*Furofuki Daikon*)

Sautéed Dried *Daikon* *Serves 5*

1 oz dried *daikon* radish
1 Tbsp sesame oil
3 pieces *agé*, slivered
2–3 Tbsp soy sauce

1) Rinse the dried *daikon* in cold water, and cut into 1-inch lengths.
2) Heat the oil in a skillet and sauté the *daikon* over a medium flame for 5 minutes.
3) Add the *agé* and shake the pan to mix the ingredients together.
4) Add water to cover, bring to a boil, then cover the pan.
5) Cook 30–45 minutes, or until the *daikon* is tender. Add a little water occasionally if necessary.
6) Season with soy sauce and simmer until dry.

Daikon Rolls (*Katsura Maki*) *Serves 5*

1 piece *daikon* radish, 8 in long
3 pinches sea salt
½ bunch watercress
1 tsp sesame oil
¾ cup carrots, thin slivered
¼ cake *tofu*, drained and mashed
1 tsp lemon juice

■ *The daikon:*
1) Cut the *daikon* into 2-inch rounds.
2) Pare each piece to half its width in a long continuous strip.
3) Roll out the *daikon* sheets and sprinkle lightly with salt.
4) Reroll, press with palm to soften, and set aside.
■ *The watercress:*
1) Bring a small pan of water to a boil and add a pinch of salt.
2) Drop in the watercress, return to a boil, and cook 1–2 minutes, or until the stems are tender.
3) Drain and allow the watercress to cool to room temperature.

4) Arrange the watercress in a neat bundle, alternating leaves and stems, and cut into 1½-inch mounds.
■ *The carrots:*
1) Heat the oil in a heavy skillet. Then sauté the carrot slices over a medium flame for 5 minutes, or until they begin to soften.
2) Sprinkle with a pinch of salt, then remove from heat.
3) When cooled to room temperature, add to the mashed *tofu*, sprinkle with a pinch of salt, and mix well.
■ *The rolls:*
1) Unroll the *daikon* sheets.
2) Spread the *tofu*-carrot mixture at the narrow edge of each sheet, and place a mound of watercress on top of the mixture.
3) Roll into a cylinder and tie with string ⅓ inch from each end of the roll.
4) Cut rolls into halves, remove strings, and sprinkle each piece with 1–2 drops lemon juice.

Daikon-Carrot Salad *Serves 5*

1 cup slivered *daikon* radish
⅓ cup slivered carrot
sea salt
½–1 tsp minced lemon rind
¼ cup soy sauce
¼ cup water
1 tsp lemon juice

1) Sprinkle the *daikon* and carrot with salt and place in separate colanders.
2) Douse each with boiling water, then press to soften and drain thoroughly.
3) Toss the *daikon*, carrot and lemon rind together.
4) Serve with a dipping sauce of equal parts soy sauce and water, and a little lemon juice.

This salad is delicious with yang animal food. It is also very refreshing in summer.

Sautéed Eggplant   *Serves 5*

1 small eggplant
1 Tbsp sesame oil
sesame seed (*goma*) *miso* (p. 135)

1) Cut the eggplant lengthwise into strips about ¾ inch wide.
2) Score the surface of each strip in a checkerboard pattern, to a depth of ¼ inch.
3) Heat the oil in a skillet.
4) Add the eggplant and sauté both sides over a low flame until browned and tender.
5) Serve with sesame seed *miso*.

Eggplant with *Miso*   *Serves 2*

1 small eggplant, sliced into thick rounds
1 Tbsp sesame oil
2–3 Tbsp *miso*

1) Heat a heavy skillet, then add the oil.
2) When oil is hot, sauté the eggplant rounds over a low flame for 2–3 minutes. Stir lightly while cooking.
3) Add enough water to half-cover, bring to a boil, and simmer 15–20 minutes, or until tender.
4) Add *miso* thinned in equal parts water, and simmer until dry. To avoid bruising the eggplant, do not stir at the end.

Variation

To deep-fry:
1) Pour 3 inches oil into a heavy skillet or deep-fryer, and heat to 350°F.
2) Cut the eggplant into 1-inch lengths, then score the skin of each piece diagonally.
3) Drop into the hot oil and deep-fry 2–3 minutes, or until cooked through and crisp.
4) Drain on absorbent paper and serve with *tsuke-jiru* sauce (p. 135).

Sautéed Leek and *Age*   *Serves 5*

½ lb leeks, sliced diagonally into 1-in lengths
1–2 pieces *age*, slivered
1 Tbsp sesame oil
soy sauce

1) Heat a heavy skillet, and coat with the oil.
2) When oil is hot, sauté the leeks in the order of greens, whites, roots, over a medium flame, for 2–3 minutes. Stir gently while cooking.
3) Add the *age* slivers, and sauté together 1 minute.
4) Add water to cover the bottom of the pan, and simmer over a low flame for 15–20 minutes.
5) Season with soy sauce to taste, and simmer until dry.

Fried *Jinenjo* in Soy Sauce   *Serves 5*

15 thin rounds *jinenjo*
oil for deep-frying
1–2 Tbsp soy sauce

1) Pour 3 inches oil into a heavy skillet or deep-fryer, and heat to 350°F.
2) Drop in the *jinenjo* rounds and deep-fry until crisp and golden.
3) Remove from oil and immediately place in a small skillet.
4) Sprinkle with soy sauce and simmer until dry.
    Delicious and very invigorating.

Jinenjo Burgers with Gravy   *Serves 5*

2½ cups grated *jinenjo*
1 tsp and 1 Tbsp sesame oil
1½ cups minced onion
1 small carrot, grated
¼ tsp sea salt
½ cup whole-wheat pastry flour, approximately
oil for frying
1 Tbsp scallion rounds

Deep-Fried *Jinenjo*
with *Nori*

■ *The burgers:*
1) Heat a heavy skillet and coat with
1 teaspoon oil.
2) When oil is hot, sauté the onions over
a medium flame for 2–3 minutes, or until
translucent. Stir gently while cooking.
3) Add carrot and sauté 2–3 minutes
more, or until carrot begins to soften.
4) Remove from heat, and add to *jinenjo*,
mixing thoroughly.
5) Season with the salt, and if necessary,
add enough of the flour to hold the mixture
together.
6) Mix well, then form into 5 patties.
7) In a skillet, heat 1 tablespoon oil, and
cook the patties 15–20 minutes, until
well cooked. Turn the patties once to cook
thoroughly.
■ *Sauce:*
1) To the oil remaining after sautéing the
patties, add 2 tablespoons flour, and cook
4–5 minutes. Stir constantly.
2) Allow flour to cool, then stir in 1 cup
water, and bring just to a boil.
3) Serve sauce as gravy, and garnish with
scallion rounds.

Deep-Fried *Jinenjo* with *Nori*   *Serves 5*

1 cup grated *jinenjo*, approximately
oil for deep-frying
¹⁄₂ sheet *nori*

1) Pour 3 inches oil into a heavy skillet or
deep-fryer and heat to 350°F.
2) Cut *nori* into 4 strips and cut each strip
into 3 rectangular pieces.
3) Coat half of each piece with the grated
jinenjo, then deep-fry until crisp and golden.
4) Drain on a wire rack or absorbent paper
before serving.

Awayuki Jinenjo   *Serves 5*

1¹⁄₂ cups grated *jinenjo*
1¹⁄₂ cups egg whites
¹⁄₄ tsp sea salt
aluminum foil, 5 pieces, 3-in square

1) Beat egg whites until they are stiff, then
fold them into the *jinenjo*, and season with
salt.
2) Spoon 1–2 heaping tablespoons of the
mixture onto the center of each piece of
foil. Then gather the corners of the foil
together, and twist closed.
3) Steam 15–20 minutes.

4) Remove from foil and serve with lemon soy sauce (p. 134) for dipping.

Lotus Root with Lemon Juice   *Serves 5*

2 cups lotus root, cut into paper-thin half-moons
1 Tbsp sesame oil
5–6 drops lemon juice
¼ tsp sea salt

1) Heat a heavy skillet and coat with the oil.
2) When oil is hot, add the lotus slices and sauté over a low flame for 5 minutes, or until the slices turn a light gray. Stir gently while cooking.
3) Add lemon juice and just enough water to prevent burning.
4) Cover pan and simmer 5 minutes.
5) Season with the salt, and serve.

Deep-Fried Lotus Root with   *Serves 5*
Kuzu-Lemon Sauce

2 cups lotus root, grated
oil for deep-frying
3 sheets *nori*
¾ cup grated carrot
1 small onion, minced
pinch of sea salt
whole-wheat pastry flour
Kuzu Lemon Sauce:
1 Tbsp *kuzu*
1 cup *kombu dashi* (p. 113)

¼ tsp sea salt
¼ Tbsp soy sauce
few drops of lemon juice

1) Pour 3 inches oil into a heavy skillet or deep-fryer, and heat to 350°F.
2) Using scissors, cut the *nori* in half, then cut each half into 3 rectangular pieces.
3) Combine lotus, carrot, onion and a pinch of salt. If mixture is too soft, add a little flour and mix well.
4) Cover the surface of each piece of *nori* with a layer of this mixture approximately ⅓ inch thick.
5) Quickly score the top of the mixture in a shallow grid pattern with the blade of a heavy knife. Then press the back of the knife across the mixture's center.
6) Nudge immediately into the hot oil from the edge of a spatula, and deep-fry 2–3 minutes, until cooked through and crisp.
7) Drain on absorbent paper and skewer 2 on each of 6 bamboo skewers.
8) Serve with *kuzu*-lemon sauce.
■ *Kuzu lemon sauce:*
1) Dissolve the *kuzu* in the *dashi* and bring to a boil.
2) Add the salt, soy sauce and lemon juice, and simmer for several minutes until thick. Stir constantly.

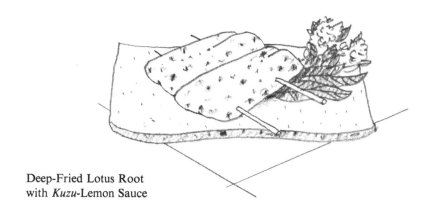

Deep-Fried Lotus Root
with *Kuzu*-Lemon Sauce

Deep-Fried Stuffed Lotus Root

Deep-Fried Stuffed Lotus Root *Serves 4*

16 ¼-in rounds lotus root
1 tsp sesame oil
1 small onion, minced
small amount of *seitan*
1 cup *kombu dashi* (p. 113)
1 Tbsp soy sauce
pinch of sea salt
½ tsp grated ginger
2 cups whole-wheat pastry flour
oil for deep-frying
grated *daikon* radish

■ *The filling:*
1) Heat a heavy skillet and coat with 1 teaspoon oil.
2) When oil is hot, sauté the onion until translucent.
3) Add the *seitan* and sauté 1–2 minutes.
4) Add the *dashi*, soy sauce, salt and grated ginger, and simmer until liquid has evaporated.
■ *To assemble:*
1) Place 1 tablespoon of this mixture on top of 8 of the lotus root rounds. Then cover with the remaining slices.
2) Squeeze the slices together so that the mixture is forced into the holes of both pieces.
3) Slowly add the water to the flour to make a batter. Stir while adding.
4) Dip each stuffed lotus root round into the batter, coating well.
5) Fill a deep-fryer or heavy skillet with 3 inches oil.
6) Drop coated rounds into the hot oil and cook until crisp and golden.
7) Drain on absorbent paper. Then cut each round in half.
8) Serve with grated *daikon* topped with several drops of soy sauce for dipping.

Sautéed Onion with Sesame Seeds *Serves 5*

3 cups onions, cut into half-moons
1 Tbsp sesame oil
¼ tsp sea salt
1–2 Tbsp sesame seeds, washed

1) Heat the oil in a heavy skillet.
2) Sauté the onions over a medium flame for 5 minutes, or until lightly browned. Stir constantly.
3) Reduce flame to low, season with the salt, and cover.
4) Simmer about 10 minutes, or until tender.
5) Dry-roast the sesame seeds over a moderately high flame until toasted and fragrant.
6) Stir the toasted seeds into the onion, mixing well, and serve.

Acorn Squash à la Mode   *Serves 4–5*

2 acorn squash or 1 Hokkaido pumpkin
4 *shiitake* mushrooms
1 oz *biifun*
4 Tbsp sesame oil
1 medium onion, cut into crescents
1 small carrot, slivered
¼ oz chopped *seitan*
¼ tsp and a pinch of sea salt
3 Tbsp whole-wheat pastry flour
1½ cups water

1)   Soak the *shiitake* 20 minutes, or until soft.
2)   Trim away the tough portions of the stems, and slice the caps fine.
3)   Drop the *biifun* into a pan of boiling water and cook 2–3 minutes.
4)   Drain *biifun* thoroughly, cut into 1-inch lengths, and set aside.
5)   Cut the top from the squash, then hollow the center by scooping out the seeds and filaments. Save the top for use later in the recipe.
■ *The stuffing:*
1)   Heat a heavy skillet and coat with 2 tablespoons oil.
2)   When oil is hot, sauté the onion over a medium flame for 5 minutes, or until lightly browned. Stir gently while sautéeing.
3)   Add mushrooms, carrot, and *seitan*, in that order, sautéeing each lightly as added.
4)   Stir in the *biifun*, mix the ingredients together, and season with ¼ teaspoon salt.
5)   Remove from heat and set aside.
■ *Baking the squash:*
1)   Heat oven to 350°F.
2)   Stuff the squash with the vegetable mixture, then recover with the squash top.
3)   Place the squash on a lightly oiled baking sheet, and lightly oil the outside of the squash.
4)   Bake 30–40 minutes, or until a food pick can be easily inserted.

■ *The sauce:*
1)   While the squash is baking, heat another skillet and coat with 2 tablespoons oil.
2)   When oil is hot, add the flour and cook 2–3 minutes, or until all lumps have been smoothed out.
3)   Remove from heat and cool. Then over a medium-low flame, add 1½ cups water, and stir until smooth.
4)   Season with a pinch of salt, and simmer 1–2 minutes.

When serving, cut the squash into individual portions and serve with the sauce.

Simmered Pumpkin with *Miso*   *Serves 5*

1 medium pumpkin, cut into 2-in cubes
1 Tbsp sesame oil
1 medium onion, cut into thin crescents
3 level Tbsp *miso*

1)   Heat a heavy skillet and coat with the oil.
2)   When oil is hot, sauté onion over a medium flame for 5 minutes, or until lightly browned. Stir gently while cooking.
3)   Add pumpkin and sauté 2–3 minutes more.
4)   Add water to cover, bring to a boil, and cover pan.
5)   Reduce flame and simmer 30 minutes, or until tender. Add water during cooking if necessary.
6)   Thin the *miso* with water, then add to the cooking vegetables.
7)   Simmer until dry.

Baked Pumpkin   *Serves 6*

1 Hokkaido pumpkin or 2 acorn squash
sesame oil
sea salt
***goma miso* sauce (p. 136)**
sprigs of parsley

1)   Preheat oven to 400°F.

2) Cut the pumpkin into 10 crescents, and place on a lightly oiled baking sheet.
3) Rub crescents with oil, then sprinkle lightly with salt.
4) Cover with aluminum foil and bake for 20 minutes.
5) Remove foil and bake until tops of crescents brown.
6) Serve with *goma miso* sauce and garnish with sprigs of parsley.

Deep-Fried Pumpkin with Peanuts

Serves 5

2 cups pumpkin purée
pinch of sea salt
1/2 cup peanuts, ground fine in a *suribachi*
1 cup brown rice flour
1/4 cup boiling water
whole peanuts
oil for deep-frying

1) Combine pumpkin purée, salt and well ground peanuts, and mix well. You can substitute 1/4 cup peanut butter for the ground peanuts if you wish.
2) In another bowl, add the flour and then enough boiling water to make a dough.
3) Add the purée to the dough, and mix well.
4) Make balls from the dough about 1 inch in diameter. Then flatten the top of each with your fingertips, and insert a whole peanut in the center.
5) Pour 3 inches oil into a deep-fryer or heavy skillet, and heat to 350°F.
6) Drop the balls into the oil and deep-fry 2–3 minutes, or until crisp.
7) Drain on absorbent paper before serving.

Pumpkin *Nori* Rolls

Serves 5

3 cups pumpkin or acorn squash purée
2 medium carrots
1 medium lotus root
1 Tbsp sesame oil
pinch of sea salt
1 tsp soy sauce
5 sheets *nori*
1–2 Tbsp *kokoh* (p. 56)

1) Quarter the carrot and lotus root lengthwise, then cut each quarter into thin sticks 1/3 inch thick.
2) Heat 1/2 tablespoon oil in a heavy skillet, then sauté carrot sticks over a medium flame for 1–2 minutes. Stir gently to coat evenly with oil and to prevent scorching.
3) Add 2–3 tablespoons water, reduce heat, and simmer until tender.
4) Season with the salt. If any liquid remains, simmer uncovered until evaporated.
5) Remove from heat and set aside.
6) Heat 1/2 tablespoon oil in another skillet, then reduce flame to low and sauté lotus sticks 2–3 minutes. Stir gently while cooking.
7) Add water to half cover, cover pan, and simmer 10 minutes.
8) Season with soy sauce, and simmer until dry. Then remove from heat.
9) Toast the *nori* by waving 1 side over a low flame for several seconds.
10) Place 1 sheet of *nori* on a *sudare* or bamboo mat.
11) Divide the pumpkin purée into 3 portions and spread 1 portion over each *nori* sheet. If purée is too moist, add 1–2 tablespoons *kokoh* to thicken.
12) Place a double row of carrot and lotus sticks across the center of the purée.
13) Roll up the mixture in the mat, lightly pressing the ingredients together into a cylinder.
14) Remove mat and repeat with remaining ingredients.
15) Use a sharp knife to slice each roll

into 1-inch rounds. Wipe the knife after each cut for neat slices.

A wonderful snack at teatime.

Simmered Pumpkin with Soy Sauce
Serves 4–5

1 medium Hokkaido pumpkin or 2 acorn squash
2 Tbsp soy sauce, approximately

1) Cut the pumpkin into 8–10 crescents, and trim away 1 inch of the peel at the center of each piece.
2) Place the crescents in a pan, and cover halfway with water.
3) Bring to a boil, and cook 15 minutes.
4) Season with 1 tablespoon soy sauce for each cup of water used, and cook 15 minutes more. Add water as needed to prevent burning.

Scallion with Sesame Sauce
Serves 5

½ lb scallions
¼ tsp sea salt
3 Tbsp sesame seeds
2 Tbsp soy sauce
½ Tbsp water

1) Bring 4–6 cups water to a boil, and add the salt.
2) Drop in the scallions and return to a boil. Cook 1–2 minutes, until vegetables are bright green.
3) Drain well and cool to room temperature. Then slice into 1-inch lengths.
4) Dry-roast the sesame seeds in a heavy skillet over a moderately high flame. Cook 5 minutes, or until lightly toasted and fragrant. Stir constantly and shake the pan to heat evenly.
5) Grind seeds to a paste in a *suribachi*, adding the soy sauce and water.
6) Add scallions to the sesame paste and toss ingredients together.

Variation

Instead of using whole sesame seeds, make a paste by using 1½ tablespoons sesame butter, 1 tablespoon soy sauce and 1–2 tablespoons water.

Scallion and *Wakame* in *Miso* Sauce
Serves 5

1 cup *wakame*
3–4 scallions, sliced into 1-in lengths
2 pinches sea salt
1 Tbsp *miso*
1 Tbsp sesame butter (*tahini*)
4–5 Tbsp water

1) Soak the *wakame* in cold water for 10–15 minutes, or until soft and pliable.
2) Separate the leaves from the tough stem, and set leaves aside.
3) Bring a small pan of water (enough to cover the scallions) to a boil, and add the salt.
4) Drop in the scallions, return to a boil, and cook 1–2 minutes, or until scallions are bright green.
5) Drain scallions in a colander, and cool to room temperature.
6) Grind the *miso* and sesame butter together in a *suribachi*, and thin with the water.
7) Add *wakame* leaves and scallions, and toss the ingredients together.

Spinach in Sesame Sauce
Serves 5

¾ lb spinach
½ tsp sea salt
4 Tbsp sesame seeds, washed
2–4 Tbsp soy sauce
4 Tbsp water

1) Bring a large pan of water to a boil and add the salt.
2) Drop in the spinach, return to a boil, and cook 1–3 minutes, or until the stems are tender.

3)   Drain spinach in a colandar, and cool to room temperature. Then cut into ½-inch long pieces.

■ *The sauce:*

1)   Dry-roast sesame seeds in a heavy skillet over a medium-high flame for 5 minutes, or until lightly toasted and fragrant. Stir constantly.

2)   Place seeds in a *suribachi* and grind to a paste, adding soy sauce and water.

3)   Add the spinach and toss the ingredients together.

Variations

A.   Other green leafy vegetables may be substituted for the spinach.

B.   Instead of sesame seeds, a sauce can be made by combining 1½ tablespoons sesame butter, 2 tablespoons soy sauce and 3 tablespoons water.

Sweet Potato Jelly   *Serves 5 or More*

> 3 cups sweet potato, steamed and puréed
> ¼ tsp sea salt

1)   Season the purée with the salt to bring out its sweetness, then press firmly into a lightly rinsed shallow mold.

2)   If the purée is too moist, blend in a little *kokoh* (p. 56) to thicken.

3)   Cool and allow to harden, then cut into small pieces and serve.

Sautéed Sweet Potato and   *Serves 5* Leeks in Broth

> 1 medium sweet potato, cut into ¾-in rounds
> ½ medium leek, cut into 1-in lengths
> 2 Tbsp sesame oil
> 4 cups *kombu dashi* (p. 113), approximately
> sea salt
> soy sauce

1)   Heat a heavy skillet and coat with the oil.

2)   When oil is hot, sauté the leeks over a medium flame for 2–3 minutes. Stir constantly.

3)   Add the sweet potato and sauté together for several minutes more.

4)   Add enough *dashi* to cover, bring to a boil, and cover pan.

5)   Cook 20 minutes, or until sweet potato is tender.

6)   Season with salt and soy sauce to taste, then simmer until dry.

Taro Potato in Sesame Sauce   *Serves 6*

> 3 small taro potatoes, washed and cut into 1½-in cubes
> pinch of sea salt
> 1 heaping Tbsp sesame butter (*tahini*)

1)   Put the taro potatoes in a pan, and add just enough water to cover, and add the salt.

2)   Cook 10–15 minutes, or until the taro are tender and the water has evaporated.

3)   Blend the sesame butter with 2½ tablespoons water to make a sauce.

4)   Coat the potatoes thoroughly and serve.

Grilled Taro Potato   *Serves 5*

> 5 small taro potatoes, washed and peeled
> pinch of sea salt
> 1 cup *goma miso* (p. 135)

1)   Bring the taro potatoes to a boil in water to cover, then add a pinch of salt.

2)   Cook 10–15 minutes, or until tender.

3)   Skewer each potato on its own bamboo skewer, and grille lightly.

4)   Coat with the *goma miso* and grill for 1 minute more.

Turnips in Broth   *Serves 5*

> 5 medium turnips
> 4 cups *kombu dashi* (p. 113), approximately
> ¼–½ cup soy sauce
> 2–4 tsp *kuzu* powder

1)   Quarter the turnips through half their depth.

2)   Bring to a boil in enough *dashi* to cover, and cook 20–30 minutes, or until tender.

3)   Season the *dashi* with soy sauce and simmer 5 minutes more.

4)   Remove the turnips and drain.

■ *The broth:*

1)   Dissolve the *kuzu* in a little water to make a thin paste, and add to the remaining *dashi*.

2)   Simmer, stirring constantly, for several minutes, or until thick.

3)   Pour over the turnips and serve.

1)   Add a pinch of salt to a saucepan of boiling water.

2)   Drop in the greens and cook until bright green. Then drain and slice into ½-in lengths. Set aside.

3)   Combine the orange juice, soy sauce and a pinch of salt. Add the grated *daikon* and mix well.

4)   Allow the mixture to stand 5 minutes.

5)   Divide the greens between 4 serving bowls, and cover with the sauce.

6)   Garnish with the orange peel.

Vegetable Greens with Orange Sauce

Serves 4

3½ oz green leaves (watercress, kale, cabbage, etc.), washed
2 pinches sea salt
juice squeezed from 4 oranges
1 Tbsp soy sauce
1 cup grated *daikon* radish
1 Tbsp minced orange skin

Vegetable Greens with
Orange Sauce

Special Dishes

Stuffed *Agé* (*Takara Zutsumi*)   *Serves 5*

5 pieces *agé*
1 oz *biifun** or *harusame**
10 green beans, rinsed and trimmed
sea salt
10 strips (3 in long) *kampyo* or *kombu* cut into thin strips
1 small carrot, slivered
1 piece *kombu*, 3-in square, wiped clean
soy sauce

1)   Douse *agé* with boiling water to remove excess oil, then drain.

2)   Cut each piece into halves. Then pull the sides apart to form a pouch, and turn inside out.

3)   Drop the *biifun* into a pan of boiling water, and cook 2–3 minutes. Then drain.

4)   Drop the green beans into a small pan of lightly salted boiling water (just enough

to cover the beans).

5)   Return to a boil, and cook 5 minutes, or until beans are bright green, and just tender.

6)   Drain the beans, and when cool, slice fine on a diagonal.

7)   Rinse the *kampyo* in lightly salted water, then squeeze dry.

8)   Sprinkle the carrot slivers with salt.

■ *Cooking:*

1)   Combine *biifun*, carrot and green beans. Then fill the *agé* pouches with the mixture.

2)   Draw the edges of the pouch together, and tie with a *kampyo* strip.

3)   Put the 3 inch *kombu* square in the bottom of a pan, and place the *agé* sacks on top.

4)   Add just enough water to cover. Season with 1 tablespoon soy sauce for each cup of water, and bring to a boil.

5)   Cover with a tight-fitting lid, or one that fits inside the pan and rests directly over the *agé* sacks, to keep them in place.

6)   Cook until half the liquid has evaporated and the *agé* are well flavored.

7)   Place 2 *agé* sacks into each of 5 individual serving dishes. Then ladle in a little

of the remaining broth.

8)   Serve hot and steaming.

*Both *biifun* and *harusame* are sold at Oriental food shops.

Chinese Spring Rolls (*Harumaki*) *Makes 10*

   1 Tbsp whole-wheat pastry flour
   1 Tbsp water
   oil for deep-frying
Shells:
   1 cup whole-wheat pastry flour
   $\frac{1}{4}$ cup water
   $\frac{1}{4}$ tsp sea salt
   1 Tbsp sesame oil
Filling:
   $\frac{1}{3}$ oz *biifun* or *seitan*
   1 Tbsp sesame oil
   $1\frac{3}{4}$ oz minced onion
   $\frac{1}{3}$ oz slivered carrot
   $\frac{1}{3}$ oz cauliflower
   $\frac{1}{4}$ tsp sea salt

■ *The shells*:*

1)   Form a soft dough by combining 1 cup flour, $\frac{1}{4}$ cup water, approximately, $\frac{1}{4}$ teaspoon salt and 1 tablespoon oil.

2)   Knead 8–10 minutes, until dough is elastic. Then roll thin on a floured cutting board.

Chinese Spring Rolls
(*Harumaki*)

3)   Preheat a heavy 7-inch skillet, and reduce flame to low.

4)   Add just enough rolled dough to cover the skillet's surface.

5)   Heat until the dough has set (not browned), then turn and heat the other side for a few seconds.

6)   Remove and set aside.

7)   Repeat with remaining dough until all is used.

■ *The filling:*

1)   Drop the *biifun* into a pan of boiling water and cook 2–3 minutes.

2)   Drain and cut the *biifun* into 1-inch lengths.

3)   Heat 1 tablespoon oil in a skillet.

4)   Sauté onion over a medium flame for 5 minutes, or until lightly browned.

5)   Add carrot, then cauliflower, sautéing each lightly.

6)   Add *biifun* and mix ingredients together.

7)   Season with ¼ teaspoon salt, and remove from heat.

■ *The rolls:*

1)   Combine 1 tablespoon flour and 1 tablespoon water to form a thin paste.

2)   Place 3–4 tablespoons of the vegetable-*biifun* mixture at the edge of one of the shells. Then roll the shell twice to cover the filling.

3)   Tuck in the edges of the shell, roll again, and seal the seam with flour paste.

4)   Repeat with remaining ingredients until all are used.

■ *Deep-frying:*

1)   Pour 3 inches oil into a heavy skillet or deep-fryer, and heat to 350°F.

2)   Drop in the filled spring rolls, and deep-fry 1–2 minutes, or until golden and crisp.

3)   Drain on a wire rack or absorbent paper before serving.

*Harumaki shells are available at Oriental food shops.

Chou Farci   *Serves 5*

1 cup buckwheat flour
¼ tsp sea salt
3 cups water
1 small cabbage
2 eggs, beaten well

1)   Combine buckwheat flour, salt and water to make a sauce.

2)   Place cabbage leaves in a strainer, and pour boiling water over them until they are tender.

3)   When cool, arrange several leaves in the

Chou Farci

bottom of an oiled casserole dish.

4)   Pour some of the flour sauce over the leaves, then some of the beaten egg over the sauce.

5)   Make alternating layers of cabbage leaves, sauce and beaten eggs until the ingredients are used up. Finish with a layer of cabbage on top.

6)   Cover the casserole dish with a tight fitting lid, and bake in a preheated 275°F oven for 40–60 minutes.

7)   Serve hot and steaming.

Variation
Substitute 2–3 cups cooked buckwheat groats for the flour, and proceed as above.

Sweet Potato and Chestnut Purée (Chestnut *Kinton*) *Serves 5*

    1 cup pumpkin purée
    7 oz sweet potato purée
    sea salt
    1 ½ cups shelled chestnuts
    4 ½ cups water

1)   Combine the pumpkin and sweet potato purées.
2)   Season the mixture with salt to taste, and set aside.
3)   Cook the chestnuts in the water for 1–1 ½ hours, or until pasty.
4)   Season with salt, then stir in the pumpkin-sweet potato mixture.
5)   Bring just to a boil, then remove from heat and serve cool.

   This is a traditional New Year's dish in Japan.

Daikon Agé Rolls *Serves 4*

    6-in piece of *daikon* radish, cut into quarters
       lengthwise
    4 pieces *agé*
    4–5 cups *kombu dashi* (p. 113)
    4 Tbsp soy sauce
    1 Tbsp whole-wheat pastry flour

    1 Tbsp water
    oil for deep-frying
    goma joyu sauce (p. 134)

1)   Bring the *dashi* (just enough to cover the *daikon*) to a boil, and season with soy sauce.
2)   Drop the *daikon* into the *dashi*, and simmer 20 minutes, or until tender. Then drain and cool.
3)   Open the *agé* by cutting open 1 long and 2 short sides. Then place on a flat surface.
4)   Combine the flour and water to make a thin paste.
5)   Place 1 stick of *daikon* near one edge of each piece of *agé*.
6)   Roll the *agé* into a tight cylinder. Then seal the seam with flour paste.
7)   In a heavy skillet or deep-fryer, heat 3 inches oil to 350°F.
8)   Drop the rolls into the hot oil, and remove as soon as they return to the surface. Drain on absorbent paper.
9)   Cut each roll into 5 slices, and serve with *goma joyu* sauce.

Daikon Roll *Serves 5*

    1 ½-in piece *daikon* radish
    pinch of sea salt
    3 tangerines or mandarin oranges, peeled and
       separated into halves

1)   Pare the *daikon* into a sheet approximately 2 feet long.
2)   Sprinkle the salt over the *daikon* sheet, and let stand 1 hour.
3)   Cut the *daikon* sheet into 6 rectangular pieces 1 ½ × 4 inches.
4)   Place an orange half at the short edge of each *daikon* sheet. Then wrap the sheet several times around the orange.
5)   Press the sheet with your palm to assure that it adheres to the orange's surface.
6)   Let stand 1–2 minutes. Then slice crosswise into sections.

Lotus Root Simmered in Soy Sauce

Serves 5

1 small lotus root
2 Tbsp sesame oil
1 cup water, approximately
2 Tbsp soy sauce
parsley, as garnish

1) Heat the oil in a skillet.
2) Sauté the whole lotus root for 2–3 minutes. Turn the lotus root to coat evenly with oil.
3) Add enough water to half-cover and bring to a boil. Then season with the soy sauce.
4) Cover pan and reduce the flame. Simmer 20–30 minutes, or until lotus root is tender enough for a chopstick to be inserted easily.
5) Uncover pan, and simmer until dry.
6) To serve, cut lotus root lengthwise into halves, then into thin half-moons. Top with parsley.

Variation

1) Grate the lotus root. Then combine with ½ cup minced onion, ¼ teaspoon salt and enough whole-wheat pastry flour to hold the mixture together.
2) Form into 1-inch balls, and deep-fry in moderately hot (300°–330°F) oil until cooked through, pale gold and crisp.
3) Drain on absorbent paper before serving.

Pumpkin Roll

Serves 6–8

½ lb pumpkin purée
2 cups whole-wheat pastry flour
¼ tsp and a pinch of sea salt
2 Tbsp sesame oil
1 cup water, approximately
1 egg yolk, well beaten (optional)

■ *The pastry:*
1) Combine flour and ¼ teaspoon salt, mixing well.

2) Add the oil, rubbing the mixture between your palms to blend evenly.
3) Add water gradually to form an elastic dough, then knead 8–10 minutes, until smooth.
4) Form dough into a ball, wrap in a damp cloth, and set aside in a cool place for 30 minutes.

■ *The roll:*
1) Season the pumpkin purée with a pinch of salt to bring out its sweetness.
2) Divide the dough into 2 parts, and roll each part into a thin rectangular sheet on a floured board.
3) Spread the purée over both sheets, and roll into cylinders. Then seal the edges of the cylinders with a few drops of water.
4) Brush tops of rolls with beaten egg yolk (if used), and place rolls on a lightly oiled baking pan.
5) Bake in a preheated 350°F oven for 30 minutes, or until nicely browned. Or the rolls can be steamed instead of baking.
6) Slice into 1-inch rounds and serve.

Variation

Substitue 2 cups *azuki* jam (p. 137) for the pumpkin purée and proceed as above.

Stuffed Onions

Serves 10

10 medium onions
1 Tbsp sesame oil
½ small carrot, diced
10 green beans, rinsed and sliced fine diagonally
5 Tbsp minced *seitan*
pinch of sea salt
1 heaping Tbsp whole-wheat flour
2 cups mock Béchamel sauce (p. 133)

1) Peel and boil the whole onions for 5–6 minutes. Then cool.
2) Cut 1 slice from the top of each onion, then scoop out the centers and chop fine.
3) Heat the oil in a skillet. Then sauté the chopped onion centers until lightly browned.

Stir gently while cooking.

4) Add the carrot, then the green beans, sautéing each lightly.

5) Add *seitan* and mix ingredients together.

6) Season with the salt, stir in the flour, then remove from heat.

7) Use the sautéed vegetable-*seitan* mixture to fill each hollowed onion.

8) Arrange onions on a lightly oiled baking pan, and bake in a preheated 450°F oven for 20–30 minutes, or until tender. Or steam the stuffed onions over *kombu dashi* (p. 113).

9) Serve topped with mock Béchamel sauce.

Steamed Turnip
Serves 4

3 cups grated turnip
3 pinches sea salt
10 thin slices of carrot, cut into flowers
1 medium scallion, cut into ³/₄-in lengths
8 cubes (¹/₂-in) *fu**, optional
1 egg white, beaten to a foam
8 cubes (¹/₂-in) *tofu*
4 slivers orange peel

1) Add a pinch of salt to a small pan of boiling water.

2) Drop in the carrot slices, and cook 2–3 minutes, or until bright orange. Then drain and set aside.

3) Bring another small pan of water to a boil, and add a pinch of salt.

4) Drop in the scallions, return to a boil, and cook 1–2 minutes, or until bright green. Then drain and cool.

5) If using *fu*, deep-fry the cubes.

6) Combine the turnip, egg white and a pinch of salt.

7) Divide the mixture among 5 custard cups with tops.

8) Arrange 2 pieces each of *tofu*, carrot slices, scallion and *fu* (if used) in each cup. Top with 1 strip of orange peel.

9) Cover and steam 15–20 minutes.

*Available at macrobiotic outlets and Oriental food stores.

Steamed Turnip

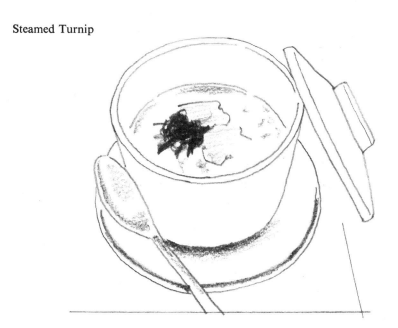

Vegetable Dumplings (*Gyoza*) *Makes 10*

2 cups whole-wheat pastry flour
¼ tsp sea salt
3 Tbsp sesame oil
½ cup boiling water, approximately
oil for frying
Filling:
2 Tbsp sesame oil
2 small onions, minced
1 small carrot, slivered
3 Tbsp minced *seitan*
pinch of sea salt

1) Combine the flour and ¼ teaspoon salt.
2) Add 3 tablespoons oil, rubbing mixture between your palms to blend evenly.
3) Add boiling water while stirring vigorously with long chopsticks.
4) When mixed well and cool enough to touch, knead 8–10 minutes, until dough is smooth and elastic.
5) Divide into 10 parts and, on a floured board, roll out into a sheet about 1/8 inch thick.
6) Using a cookie cutter or an inverted tea cup, cut into rounds about 3 inches in diameter.

■ *The filling:*
1) Heat a heavy skillet and coat with 2 tablespoons oil.
2) When oil is hot, sauté the onions over a medium flame for 5 minutes, or until lightly browned.
3) Add carrot slivers, then the *seitan*, and mix all ingredients together.
4) Taste before seasoning with salt (the *seitan* is salty). Then turn off heat.

■ *The dumplings:*
1) Place 1–2 tablespoons of the vegetable mixture at the center of each dough round.
2) Moisten the edges with a mixture of equal parts water and flour.
3) Bring up sides of dough to form half-moon shapes. Then seal the edges by pinching the dough with your fingers.
4) Heat a heavy skillet and brush lightly with oil.
5) Stand dumplings up in pan, cover, and cook over a medium flame.
6) When bottom is lightly browned, sprinkle several drops of water on the skillet's surface, recover, and cook 5 minutes more.

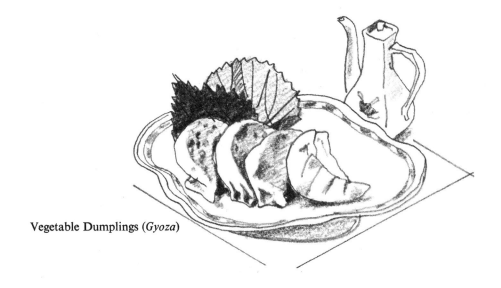

Vegetable Dumplings (*Gyoza*)

Variation

Make *kombu dashi* (p. 113) and bring to a boil. Drop the dumplings into the boiling *dashi*, and cook until they rise to the surface.

Zwiebelkuchen   *Serves 5*

  3 cups whole-wheat pastry flour
  ¾ tsp sea salt
  4 Tbsp sesame oil
  ½ cup water, approximately
  2 medium onions, cut into half-moons
  1 cup shredded cabbage
  2 cups slivered carrot
  1 egg, beaten well

■ *The pastry:*

1) Combine flour and ½ teaspoon salt, mixing well.
2) Add 3 tablespoons oil, rubbing mixture between your palms to blend evenly.
3) Add water gradually to form an elastic dough, and knead 8–10 minutes, until smooth. Then set aside ½ cup of dough.
4) Roll out remaining dough on a floured board, and line a 9-inch pie plate with it.
5) Roll reserved dough into a thin round sheet, and set aside.

■ *The filling:*

1) Heat 1 tablespoon oil in a heavy skillet.
2) Sauté onions over a medium flame for 5 minutes, or until lightly browned, stirring gently.
3) Add cabbage, then carrot, sautéing each as added.
4) Mix ingredients together, and season with ¼ teaspoon salt.
5) Remove from heat, and allow to cool. Then stir in the beaten egg.

■ *Baking:*

1) Preheat oven to 450°F.
2) Fill dough-lined pan with vegetable-egg mixture.
3) Line the edge of the pie pan with the extra dough. Use a fork to make impressions along the edges.
4) Bake 30 minutes, or until nicely browned.

Sea Vegetables

Hijiki with Sesame Seeds   *Serves 5*

  1 oz dried *hijiki*
  1½ Tbsp sesame oil
  3 Tbsp soy sauce
  3 Tbsp sesame seeds

1) Wash *hijiki* quickly under cold running water, then cut into 1-inch lengths.
2) Heat the oil in a heavy skillet, then sauté the *hijiki* over a medium flame for 10 minutes, or until its strong aroma is gone.
3) Add water to cover pan, and cook 30–40 minutes, or until *hijiki* is swollen and tender.
5) Remove cover, season with soy sauce, and simmer until dry.

6) Just before serving, toast the sesame seeds over a medium-high flame for 4–5 minutes. Stir constantly and shake pan to heat evenly.
7) When the seeds turn light brown and fragrant, remove from heat, and chop with a heavy knife.
8) Sprinkle the chopped sesame seeds over individual portions of *hijiki* and serve.

Hijiki with Lotus Root   *Serves 5*

  ⅔ oz dried *hijiki*
  3 Tbsp sesame oil
  3 oz lotus root, cut into quarter slices
  soy sauce

Hijiki with Lotus Root

1) Wash *hijiki* quickly under cold running water, then cut into 1-inch lengths.
2) Heat the oil in a heavy skillet. Then sauté the lotus root over a low flame for 1–2 minutes, stirring gently. To prevent the lotus root from getting sticky, do not over-cook.
3) Add the *hijiki*, and sauté together for 5–10 minutes, or until *hijiki* no longer releases its strong aroma.
4) Add enough water to cover, and bring to a boil.
5) Simmer 25–30 minutes. Then season with soy sauce, and cook until dry.

Variation
When using dried lotus root, soak it overnight, then proceed as above.

Kombu with Soy Sauce

**1 strip *kombu*, 10 in long, wiped clean
soy sauce
minced ginger**

1) Cut *kombu* into 1-inch squares.
2) Place *kombu* in a deep skillet or heavy saucepan, and add more than enough water to cover.

3) Bring to a boil, and cook 30–40 minutes. Add water if necessary, to keep *kombu* covered.
4) Add 1 part soy sauce to the remaining liquid, and simmer until dry.
5) Cover the *kombu* with equal parts water and soy sauce, and again simmer until dry.
6) Repeat this step once more. Then turn off heat, and add the minced ginger.
7) Serve only 1–2 pieces of this salty condiment per person.
8) Store in an airtight container.

Kombu Root with Soy Sauce

**½ lb *kombu* root (*nekombu*), wiped clean
soy sauce**

1) Place the *kombu* root in a pressure cooker, and add enough water to twice cover.
2) Bring to full pressure over a high flame, reduce flame to low, and simmer 30–40 minutes.
3) Remove from heat, and allow pressure to return to normal.
4) Place *kombu* root in a saucepan, and cover with equal parts soy sauce and water.
5) Bring to a boil, cover, and simmer until

root is tender. Add more water and soy sauce if necessary.

6)   When root is tender, uncover, and simmer until dry.

7)   Serve only 1 piece per person because *kombu* root is very yang.

Fried *Kombu* (*Musubi Kombu*)

1 strip *kombu*, 6 in long, wiped clean with a dry
    towel
oil for deep-frying
sea salt

1)   Pour 3 inches oil in a heavy skillet or deep-fryer, and heat to 350°F.

2)   Cut the *kombu* into strips $1/3 \times 1\frac{1}{2}$ inch.

3)   Tie each strip into a loose knot. Or cut a short slit in the middle of each strip and thread one end of the strip through the slit.

4)   Drop into the hot oil, and deep-fry until swollen and crisp.

5)   Drain on absorbent paper, and sprinkle with salt.

A delicious relish with beer or *saké*.

Simple *Nori* Condiment

1 sheet of *nori*

1)   Toast 1 side of the *nori* by waving it over a low flame until crisp.

2)   Crumble and use as a garnish with rice, vegetables, soups, etc. Or cut into strips and use to wrap rice balls (p. 35).

Roasted *Wakame*

1)   Roast *wakame* directly over an open flame until crisp.

2)   Crumble, and serve as a mineral-rich condiment over rice.

Tempura

Vegetable *Tempura*   *Serves 5*

8–10 half-moon slices ($\frac{1}{4}$-in thick) lotus root
10 green beans, cut in halves diagonally
10-in long piece burdock root, cut in 3-in slivers
1 small carrot, cut into 3-in slivers
oil for deep-frying
tsuke-jiru dipping sauce (p. 135)
Tempura Batter:
2 cups whole-wheat pastry flour
$\frac{1}{2}$ tsp salt
$1\frac{1}{2}$ cups water, approximately

■ *The batter:*

1)   Combine the flour and salt and mix well.

2)   Stir in the water to make a batter.

■ *Cooking:*

1)   Pour 3 inches oil into a heavy skillet or deep-fryer, and heat to 375°F.

2)   Using chopsticks, dip the lotus root and green beans, one at a time, into the batter.

Then drop them immediately into the hot oil.

3)   After 1–2 minutes, turn the pieces over, and fry 1 minute longer, or until golden and crisp. Then drain on absorbent paper.

4)   Mix the burdock and carrot slivers together.

5)   Place small batches of these mixed vegetables on a rice paddle or spatula. Using chopsticks to hold the vegetables in place, dip them into the batter, and then drop into the hot oil.

6)   Deep-fry as in step 3 above. Occasionally remove any bits of batter that remain in the oil, and adjust the temperature of the oil to keep it at 375°F.

7)   Arrange on serving dishes, or in shallow bamboo baskets, and keep warm in a preheated 250°F oven.

Vegetable *Tempura*

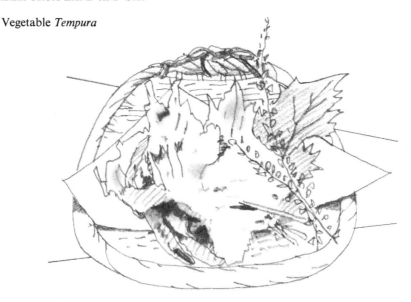

8) Serve with a *tsuke-jiru* dipping sauce, or accompany each serving with 1 tablespoon grated *daikon* seasoned with soy sauce.

Mixed Vegetable *Tempura* Serves 5

1 cup slivered burdock
1 cup slivered carrot
1 cup lotus root, cut into thin half-moons
oil for deep-frying
⅔ oz grated *daikon* radish
soy sauce
Tempura Batter:
1½ cups whole-wheat pastry flour
¼ tsp sea salt
1½ cups water, approximately

1) Fill a heavy skillet or deep-fryer with 3 inches oil, and heat to 370°F.
2) Combine the flour, salt, and enough water to form a thick batter.
3) Add the burdock, carrot and lotus root to the batter, and mix thoroughly.
4) Scoop bunches of the vegetables onto a rice paddle or spatula, and gently drop into the hot oil. Use chopsticks to scrap the mixture off the paddle.
5) After 1–2 minutes, turn the *tempura*

over and fry 1 minute more, or until crisp and golden.
6) Drain on absorbent paper, and keep individual servings warm in a preheated 250°F oven.
7) Serve with mounds of grated *daikon* lightly seasoned with soy sauce.

For special occasions add diced raw shrimp to the batter.

Variation
Substitute a mixture of precooked chestnuts (p. 138) and snow peas for the.vegetables used above. Deep-fry by the spoonful. Or stir 2 cups precooked corn kernels into the batter, and serve with deep-fried *harusame*.

Chestnut *Tempura* Serves 5
(*Kuri Igaguri*)

20 medium chestnuts, cooked
oil for deep-frying
1–2 oz *somen* noodles, broken into ⅓-in lengths
Tempura Batter:
1 cup whole-wheat pastry flour
1–2 Tbsp *yannoh* (grain coffee)

Chestnut *Tempura*
(*Kuri-Igaguri*)

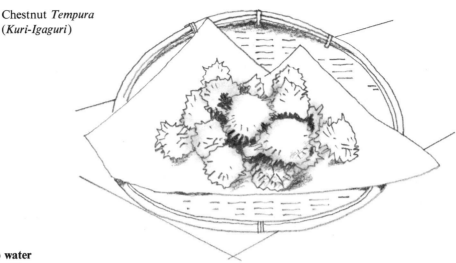

½–¾ **cup water**
¼ **tsp sea salt**

1)   Pour 3 inches oil into a heavy skillet or deep-fryer, and heat to 350°F.
2)   Combine flour, *yannoh*, water and salt to form a thick batter.
3)   Dip each chestnut into the batter, coating thoroughly. Then cover with pieces of *somen*.
4)   Drop into the hot oil, and deep-fry both sides until browned and crisp.
5)   Drain on absorbent paper before serving.

Miso **Stuffed Lotus Root** *Tempura* (*Renkon Miso Inro*)   *Serves 5*

1 lotus root
pinch of sea salt
2 Tbsp sesame oil
1 large onion, minced
2 Tbsp *miso*
oil for deep-frying
5 Tbsp grated *daikon* **radish**
5 tsp soy sauce
Tempura Batter:
  1 cup whole-wheat pastry flour
  ¾ **cup water, approximately**
  ¼ **tsp sea salt**

Miso Stuffed Louts Root *Tempura*
(*Renkon Miso Inro*)

■ *The stuffing:*
1)   Bring a pan of water to a boil, and add a pinch of salt.
2)   Add the whole lotus root, and return to a boil.
3)   Cook 15 minutes, or until tender. Then drain and allow to cool.
4)   Heat 2 tablespoons oil in a skillet, then sauté the onion until translucent.
5)   Place the *miso* on top of the onion without mixing. Then add 1 tablespoon water.
6)   Cover and simmer over a very low flame until water has evaporated, about 10–15 minutes.
7)   Uncover, and stir gently for the first time.

■ *Cooking:*
1)   Pour 3 inches oil into a heavy skillet or deep-fryer, and heat to 350°F.
2)   Combine the flour, water and a ¼ teaspoon salt to form a batter.
3)   Cut a thin slice from one end of the lotus root. Then use the onion-*miso* mixture to stuff the lotus root through its holes.
4)   Dip the stuffed, whole lotus root into the batter, and coat thoroughly.
5)   Drop into the hot oil, and deep-fry until golden and crisp.
6)   Drain on absorbent paper. Then cut into ⅓-inch rounds.
7)   Serve with small mounds of grated *daikon* lightly seasoned with soy sauce.

Onion and Cauliflower Tempura   Serves 5

> 2 medium onions, cut into half-moon slices
> ½ medium cauliflower, separated into flowerets
> oil for deep-frying
> 5 Tbsp grated *daikon* radish
> 5 tsp soy sauce
> *Tempura Batter:*
>   1½ cups whole-wheat pastry flour
>   ½ tsp sea salt
>   1 cup water, approximately

1)   Pour 3 inches oil into a heavy skillet or deep-fryer, and heat to 350°F.
2)   Combine flour, salt and water to form a batter.
3)   Stir the onions and cauliflowerets into the batter, then drop by the spoonful into the hot oil.
4)   Deep-fry until golden and crisp. Then drain on absorbent paper.
5)   Serve with small mounds of grated *daikon* lightly seasoned with soy sauce.

Pumpkin *Tempura*   Serves 5

> 1 small pumpkin or acorn squash
> oil for deep-frying
> 1 cup whole-wheat pastry flour
> ¾ cup water, approximately
> ¼ tsp sea salt
> 5 Tbsp grated *daikon* radish
> 5 tsp soy sauce

1)   Peel pumpkin, then cut into half-moons ⅓ inch thick.
2)   Pour 3 inches oil into a skillet or deep-fryer, and heat to 350°F.
3)   Combine flour, water and ¼ teaspoon salt to form a batter.
4)   Dip pumpkin into batter, and drop into the hot oil.
5)   Deep-fry until crisp and golden. Then drain on absorbent paper.
6)   Serve accompanied with small mounds of grated *daikon* lightly seasoned with soy sauce for dipping.

Pumpkin Peel *Tempura*   Serves 5

> peel from 1 organic pumpkin or acorn squash
> ½ medium onion, minced
> 1 cup whole-wheat flour
> ¾ cup water, approximately
> 2 pinches sea salt
> oil for deep-frying

1) Cut the pumpkin peel into thin strips, and mix with the minced onions.

2) Add enough flour and water to the vegetables to form a batter. Then add the salt.

3) Pour 3 inches oil into a heavy skillet or deep-fryer, and heat to 350°F.

4) Spoon the batter-mix into the hot oil, and deep-fry until golden and crisp.

5) Drain on a wire rack or absorbent paper before serving.

This dish is a delicious way to prevent waste.

Sweet Potato Ball *Tempura*   *Serves 5*

    3 cups sweet potato purée
    1 cup minced onion
    oil for deep-frying
    1 cup whole-wheat pastry flour
    1 cup water
    $\frac{1}{2}$ tsp sea salt
    5 Tbsp grated *daikon* radish
    5 tsp soy sauce

1) Combine sweet potato and onion, mixing thoroughly.

2) Form mixture into 1-inch balls and set aside.

3) Pour 3 inches oil into a heavy skillet or deep-fryer, and heat to 350°F.

4) Combine the flour, water and salt to form a batter.

5) Dip the balls into the batter, coating thoroughly.

6) Drop the balls into the hot oil, and deep-fry until golden and crisp.

7) Drain on absorbent paper, and serve with grated *daikon* lightly seasoned with soy sauce for dipping.

Nut Snack *Tempura*

Dip whole almonds, cashews or walnuts, olives or pitted *umeboshi* into the tempura batter and deep-fry.

Delicious as snacks with beer.

Pumpkin Croquettes   *Serves 5*

    3 cups pumpkin or acorn squash purée
    $\frac{1}{2}$ cup minced onion
    $\frac{1}{4}$ cup grated carrot
    $\frac{1}{4}$ tsp sea salt
    1 heaping Tbsp whole-wheat pastry flour
    oil for deep-frying
    2 cups bread crumbs

Sweet Potato Ball *Tempura*

Batter:
  1 cup whole-wheat pastry flour
  ¼ tsp sea salt
  1 cup water, approximately

1) Combine the vegetables, and add ¼ teaspoon salt.
2) Form into 10 croquettes, using flour if necessary to hold the mixture together.
3) Pour 3 inches oil into a heavy skillet or deep-fryer, and heat to 350°F.
4) Combine 1 cup flour, ¼ teaspoon salt and enough water to form a batter.
5) Dip the croquettes into the batter, then roll in bread crumbs.
6) Drop the croquettes into the hot oil, and deep-fry until crisp and golden.
7) Drain on absorbent paper before serving.

Variation

Instead of deep-frying, brown the croquettes in a well oiled skillet. Serve with gravy (p. 133).

Deep-Fried Turnip with Egg White (*Kabu Awayuki Agé*)   *Serves 5*

  3 cups grated turnip
  oil for deep-frying
  3 Tbsp whole-wheat pastry flour, approximately
  1 egg white, beaten until stiff
  2½ Tbsp grated *daikon* radish
  2½ Tbsp grated carrot
  5 tsp soy sauce

1) Pour 3 inches oil into a heavy skillet or deep-fryer, and heat to 350°F.

2) Mix the turnip with enough flour to form a thick batter, then fold in the egg white.
3) Drop the mixture into the hot oil by the spoonful, and deep-fry 2–3 minutes, or until browned and crisp.
4) Drain on absorbent paper.
5) Serve with a mixture of grated *daikon* and carrot lightly seasoned with soy sauce for dipping.

Deep-Fried Vegetable Balls   *Serves 5*

  1 medium onion, minced
  5 green beans, rinsed, trimmed and chopped into small pieces
  3 cups pumpkin or squash purée
  oil for deep-frying
  3 Tbsp minced *seitan*
  ½ tsp sea salt
  1 cup whole-wheat pastry flour
  2 cups bread crumbs

1) Fill a heavy skillet or deep-fryer with 3 inches oil, and heat to 360°F.
2) Combine onion, beans, pumpkin and *seitan*, and season with the salt.
3) Add enough flour to hold the mixture together, and form into 15 or so 1-inch balls.
4) Coat balls with bread crumbs, and drop into the hot oil.
5) Fry both sides until crisp and golden.
6) Drain on a wire rack or absorbent paper before serving.

Wild Vegetables

Bracken   *Serves 5*

Use the young shoots or fiddleheads found in early spring.

  ¼ lb bracken
  ¼ tsp sea salt
  1 Tbsp sesame oil
  ⅔ Tbsp soy sauce

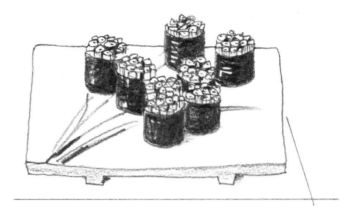

Bracken

1)   Wash the bracken thoroughly, and trim off discolored (brownish) areas.

2)   Bring a small pan of water (just enough to cover the bracken) to a boil, then add the salt.

3)   Drop in the bracken, return to a boil, and cook 10 minutes.

4)   Drain in a colander, and cut into 1-inch lenghts.

5)   Heat the oil in a heavy skillet. Then sauté the bracken over a medium flame for 5 minutes, stirring gently.

6)   Season with soy sauce, reduce flame to very low, and simmer dry.

7)   Serve in small portions.

Variations

A.   Bracken Nori Roll:

1.   Cut a sheet of toasted *nori* into halves, and place on a *sudare* or bamboo mat.

2)   Arrange the sautéed bracken along one edge of each piece of *nori*.

3)   Sprinkle the opposite edge of each *nori* sheet with a few drops of water. Then roll into a tight cylinder.

4)   Remove mat, and slice rolls into rounds.

B.   Bracken Agé Roll:

1)   Douse 1 piece of *agé* with boiling water, and drain.

2)   Using scissors, open the *agé* by cutting open 1 long and 2 short sides.

3)   Lay the *agé* out flat, and cut into halves. Then place on a *sudare* or bamboo mat.

4)   Arrange the sautéed bracken along one edge of each piece of *agé*.

5)   Roll into a cylinder, and tie at 4 equidistant points with strips of *kampyo* (gourd) rinsed in lightly salted water.

6)   Bring 2 cups *kombu dashi* (p. 113) to a boil, and season to taste with soy sauce.

7)   Drop in the rolls, and cook 15 minutes, or until the liquid is gone and the *agé* are well flavored.

8)   Drain rolls and allow to cool. Then slice each roll crosswise into 5 pieces.

Dandelion with Soy Sauce   *Serves 5*

Pick dandelions while the leaves are still tender and before the flower blooms.

½ lb dandelion greens
1 Tbsp sesame oil
3 Tbsp soy sauce
3 Tbsp water
1 Tbsp sesame seeds, roasted and chopped with a knife

1)   Wash the greens, and chop fine.
2)   Heat the oil in a heavy skillet, then sauté the greens over a medium flame for 2–3 minutes.
3)   Thin the soy sauce with the water, and add to the pan of greens.
4)   Simmer until liquid is completely absorbed.
5)   Serve sprinkled with roasted, chopped sesame seeds.

For variety, use 3 tablespoons of *miso* instead of soy sauce.

Variation

Dandelion Roots:
1)   Scrub roots well, then mince.
2)   Sauté in a little sesame oil over a medium flame for 3–4 minutes.
3)   Season with soy sauce or thinned *miso*, and simmer until dry.

Use sparingly as a garnish with rice.
This is a traditional dish for arthritis.

Mustard Greens in Sesame Sauce
Serves 5

½ lb mustard greens, washed thoroughly
¼ tsp sea salt
1 Tbsp sesame butter
⅔ Tbsp soy sauce

1)   Bring a pan of water to a boil, then add the salt.
2)   Drop in the greens, and cook until tender and bright green.
3)   Drain greens in a colander, and cool to room temperature. In Japan this is done by fanning the greens with a paper fan. The bright green color of the vegetables are preserved in this way.
4)   Mix sesame butter and soy sauce to make a sauce.

5)   Serve individual portions of the greens topped with sesame sauce.

Wild Scallions
Serves 5

¼ lb wild scallions
1 Tbsp sesame oil
2–3 Tbsp soy sauce

1)   Wash scallions, and cut into 1-inch lengths.
2)   Heat the oil, and sauté scallions over a medium flame for 3–4 minutes.
3)   Season with soy sauce, and simmer until liquid is completely absorbed.

Variations

A.   Skipping step 3 above, add the sautéed scallions to a *miso* soup stock about 5 minutes before adding the *miso*.
B.   After step 1 above, dip the scallion pieces into *tempura* batter and deep-fry.

Wild Spinach in Sesame Sauce *Serves 5*

¼ lb wild spinach
2 pinches sea salt
1 Tbsp sesame butter
2 Tbsp water
soy sauce

1)   Bring a large pan of water to a rolling boil, and add the salt.
2)   Drop in the spinach, return to a boil, and cook 5 minutes, or until leaves are bright green.
3)   Drain spinach thoroughly in a colander, and cool. Then cut into 1½-inch lengths.
4)   Thin the sesame butter with 2 table-spoons water, and season with soy sauce.
5)   Add drained spinach to the *suribachi*, and toss with the sesame sauce.
6)   Serve in small portions.

Salads

Pressed Salad

Salting, then pressing raw vegetables, removes excess liquid, thus making them more yang. The type of vegetables, and the amount of salt, time and pressure used are factors which influence the quality of pickles. Short time, yin, pickles are refreshing in the hot, yang, summer. Long time pickles, yang, are more suited for the cold, yin, winter. Cabbage, lettuce, cucumber, carrot, onion and many other vegetables are delicious prepared in this way.

1)   Cut roots into thin slices or slivers. Chop green leaves fine, and cut cabbage heads into 1-inch wide pieces.
2)   Place the vegetables in a large bowl, sprinkle with salt, and cover with a dish that sits directly on top of the ingredients.
3)   Place a stone or other heavy weight on top of the plate for added pressure. Or combine the vegetables and salt in a salad press.
4)   Allow the vegetables to pickle 30 minutes to 3 days, depending on the strength of pickle desired.

6)   Serve small portions—1–2 tablespoons—to each person.

Endive Salad   *Serves 5*

3 small endives
1 medium cucumber
5 small red radishes
2 Tbsp olive or corn oil
¼ tsp sea salt
⅔ drops lemon juice or 1 Tbsp *umeboshi* juice (p. 166)

1)   Cut the endives into ½-inch pieces, and the cucumber into diagonal slices.
2)   Cut radishes into flower shapes, and soak in cold water until they open.
3)   Combine oil, salt, and lemon juice in a large bowl.
4)   Add the vegetables and toss the ingredients together lightly.

Biifun Salad   *Serves 5*

6 oz *biifun*
¼   tsp and 4 pinches sea salt

Biifun Salad

1 small cauliflower, separated into flowerets
½ bunch watercress
1 small carrot, slivered
3 Tbsp corn or olive oil
1 tsp fresh orange juice
1 hard boiled egg, yolk and white separated
  (optional)

■ *The noodles:*

1) Bring 1 quart water to a rolling boil, and add 2 pinches salt.

2) Drop in the *biifun* noodles, return to a boil, and cook 3–4 minutes.

3) Drain in a strainer, and set aside to cool.

■ *The vegetables:*

1) Bring a second pan of water to a boil, and add 2 pinches salt.

2) Drop in the cauliflowerets, and return to a boil. Then cook 5 minutes, or until just tender, but still crisp.

3) Remove the cauliflower, and set aside to drain.

4) Drop in the watercress, and cook 2–3 minutes, or until the leaves are bright green.

5) Drain in a colander, and allow to cool.

6) Drop in the carrot slivers, and cook 2–3 minutes, or until bright orange.

7) Drain and set aside.

■ *The salad:*

1) Combine oil, ¼ teaspoon salt and the orange juice in a large bowl.

2) Add noodles and vegetables, and toss ingredients together.

3) Place salad on a large platter. Garnish with egg white and yolk, grated separately, and parsley sprigs.

Boiled Salad

Another way to "yangize" raw vegetables for use in salads is to steam or boil them in lightly salted water. Cook until just tender but still crisp. Cut vegetables fine to cook quickly. Save the cooking water for baking, or as a weak *dashi* or broth for cooking other vegetables.

Cauliflower Salad   *Serves 5*

3 pieces *koya-dofu*, grated
1 tsp sesame or corn oil
6 pinches sea salt
1–2 Tbsp soy sauce
3 small carrots, grated
1 small cauliflower, separated into flowerets
½ 1b watercress
2–3 red radish, cut into flower-shapes
Lyonnaise Sauce:
3 tsp sesame oil
½ cup whole-wheat pastry flour
1 cup minced onion
2 cups water, approximately
¼ cup white wine

■ *The koya-dofu:*

1) Place grated *koya-dofu* at the center of 3 layers of cheesecloth or a piece of unbleached muslin about 1 foot square. Then gather in the corners to form a sack.

2) Hold sack in a pan of boiling water for 2–3 minutes, then cool under running cold water.

3) Press sack between your palms while continuing to rinse until white foam is no longer released. Then squeeze out excess liquid.

4) Heat a heavy skillet, and coat with the oil.

5) Sauté the *koya-dofu* over a medium flame for 2–3 minutes, stirring constantly.

6) Add water to cover, and cook until dry.

7) Season with 3 pinches salt and the soy sauce, trying to keep the color of the *koya-dofu* light.

8) Remove from heat, and cool to room temperature.

9) Blend in grated carrots, and set mixture aside.

■ *The vegetables:*

1) Bring a large pan of water to a boil, and add 2 pinches of salt.

2) Drop in the cauliflower, return to a boil, and cook 5 minutes, or until tender but still crisp. Then drain in a colander.

3) Drop in the watercress, and cook until leaves are bright green and stems are tender. Then drain.

4) When cool, squeeze the excess liquid out of the leaves. Then chop, and sprinkle with a pinch of salt.

■ *The sauce:*

1) Heat 2 teaspoons oil in a heavy skillet, and add ½ cup flour.

2) Roast about 5 minutes, stirring briskly. Then set aside to cool.

3) Heat 1 teaspoon oil in another skillet, then sauté the minced onions until browned, about 5 minutes. Stir constantly to prevent burning.

4) Return the roasted flour to a medium-low flame, and add 1 cup water.

5) Stir briskly with a whisk, and add enough water to reach a creamy consistency, about ½–1 cup.

6) Add the sautéed onions, and flavor with ¼ cup white wine.

■ *The salad:*

1) Arrange cauliflower at the center of a large platter. Then pour on the lyonnaise sauce.

2) Surround the cauliflower with the *koya-dofu*-carrot mixture, and then with the watercress.

3) Garnish with a few red radishes.

Chick-Pea Salad   *Serves 5*

2 cups cooked chick-peas (p. 138)
2 oz *harusame* or 2 oz cooked vermicelli
¼ tsp and a pinch of sea salt
½ small carrot, cut into thin half-moons
1 Tbsp minced onion
2 Tbsp corn or olive oil
few drops of fresh orange juice
1 medium cucumber, sliced fine on a diagonal

1) Bring 4–6 cups water to a boil, then

cook *harusame* 3–4 minutes.

2) Drain noodles, and cool thoroughly under cold running water. Then cut into 1-inch lengths.

3) Bring another pan of water to a boil, and add a pinch of salt.

4) Drop in carrot slices, and return to a boil. Cook several minutes, or until bright orange and just tender.

5) Drain carrot and set aside.

6) Place minced onions in a large bowl. Then add oil, ¼ teaspoon salt and the orange juice.

7) Let the mixture sit for 10 minutes.

8) Add noodles, carrot, cucumber and chick-peas, and toss together.

Fruit Salad   *Serves 5*

1-in piece lotus root
4 pinches sea salt
1 tsp minced onion
1 tsp corn or olive oil
1 small carrot, thin slivered
2 medium apples, chopped fine
2 small cucumbers, cut in thin half-moons
20 strawberries, rinsed in salted water
5 small radishes, cut into flower-shapes
1 hard boiled egg, yolk and white separated (optional)

1) Bring a small pan of water to a boil, and add 2 pinches salt.

2) Cook lotus root 2–3 minutes, or until tender.

3) Drain and allow to cool. Then mince.

4) Place minced onion in a large bowl.

5) Add oil and 2 pinches salt, and allow to stand 10 minutes.

6) Add carrot slices, lotus root and apples, and toss ingredients together.

7) Arrange on a large platter, and surround with cucumber slices, strawberries and radishes.

8) Top with egg white and yolk, grated separately.

Wakame and Cucumber Salad   *Serves 5*

1½ oz *wakame*
pinch of sea salt
1 medium cucumber, sliced very fine on a diagonal
juice of one orange
¼ cup *umeboshi* juice (p. 166)

1) Wash *wakame* quickly, and soak 10–15 minutes.
2) Strain *wakame*, and press between your palms to remove excess liquid. Then cut into ⅔-inch squares.
3) Rub the salt into the cucumber slices, and let stand 10 minutes. Then squeeze out excess liquid.
4) Combine *wakame*, cucumber and orange juice in a large bowl.
5) Pour in *umeboshi* juice, and toss.

Delicious on a hot summer day.

3. SOUPS AND STEWS

Dashi Number One (*Ichiban Dashi*)   *Makes 2½ Quarts*

7-in strip *kombu*, wiped clean with a dry cloth
10 cups water
1 cup dried bonito flakes (*katsuo bushi*)

1) Bring *kombu* and all the water to a boil over a high flame.
2) Boil 2–4 minutes, then remove *kombu* and save for use in another dish. Or leave *kombu* in the pan and proceed to step 3.
3) Stir in the dried bonito flakes, return to a boil, then turn off heat.
4) Let stand 2–3 minutes, or until bonito flakes sink to the bottom.
5) Strain, and save the bonito flakes (and *kombu* if still in the pan) for use in *dashi* No. 2 or for other dishes.

Dashi Number Two (*Niban Dashi*)   *Makes 2½ Quarts*

10 cups water
leftover *kombu*
leftover bonito flakes (*katsuo bushi*)
vegetable trimmings

1) Add 10 cups water to the *kombu* and bonito flakes left from making *dashi* No. 1. Include any vegetable trimmings that you have.
2) Bring to a boil over a high flame, and cook with the lid slightly ajar for 5 minutes.
3) Turn off heat and set aside until the bonito flakes sink to the bottom.
4) Strain, discarding *kombu*, bonito and vegetables.

Use as a weak stock for cooking vegetables.

Kombu Dashi   *Makes 1 Quart*

1 strip *kombu*, 7×3 in
4 cups cold water

1) Wipe the *kombu* clean with a dry cloth.
2) Soak the *kombu* in water for 2–3 hours. Or boil 1 hour.
3) Strain to remove the *kombu*.
4) Use this *dashi* in place of water for extra flavor and nutrition in cooking.

Vegetable Stock   *Makes 2 Quarts*

10 cups water
1 piece *kombu*, 3-in square
3 cups vegetable trimming* (onion, carrot, celery, etc.)
2–3 eggshells (optional)

1) Bring the water to a boil, and add *kombu*, trimmings, and eggshells if using.
2) Return to a boil, and cook 30–40 minutes, leaving the lid slightly ajar to prevent boiling over.
3) Turn off heat, and allow to stand 2–3 minutes. Then strain, reserving the liquid for use as cooking stock.

*Never discard the skins or odd ends of vegetables not used when preparing other dishes. A delicious, nutritious stock can be made from carrot crowns, onion skins and other trimmings.

Wakame Miso Soup   *Serves 5*

½ oz dried *wakame*
5 cups *kombu dashi*
½ cake *tofu*, cubed (optional)
5 level Tbsp *miso*

1) Soak the dried *wakame* in water to cover for 10 minutes. Then cut into small pieces.
2) Bring the *dashi* to a boil, then remove

the *kombu* if still in the *dashi*.

3) Add *wakame* and cook 5–10 minutes. Then add *tofu* cubes if using.

4) Thin the *miso* with several tablespoons of the cooking broth, and add, stirring until smooth.

5) Return just to a boil and turn off heat.

Mugi (Barley) *Miso* Soup   *Serves 5*

> 1 oz *wakame*
> 1 Tbsp sesame oil
> greens from 1 medium turnip, finely chopped
> 1 medium turnip, cut in thin half-moons
> 4–5 cups *kombu dashi* (p. 113)
> ⅔ Tbsp *mugi miso*

■ *The vegetables:*

1) Rinse the *wakame* quickly under cold running water. Then soak it for 10 minutes.

2) When soft, cut the *wakame* into ⅓-inch lengths and set aside.

3) Heat a saucepan and add the oil.

4) When oil is hot, sauté the turnip greens over a medium flame for 1 minute. Stir constantly.

5) Add the turnip half-moons, and sauté together for a few minutes.

6) Add the *dashi* and bring to a boil over a high flame.

7) Reduce flame to medium, add the *wakame*, and cover pan.

8) Cook 15–20 minutes, or until vegetables are tender.

■ *The soup:*

1) Put the *miso* in a *suribachi* and add ½ cup cooking stock.

2) Grind *miso* smooth. Then add to the cooking broth and stir to distribute evenly.

3) Bring just to a boil, and turn off heat.

4) Serve immediately.

Miso Soup with *Saké* Lees   *Serves 5*

> 1 cup scallions or leeks, sliced diagonally into
>   1-in lengths
> 1 Tbsp sesame oil
> 2 cups *daikon* radish, cut into thin rectangles
> 5 small taro potatoes, sliced lengthwise into halves
> carrot, 5 flower-shaped pieces
> 5 cups water
> 2 heaping Tbsp *miso*
> ½–1 cup *saké* lees*

1) Heat the oil in a heavy saucepan. Then sauté the scallions or leeks over a medium flame for 1–2 minutes. Stir constantly.

2) Add in order *daikon*, taro and carrot.

3) Mix vegetables together and sauté 1 minute.

4) Pour in 5 cups water and bring to a boil over a high flame.

5) Reduce flame to medium, cover, and cook 30 minutes, or until tender.

■ *The soup:*

1) Thin the *miso* in 4–5 tablespoons cooking broth.

2) Thin the *saké* lees in 3–4 tablespoons water.

3) Blend the *miso* and then the lees into the soup, stirring until smooth.

4) Bring just to a boil and turn off heat.

5) Serve immediately.

Saké lees can be found at Oriental food stores.

Corn Soup   *Serves 5*

> 3 medium ears of corn, kernels cut from cobs
> 2 Tbsp corn oil
> 1 small onion, minced
> 1 piece *kombu*, 3-in square
> 6 cups water
> pinch of sea salt
> ½ medium cauliflower, separated into flowerets
> 1 Tbsp *kuzu*
> 2 Tbsp water
> 2 Tbsp croutons
> 2 Tbsp minced parsley

■ *The broth:*

1) Heat a heavy saucepan, then coat with the oil.

2) When oil is hot, sauté the onion over a medium flame for 2–3 minutes, stirring gently.

3) Add the corn kernels and sauté together for 1 minute. Do not let the kernels brown.

4) Add the *kombu*, pour in 6 cups water, and bring to a boil over a high flame.

5) Reduce flame to medium, cover, and cook 20–30 minutes.

■ *The cauliflower:*

1) While broth is cooking, bring a small pan of water (enough to cover the flowerets) to a boil over a high flame. Then add a pinch of salt.

2) Drop in the cauliflowerets, return to a boil, and cook 5 minutes, or until tender but still crisp.

3) Remove flowerets with a slotted spoon, and drain in a colander.

■ *The soup:*

1) Dissolve the *kuzu* in 2 tablespoons cold water.

2) When broth is done, season with salt to taste. Then pour in the *kuzu*.

3) Simmer 1–2 minutes, stirring while the soup thickens.

4) Serve topped with cauliflowerets, croutons, and a sprinkling of minced parsley.

Corn Cream Soup 1   *Serves 5*

2 Tbsp corn oil
1 small onion, minced
1 cup corn flour
1 small carrot, slivered
6 cups *kombu dashi* (p. 113)
1 Tbsp sesame oil
¼ cup unbleached white flour
¾ cup water
sea salt
2 Tbsp croutons
2 Tbsp minced parsley

■ *Corn cream:*

1) Heat a heavy skillet and coat with the corn oil.

2) When oil is hot, sauté the onion over a medium flame until lightly browned, stirring gently.

3) Add the corn flour and sauté until golden.

4) Add the carrot and *dashi*, and bring to a boil.

5) Cover and simmer 30 minutes, stirring occasionally.

■ *The sauce:*

1) While the cream is cooking, heat the sesame oil in a heavy skillet.

2) When oil is hot, add the white flour and cook until lightly browned and fragrant. Stir constantly to heat evenly.

3) Remove from stove and cool. Then gradually add the water, stirring until smooth.

4) Return pan to stove and cook 2–3 minutes, or until edges of sauce bubble. Stir constantly.

■ *The soup:*

1) When the corn cream is ready, blend in the flour sauce.

2) Season with salt to taste, and simmer 5 minutes.

3) Serve topped with croutons and sprinkled with minced parsley.

Corn Cream Soup 2   *Serves 5*

2 Tbsp corn oil
1 medium onion, minced
3 ears of corn, kernels removed
6 cups *kombu dashi* (p. 113)
sea salt
1 heaping Tbsp *kuzu*
2–3 Tbsp water
1 egg, beaten
2 Tbsp parsley, chopped
5 thin strips lemon peel

1) Heat a heavy saucepan and coat with the oil.

2) When oil is hot, sauté the onion over a medium flame for 2–3 minutes, stirring gently.

3) Add corn and sauté together for 1 minute. Do not allow the kernels to brown.

4)   Pour in the *dashi* and bring to a boil over a high flame.

5)   Reduce flame to medium, cover, and cook 30–45 minutes.

6)   When done, season with salt to taste.

■ *The thickener:*

1)   Dissolve the *kuzu* in the water, then add the egg and mix well.

2)   Add this mixture to the soup, and stir constantly while it thickens. Add more salt if necessary.

3)   Serve sprinkled with parsley and garnished with lemon peel.

Clear Soup with Brown Rice Dumplings (*Genmai Suiton*)   *Serves 4*

> 20 green beans, rinsed and trimmed
> oil for deep-frying
> 2 Tbsp sesame oil
> 1 cup scallions or leeks, cut into 1-in diagonal slices
> 5 small turnips, cut into quarters
> 5 cups *kombu dashi* (p. 113)
> ½ cup boiling water
> 1 cup brown rice flour
> 1 tsp sea salt
> 1½ Tbsp soy sauce
> 1 sheet *nori* or *aonori* (green *nori*) flakes

■ *The beans:*

1)   Fill a heavy skillet or deep-fryer with 2–3 inches oil, and heat to 350°F.

2)   Drop in the green beans and deep-fry until crisp.

3)   Drain on absorbent paper, and slice on a diagonal into thirds. Then set slices in a warm oven until ready to use.

■ *The broth:*

1)   Heat a heavy saucepan and coat with the sesame oil.

2)   When oil is hot, sauté the scallions or leeks over a medium flame for 4–5 minutes, or until lightly browned.

3)   Add the turnips and sauté together for 1 minute.

4)   Cover with the *dashi* and bring to a boil over a high flame.

5)   Reduce flame to medium, cover, and cook 20–30 minutes, or until tender.

■ *The dumplings:*

1)   While broth is cooking, add boiling water to the rice flour while stirring vigorously with 4 long chopsticks held in your fist. Or use a long fork with 4 tines.

2)   Knead 3–4 minutes, until dough is smooth and somewhat stiff.

3)   Divide the dough into 8 portions and roll each into a small dumpling.

■ *The soup:*

1)   When vegetables are tender, season the broth with the salt and soy sauce.

2)   Drop in the 8 dumplings. They will sink to the bottom of the pan. When they rise to the surface remove the dumplings with a slotted spoon.

■ *Just before serving:*

1)   Toast 1 side of the *nori* by waving it over a low flame for several seconds, or until crisp.

2)   Using scissors, cut the *nori* in half, then crosswise into thin strips.

3)   Ladle the soup into individual serving bowls, and garnish each with several green beans and toasted *nori* strips or *aonori* flakes.

Borscht   *Serves 5*

> 3 Tbsp sesame oil
> 3 small onions, quartered
> 5 small cabbage leaves, cut into 2-in squares
> 1 small tomato (optional), quartered
> 1 small beet, cubed
> 2 small carrots, cubed
> ¼ tsp sea salt
> 5–6 cups water
> 2 bay leaves
> 2 small celery stalks, cubed

1)   Heat a heavy skillet and coat with the oil.

2) When oil is hot, sauté the onion over a medium flame for 5 minutes, or until lightly browned.

3) Add in order, the cabbage, tomato (if used), beet and carrot. Then mix the ingredients together.

4) Season with the salt to keep the vegetables firm and to help hold their color.

5) Add enough water to cover, and drop in the bay leaves.

6) Bring to a boil over a high flame, then reduce flame to medium. Cook, covered, for 20–30 minutes, or until vegetables are tender.

7) Add the celery and cook 5 minutes more.

8) Season with salt to taste, and serve.

Mountain Potato (*Jinenjo*) Soup

1) Prepare a soup using your favorite vegetables.

2) When done, add 1 tablespoon finely grated *jinenjo* per cup of soup.

3) Simmer 1–2 minutes, then season with soy sauce to taste.

Jinenjo, or mountain potato, grows wild in the mountains of Japan. When grated, it clings together strongly, telling us that it is very yang. It is available at macrobiotic outlets and Oriental food stores. Try it. It is delicious and invigorating.

Kokoh Soup   *Serves 5*

½ small cauliflower, separated into flowerets
¼ tsp and a pinch of sea salt
1 Tbsp sesame oil
2 small onions, cut into thick crescents
2 cups cubed Hokkaido pumpkin or acorn squash
1 small carrot, diced
3 Tbsp minced *seitan*
5¾ cups water
5 Tbsp *kokoh* (p. 56)

2 Tbsp minced parsley
1 tsp minced orange peel

■ *The cauliflower:*

1) Bring a small pan of water to a boil over a high flame, and add a pinch of salt.

2) Drop in the cauliflowerets, return to a boil, and cook 3 minutes, or until flowerets are tender but still crisp.

3) Set flowerets aside in a colander to drain.

■ *The stock:*

1) Heat a heavy saucepan and coat with the oil.

2) When oil is hot, sauté the onions over a medium flame, stirring gently, for 5 minutes, or until well browned.

3) Add pumpkin or squash, carrot and *seitan.*

4) Pour in enough water to cover (about 5 cups), and season with ¼ teaspoon salt.

5) Bring to a boil over a high flame. Then reduce flame to medium, cover, and cook 25 minutes, or until tender.

■ *The soup:*

1) Thin the *kokoh* in ¾ cup water.

2) When the stock is ready, blend in the *kokoh.*

3) Cook 5 minutes, stirring constantly. Then season with salt to taste.

4) Serve topped with cauliflowerets, minced parsley and a sprinkling of the orange peel.

Mochi Soup   *Serves 5*

8 pieces *mochi*
¼ tsp sea salt
1 cup scallions or leeks, sliced diagonally into 1-in lengths
4 small taro potatoes, boiled and cut in half
carrot, 8 thin flower-shaped pieces
1 bunch spinach or watercress, washed and trimmed
3 Tbsp and 2 tsp sesame oil
½ small onion, minced
3-in piece *kombu*, wiped clean
4 rolls *maki-yuba*, optional
oil for deep-frying

½ cup whole-wheat pastry flour
2 Tbsp minced parsley

■ *The vegetables:*

1)   In a 2-quart saucepan, bring 6 cups water to a boil. Then add ¼ teaspoon salt.

2)   Drop in the scallions, return to a boil, and cook 5 minutes, or until vegetables are tender.

3)   Remove, drain, and set aside.

4)   In the same water, boil the taro potatoes until tender. Then remove and set aside.

5)   Drop in the carrot flowers and cook 2–3 minutes, or until just tender. Then remove, drain and set aside.

6)   Drop in the spinach, and cook 1–3 minutes, until stems are tender.

7)   Then squeeze lightly to remove excess water. Save the cooking water.

8)   Arrange spinach in a bundle, and slice into 1-inch lengths. Then set aside.

■ *The stock:*

1)   Heat a heavy saucepan and coat with 1 teaspoon sesame oil.

2)   When oil is hot, sauté the onion over a medium flame for 1–2 minutes, or until its strong aroma is gone.

3)   Add 5 cups of the water used to cook the vegetables, and bring to a boil over a high flame. Then drop in the *kombu*.

4)   Reduce flame to medium, cover, and cook 20 minutes.

5)   Remove *kombu*, and season the broth with salt to taste.

■ *The maki-yuba (if using):*

1)   Fill a heavy skillet or deep-fryer with 2–3 inches oil, and heat to 350°F.

2)   Drop in the *maki-yuba* and deep-fry 2–3 minutes, or until crisp and golden.

3)   Drain on absorbent paper, and set aside in a warm oven until ready to use.

■ *The sauce:*

1)   Heat a heavy skillet and coat with 3 tablespoons sesame oil.

2)   When oil is hot, add the flour and cook over a medium flame until browned and fragrant. Stir constantly.

3)   Remove from heat and cool, or dip bottom of pan into cold water.

4)   Stir in 2 cups water, blending smooth.

5)   Return to heat, bring to a boil, and simmer 10–15 minutes, stirring constantly.

6)   Season with salt to taste, and continue to simmer the sauce until ready to use.

■ *The mochi:*

1)   Heat 1 teaspoon sesame oil in a heavy skillet.

2)   Brown 1 side of the *mochi*, then turn it over and brown the other side. Then remove from pan and set aside.

■ *To assemble:*

1)   Place 2 pieces of *mochi* in each of 5 serving bowls.

2)   Arrange the scallions, carrot and watercress around the *mochi*.

3)   Pour in the hot broth and spoon some of the thickened sauce on top of each serving.

4)   Crown the sauce with a piece of *maki-yuba* (if using), sprinkle with minced parsley, and serve.

Soybean Potage (*Go Jiru*)   Serves 5

1 cup soybeans, soaked overnight
2 pieces *agé**
1 Tbsp sesame oil
½ cup scallions or leeks, sliced diagonally into
    1-in lengths
1 small carrot, diced
½ tsp and a pinch of sea salt
5 green beans, rinsed and trimmed
soy sauce

1)   Grind the soaked soybeans to a smooth paste in a *suribachi* or electric mixer. Please note that this is one of the few times that an electric mixer is used in macrobiotic cooking.

2)   Place the *agé* in a colander, and pour

5–6 cups boiling water over it to remove excess oil.

3) Drain and then cut the *age* into 2-inch squares.

■ *The soup:*

1) Heat a heavy saucepan and coat with the oil.

2) When oil is hot, sauté the scallions or leeks over a medium flame for 2–3 minutes, stirring constantly.

3) Add soybean paste, carrot and *age* squares.

4) Add enough water to twice cover the ingredients, season with ½ teaspoon salt, and bring to a boil over a high flame.

5) Reduce flame to medium, cover, and cook 30 minutes, stirring occasionally.

■ *The green beans:*

1) While soup is cooking, bring a small pan of water to a boil over a high flame. Then add a pinch of salt.

2) Drop in the green beans, return to a boil, and cook 4–5 minutes, until beans are bright green and just tender.

3) Drain the beans in a colander, then slice diagonally into thirds.

■ *Serving:*

1) When soup is done, season with soy sauce to taste.

2) Serve garnished with green beans.

*As a substitute for *age*, slice dry pack *tofu* into ¼-inch thick slices. Then deep-fry and drain on absorbent paper.

Japanese-Style Stew   *Serves 4*

> 8 pieces *mochi*
> 6 taro potatoes, peeled
> 7 cups *kombu dashi* (p. 113)
> 4½ Tbsp soy sauce
> ½ tsp and a pinch of sea salt
> 5¼ oz green vegetables (watercress, kale, cabbage, etc.)
> 4 *shiitake* mushrooms
> 4 slices of carrot, cut into flower shapes
> 1 Tbsp *sake*
> green *nori* (*aonori*)

1) Rub the taro potatoes with salt. Then rinse under running water.

2) Bring a pan of water to a boil, add the taro and cook 5 minutes. Then wash the taro under cold running water to remove their stickiness.

3) Combine 2 cups *dashi*, 1½ tablespoons soy sauce, and ¼ teaspoon salt in a saucepan.

4) Add the taro potatoes and cook until tender. Then drain and cut into halves.

Japanese-Style Stew

5)   Add a pinch of salt to a pan of boiling water. Drop in the greens and cook until bright green. Then drain and cut in ¾-inch lengths.

6)   Soak the *shiitake* in lightly salted cold water until tender, about 20 minutes. Then remove their hard stems.

7)   Cook the *shiitake* in 1 cup *dashi* combined with 1 tablespoon soy sauce. Simmer until liquid has evaporated.

8)   Place the carrot slices in a skillet. Sprinkle with salt. The salt will draw liquid from the carrots.

9)   Sauté the carrot slices in their own liquid until dry. Then add a little water, and cover. Cook over a low flame until tender, adding more water if necessary.

10)   Toast the *mochi* over a low flame until puffed and brown. Turn once while cooking.

11)   Combine 4 cups *dashi*, ¼ teaspoon salt, 2 tablespoons soy sauce and 1 tablespoon *saké* in a saucepan.

12)   Add the *mochi* and bring just to a boil.

13)   Put 2 pieces of *mochi* in each of 4 serving bowls.

14)   Divide the vegetables between the 4 bowls and pour in the soup stock.

15)   Serve garnished with the green *nori* flakes.

Vegetable Stew (*Kenchin Jiru*) *Serves 5*

1 cup scallions or leeks, sliced diagonally into 1-in lenghts
1 Tbsp sesame oil
1 cup shaved burdock
2-in long piece *daikon* radish, cut into ¼-in rounds, then into quarters
½ small carrot, cut into ¼-in thick half-moons
¼ cake *konnyaku** (optional), cut in ½ × ½-in rectangular slices
1 piece (3-in square) *kombu*
sea salt
5–6 Tbsp soy sauce

1)   Heat a heavy pot and coat with the oil.

2)   When oil is hot, sauté the scallion over a medium flame for 5 minutes, or until lightly browned.

3)   Add in order, the burdock, *daikon*, carrot and *konnyaku* (if used).

4)   Mix the ingredients together, and sauté 1–2 minutes.

5)   Drop in the *kombu*, add slightly more than enough water to cover, and bring to a boil over a high flame

6)   Reduce flame to medium, cover with lid slightly ajar, and cook 40 minutes or more.

Vegetable Stew (*Kenchin Jiru*)

7) Season with salt and soy sauce to taste, simmer 1–2 minutes more, and serve.

Konnyaku is a translucent jelly made from starch of the devil's-tongue plant.

Seasonal Stew (*Um-Pen*) *Serves 4*

4 small *shiitake*, soaked in cold water 20–30
    minutes or 10 fresh mushrooms, medium size
2 Tbsp sesame oil
1 medium celery stalk, sliced diagonally into ¾-in
    lengths
2 cups lotus root, cut into quarters, then thin sliced
1 cup carrot, cut in 1 × 2-in rectangles then into
    ¼-in slices
pinch of sea salt
8 medium green beans, rinsed and trimmed
2 Tbsp soy sauce
2 Tbsp *kuzu*
3 Tbsp water
4 fine slivers lemon peel, 1 in long

■ *The stew:*

1) Remove the hard stems from the *shiitake*, and slice the caps fine. If using fresh mushrooms, use whole.

2) Heat a heavy pot and coat with the oil.

3) When oil is hot, sauté the mushrooms over a medium flame for 2–3 minutes, stirring gently.

4) Add the celery, lotus root and carrot, and mix well.

5) Sauté 1–2 minutes, then add enough water to cover and bring to a boil over a high flame.

6) Reduce flame to medium, cover with lid slightly ajar, and cook 40 minutes or more.

■ *The green beans:*

1) While the stew is cooking, bring a small pan of water (enough to cover the green beans) to a boil over a high flame, and add a pinch of salt.

2) Drop in the beans, return to a boil, and cook 5 minutes, or until beans are bright green and tender, but still crisp.

3) Drain, then cool the green beans under running cold water. Then slice them on a diagonal and set aside in a colander.

■ *Serving:*

1) When the stew is ready, season with soy sauce to taste.

2) Dissolve the *kuzu* in 3 tablespoons cold water. Then add to the stew.

3) Simmer 2–3 minutes more, stirring while the broth thickens.

4) Serve individual portions garnished with several of the green beans and a sliver of lemon peel.

Chinese Stew (*Happosai*) *Serves 5*

2 small onions, quartered
2 Tbsp sesame oil
2 cups ¼-in thick rounds lotus root
½ small carrot, cut into 4 irregular chunks
1½ cups cubed *seitan*
¼ tsp and 2 pinches sea salt
½ small cauliflower, separated into flowerets
20 green beans, rinsed and trimmed
soy sauce to taste
2 Tbsp *kuzu*
3 Tbsp water

1) Heat a heavy pot (cast iron if available) and coat with the oil.

2) When oil is hot, sauté the onions over a medium flame for 5 minutes, or until lightly browned.

3) Add the lotus root, carrot and *seitan*.

4) Half cover the ingredients with water, add ¼ teaspoon salt, and bring to a boil over a high flame.

5) Reduce flame to medium, cover with the lid slightly ajar, and cook 40 minutes or more.

■ *While stew is cooking:*

1) Bring a pan of water (enough to cover the cauliflower) to a boil over a high flame, and add 2 pinchs of salt.

2) Drop in the cauliflower, return to a boil, and cook 5 minutes, or until tender but still crisp. Then drain and set aside.

3) Drop the green beans into the same water, and cook 5 minutes, or until bright green and just tender.

4) Place the green beans in a colander to drain, and fan to cool. Then cut diagonally into halves.

■ *To serve:*

1) When stew is ready, season it with soy sauce to taste.

2) Dissolve the *kuzu* in 3 tablespoons water, and add to the stew.

3) Simmer 2–3 minutes, stirring as the broth thickens.

4) Serve individual portions garnished with cauliflowerets and green beans.

White Fish Stew (*Noppei Jiru*) *Serves 5*

2-in long piece *daikon* radish, cut into ½-in
   rounds, then into quarters
1 Tbsp sesame oil
5 small taro potatoes, quartered
1 small carrot, cut into ¼-in rounds
2 *gammodoki* (deep-fried balls of mashed tofu
   and slivered vegetables), each cut into 4 pieces,
   optional
½ lb white-fleshed fish, cut into 5 pieces
3-in piece *kombu*, wiped clean
5 cups and 3 Tbsp water
½ tsp sea salt
soy sauce to taste
1 Tbsp *kuzu*

1) Heat a heavy pot and coat with the oil.

2) When oil is hot, sauté the *daikon* over a medium flame for 2–3 minutes, stirring constantly.

3) Add in order, the *taro* potatoes, carrots and *gammodoki* (if using). Then mix together well.

4) Drop in the fish and *kombu*, and add enough water to slightly more than cover.

5) Season with the salt, and bring to a boil over a high flame.

6) Reduce flame to medium, cover with lid slightly ajar, and cook 40–50 minutes.

7) Season with soy sauce to taste, then

add *kuzu* thinned in 3 tablespoons cold water.

8) Simmer for several minutes more, stirring while the broth thickens.

Bouillabaisse of Fish *Serves 4*

½ lb red snapper, cut into 4 pieces
8 medium shrimp, shelled and deveined
4 medium clams, washed carefully
1 Tbsp sesame oil
4 small onions, cut into halves
6 cups water
4 bay leaves
½ tsp sea salt
2 medium celery stalks, sliced diagonally into
   1-in lengths
½ tsp ground saffron

1) Heat a heavy pot and coat with the oil.

2) When oil is hot, sauté the onion over a medium flame for 2–3 minutes, or until its strong aroma is gone.

3) Add 1 cup water and bring to a boil. Then drop in the red snapper, shrimp and clams.

4) Add the bay leaves, season with the salt, and pour in 5 cups water.

5) Bring to a boil over a high flame, then reduce flame to medium. Cover with the lid slightly ajar, and cook 40 minutes.

6) Add celery and saffron, and cook 5 minutes more.

7) Season with salt to taste, and serve.

Vegetable Bouillabaisse *Serves 10*

10 large *shiitake* mushrooms, soaked in cold water
   for 20–30 minutes
20 strips *kampyo*
5 pieces *agé*
1 medium burdock root, shaved into slivers
2 Tbsp sesame oil
10 small onions, quartered
2 small carrots, cut into thick diagonal slices
4 bay leaves
6 cups *kombu dashi* (p. 113)
¼ tsp sea salt
2 stalks celery, sliced diagonally into 1-in lengths

1 cake *tofu*, grilled and cut into 10 blocks
½ tsp ground saffron

1) After soaking the *shiitake*, trim away the hard stems and set the mushrooms aside.
2) Rinse the *kampyo* strips in lightly salted water, squeeze dry, and set aside.

■ *The agé rolls:*
1) Pour boiling water over the *agé* to remove excess oil.
2) Using scissors, open the *agé* by cutting along 2 of the short sides, and 1 of the long sides.
3) Spread the pieces open lengthwise with their outsides facing up.
4) Arrange a row of burdock slivers along 1 edge of each piece of *agé*
5) Roll into a cylinder and tie with *kampyo* strips at 4 equidistant points.
6) Slice the roll at points midway between strips. This will produce 4 *agé* rolls, each held closed at its center by a gourd strip.

■ *The bouillabaisse:*
1) Heat a heavy pot and coat with the oil.
2) When oil is hot, sauté the onions over a medium flame until their strong aroma is gone.
3) Add *shiitake* and then carrots, sautéing each lightly.
4) Add the *agé* rolls, bay leaves and enough of the *dashi* to cover.
5) Season with ¼ teaspoon salt, and bring to a boil over a high flame.
6) Reduce flame to medium, cover with lid ajar, and cook 40 minutes.
7) Add celery, *tofu* and saffron, and simmer 5 minutes more.
8) Season with salt to taste, and serve.

Oden   *Serves 10*

12 strips *kombu*, 3-in long
20 strips *kampyo*, 3-in long
1 medium burdock root
10 pieces *agé*

6 cups water
½ tsp and 3 pinches sea salt
10 leaves cabbage
1 Tbsp sesame oil
3 small onions, cut into crescents
2 small carrots, slivered
3 small carrots, quartered lengthwise then each quarter cut into 1½-in lengths
oil for deep-frying
6-in length lotus root, grated
½ small carrot, grated fine
1 cup unbleached flour
10 medium Brussels sprouts
2 blocks *konnyaku*, cut into triangular pieces
5-in long piece *daikon* radish cut into 10 rounds
1 lb *shirataki*, soaked overnight
10 small turnips
1–2 strips lemon peel
soy sauce to taste

1) Soak the *kombu* in cold water for 20–30 minutes, or until soft and pliable. Save the soaking water.
2) Rinse the gourd strips in salted water, squeeze the strips dry, and set aside.
3) Cut the burdock into logs 1½ in long, quarter each log lengthwise, and set aside.
4) Pour boiling water over the *agé* to remove excess oil.
5) Drain, then cut the pieces in half.
6) Pull open the center of each to make a pouch, then set aside.
7) Bring 6 cups water to a boil, and add 2 pinches of salt.
8) Using long chopsticks, hold the stems of the cabbage leaves in the water, and cook until just tender.
9) Submerge the upper portion of the leaves for an instant. Then drain the leaves, trim the cores smooth, and set aside.

■ *The rolls:*
1) Heat a heavy skillet and coat with the oil.
2) When oil is hot, sauté the onions over a medium flame for 2–3 minutes, or until the strong aroma is gone.
3) Add carrot slivers and sauté together for 1 minute.

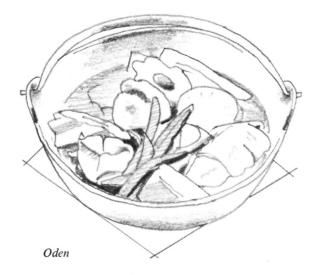

Oden

4)   Mix ingredients together, sprinkle with a pinch of salt, and remove from heat.
5)   When cool, divide the mixture into 2 parts. Use 1 part to fill the *agé* pouches.
6)   Fold over the lip of each pouch to form a flap, and tie with gourd strips.
7)   Divide the remaining sautéed vegetables among the cabbage leaves. Then roll up the leaves, tucking in the edges.
8)   Tie each cabbage roll with a gourd strip.
■ *Kombu rolls:*
1)   Roll 1 piece of *kombu* into a tight cylinder, and slice crosswise into thin strips to be used as threads.
2)   Arrange 2 pieces of carrot and 2 pieces of burdock along the short edge of each of 10 pieces of *kombu*.
3)   Roll into a tight cylinder, and tie each with the *kombu* threads.
■ *Next:*
1)   Fill a heavy skillet or deep-fryer with 3 inches oil, and heat to 350°F.
2)   Combine the lotus root and grated carrot, adding enough of the flour to hold the mixture together.

3)   Form into 20 balls, 1 inch in diameter, and drop into the hot oil.
4)   Deep-fry until golden and crisp, then drain on absorbent paper.
5)   Skewer 2 lotus balls and 1 Brussels sprout on each of 10 bamboo skewers. Then set aside.
■ *To assemble:*
1)   Place the remaining piece of *kombu* in the bottom of a shallow cast-iron pot.
2)   Put the ingredients that require long cooking (*kombu* rolls, *konnyaku*, *daikon*, *shirataki*, and turnips) in the center of the pot.
3)   Arrange the ingredients that have already been partially cooked, or that cook quickly, near the sides.
4)   Add the *kombu* soaking water, and enough freshwater (if necessary) to cover.
5)   Bring to a boil over a high flame, and add ½ teaspoon salt.
6)   Reduce flame to low, cover with lid ajar, and drop in the lemon peel.
7)   Simmer 2–4 hours. Do not stir while cooking.
8)   Remove the ingredients arranged near

the sides of the pot as soon as they are done. To reheat, replace them when the other ingredients are ready.

9) Season with soy sauce to taste, and serve steaming hot.

Cooking at the Table (*Nabe Ryori*)

Serves 5

16 oz *udon* noodles
2 pinches sea salt
9 leaves Chinese cabbage
1 bunch watercress or spinach
1 cake *tofu*, grilled
3 pieces *agé*
15 strips *kampyo*, 3-in long
2 cups scallions or leeks, sliced diagonally into
   1½-in lengths
5 rolls *maki-yuba*, soaked in water until soft
1 piece *kombu*, 3-in square
soy sauce to taste

■ *The udon:*

1) Bring 2 quarts unsalted water to a rolling boil, and drop in the noodles.

2) Return to a boil, and add 1 cup cold water.

3) Cook 10 minutes, or until noodles are

tender and crisp.

4) Remove, rinse in a colander under running cold water, and set aside to drain.

■ *The green vegetables:*

1) Bring 6 cups water to a boil, and add 2 pinches of salt.

2) Using long chopsticks, hold the stems of the Chinese cabbage in the water, and cook until just tender.

3) Submerge the upper portion of the leaves for an instant, then remove from pot.

4) Drain the leaves, then trim the cores smooth.

5) Into the same pan, drop the watercress, return to a boil and cook 1–2 minutes, or until the stems are tender.

6) Remove from pot, and drain.

■ *Vegetable rolls:*

1) Place 3 Chinese cabbage leaves, edges overlapping, on a *sudare*, or bamboo mat. Arrange the leaves with stems and leaves overlapping alternately.

2) Lay the watercress leaves in a neat double row, alternating stem and leaf, horizontally across the center.

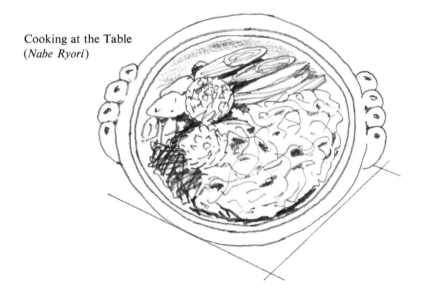

Cooking at the Table
(*Nabe Ryori*)

3) Roll from the wide edge of the mat into a tight cylinder.

4) Remove *sudare* and repeat with remaining ingredients. Then slice each roll into 1-inch thick sections, and set aside.

■ *Agé rolls:*

1) Slice the *tofu* into 6 long blocks.

2) Using scissors, open the *agé* by cutting along 2 of the short and 1 of the long sides.

3) Spread the *agé* pieces open lengthwise, and arrange 2 *tofu* blocks along 1 edge of each piece.

4) Roll into a cylinder, and tie with gourd strips at 5 equidistant points.

5) Slice the roll at points midway between the gourd strips to produce 5 *agé-tofu* rolls. Each roll should be held closed at its center by a strip of gourd.

■ *To assemble:*

1) Center the boiled noodles on a large platter. Then arrange the Chinese cabbage rolls and the *agé* rolls, the scallions and the *maki-yuba* attractively around them.

2) Place a piece of *kombu* into a shallow cast-iron pot and cover with 6 cups water.

3) Bring to a boil (in the kitchen) and season with salt and soy sauce.

Traditionally *nabe* is cooked at the table in front of everyone. If you have an electric hot plate or gas burner:

1) Place the pot on the burner, and arrange the vegetables in the pot.

2) Put the extra ingredients on a platter by the table, and replenish the pot as needed.

3) Provide each guest with a small dish of dipping sauce made of soy sauce and lemon juice.

4) Guests should help themselves directly from the cooking pot.

Variations

A. Substitute ¼ pound *harusame* (transparent bean noodles) for the *udon.* Drop the *harusame* into boiling water for 3–4 minutes, and rinse under cold water. *Gammodoki* (deep-fried balls of mashed *tofu* and slivered vegetables) and deep-fried *kurumabu* (1 of the many kinds of *fu*) may be used in addition to or in place of the *agé-tofu* rolls. Use whatever seasonal vegetables are at hand.

B. One third of the ingredients may consist of your favorite seafood.

C. Miso Nabe:

1) Arrange ingredients on a large platter.

2) Fill the cooking pot halfway with water, and coat the upper half of the pot with a thick layer of *miso.* As the water simmers, the *miso* will slowly dissolve into the broth.

3) If broth is too thin at first, add a little *miso* directly to the cooking water.

D. For an even more tempting soup, add 1 cup mock Béchamel sauce (p. 133) and some *saké* or white wine to the remaining broth.

4. CONDIMENTS AND PICKLES

Sesame Salt (*Gomashio*)

1 Week's Supply for 5

1 cup sesame seeds (white or black)
1 level Tbsp and a pinch of sea salt

■ *The salt:*

1) Roast the salt in a heavy skillet over a medium flame, stirring constantly to heat evenly.

2) When salt no longer releases a strong chlorine odor, place it in a *suribachi*.

3) With a wooden pestle, crush the roasted salt to a fine grain.

■ *The sesame seeds:*

1) Wash the sesame seeds in a fine-mesh strainer. Then drain.

2) Dab the strainer with a dry sponge to draw off excess water. Then let stand for several minutes.

3) Put the sesame seeds in the skillet, and toast over a moderately high flame for 3–5 minutes. Stir constantly and shake the pan to warm the seeds evenly.

4) When seeds turn light brown and fragrant, remove from heat, and add to the roasted salt in the *suribachi*.

■ *Grinding:*

1) Place the *suribachi* in your lap, grasp the lower third of the pestle with one hand, and gently lay your other palm on the pestle's top.

2) Using only the weight of the pestle, grind the toasted sesame seed-salt mixture in a steady circular motion. Do not use your strength to put extra pressure on the pestle.

3) Crush 70–80 percent of the seeds. Be sure not to crush the seeds to the extent that their oil is expressed.

4) Store the *gomashio* in an airtight container.

Gomashio is a versatile condiment used in place of table salt. Sea salt alone is very yang. The yin oil of the sesame seeds helps

Sesame Salt (*Gomashio*)

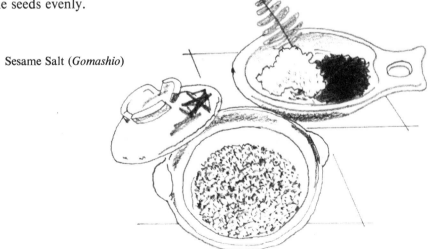

balance it in our body. The combination makes for a delicious harmony, perfect for use with grain or vegetable dishes.

The better it is made, the longer *gomashio* will keep. I have made *gomashio* that stood the test of a six-month voyage, but only after years of practice. At first, make just enough to last a week.

It is in the preparation of simple foods like rice and *gomashio* that a cook's real skill is tested. It is far easier to assemble a gourmet feast than to produce consistently delicious, well-balanced sesame-salt. Mastery of this simple condiment means mastery of the center of your life.

Most people, children and adults alike, develop a special affection for *gomashio* and may overindulge. As a result they grow thirsty and then drink excessively. The proportion of 15 parts sesame seeds to 1 part salt that I have recommended is moderate. Modify it to suit your needs and taste.

Sautéed Vegetables with Miso (*Tekka Miso*) *Makes 2 Cups*

 ²⁄₃ cup sesame oil
 3 oz burdock, minced fine
 2 oz lotus root, minced fine
 1½ oz carrot, minced fine
 10 oz *miso*
 1 Tbsp ginger root, minced fine

1)   Heat the oil in a heavy skillet.
2)   Add the burdock, and sauté over a medium flame until its strong earthy aroma is gone.
3)   Add lotus root, then carrot, sautéing each as added.
4)   Add the *miso*, and mix the ingredients well.
5)   Reduce the flame to low, and sauté for 1–2 hours, stirring constantly.
6)   Stir in the ginger root and reduce flame to very low.

7)   Sauté 2 more hours, or until dry and crumbly. Stir often.
8)   Serve in small amounts with rice or other grains. This condiment is quite strong, and should be used in moderation.

Tekka is also available prepackaged at macrobiotic outlets.

Moist *Tekka* (*Shigure Miso*) *Makes 2–3 Cups*

 1 lb onions
 2 oz burdock root
 2 oz lotus root
 1½ oz carrot
 ½ cup sesame oil
 10 oz *miso*
 1½ cups water
 1 Tbsp finely minced ginger root
 1 tsp finely minced orange peel

1)   Mince the vegetables very fine.
2)   Heat the oil in a heavy skillet.
3)   Sauté the onions over a medium flame, stirring gently, for 5 minutes, or until lightly browned.
4)   Add in order, the burdock root, lotus root and then the carrot. Sauté each lightly as added.
5)   Thin the *miso* in the water, and add to the vegetables.
6)   Stir in the ginger root and orange peel.
7)   Reduce flame to low, and cover pan.
8)   Simmer for 1 hour or more. Stir occasionally.

Miso Sauté *Makes ⅓ Cup*

 3 Tbsp *miso*
 1 Tbsp sesame oil
 1 Tbsp sesame seeds

1)   Heat the oil in a heavy skillet.
2)   Add the sesame seeds, and sauté for about 30 seconds.
3)   Add the *miso*, and sauté over a medium flame for 3–5 minutes, or until fragrant.
4)   Serve as a garnish with rice.

Soybeans with *Miso* and Burdock
Makes 2–3 Cups

    1 cup soybeans, washed and soaked overnight
    3–4 cups water, approximately
    2 cups fine-shaved burdock root
    1 heaping Tbsp *miso*

1) Combine the soybeans with 2 cups water in a heavy saucepan.
2) Bring to a boil, then cook 40–50 minutes. Add a little water occasionally to prevent burning.
3) Add the burdock root and enough water to cover. Then cook 30 minutes more, or until the burdock is tender.
4) Thin the *miso* in 2–3 tablespoons of the cooking liquid. Then add to the pot, blending smooth.
5) Simmer 10 minutes more, then turn off heat.
6) Serve as a garnish with grains.

Soybeans with *Miso*
Makes 1½ Cups

    1 cup soybeans, washed
    2 Tbsp sesame oil
    1¼ cups water
    ¼ cup *miso*

1) Heat a heavy skillet and coat with the oil.
2) When the oil is hot, sauté the soybeans over a medium flame until slightly tender. Stir constantly to heat evenly and prevent scorching.
3) Add 1 cup water, reduce flame, and simmer until water is completely absorbed by beans.
4) Thin *miso* in remaining ¼ cup water, and add to the beans.
5) Simmer again until liquid is completely absorbed.
6) Serve as a garnish with rice.

Miso Pickles (Fall and Winter)

Insert the vegetables to be pickled in a crock of *miso*. Be sure to completely cover the vegetables.

• **Carrot or Burdock:**
1) Use these vegetables whole or cut them into lengths that will fit the container.
2) Drop pieces into boiling water for 30 seconds, remove and allow to cool.
3) Embed in *miso*, and wait at least 10 days.

• *Daikon:*
1) Dry a whole *daikon* (p. 130, Pickled *Daikon*, step 1), then cut lengthwise into halves. If necessary, cut the lengths crosswise to fit the container.
2) Embed in *miso* and wait for 1 month.

• **Cucumber:**
1) Use whole or cut into lengths that will fit the container.
2) Sprinkle with sea salt, and press in a bowl under a heavy weight for 1 day.
3) Discard excess liquid, and embed in *miso* for 1 month.

• **Ginger Root:**
1) Sprinkle with sea salt, and press in a bowl under a heavy weight for 1 day.
2) Discard excess liquid and embed in *miso* for 1 month.

Delicious served with pickled *daikon* and cucumber.

To serve, rinse off the *miso* under cold running water, and cut pickles into small pieces.

The longer the pickles remain in the *miso*, the stronger (and more yang) they become. Try pickling yin vegetables like green peppers or tiny eggplants.

Pickled *Daikon* (*Takuwan*)

Makes 1–2 Pounds

5 lb *daikon* radish, root and greens
5 lb rice bran (*nuka*) or wheat bran
2–2½ lb sea salt

1)   Hang the whole *daikons*, leaves intact, in a cool dry place for 2 weeks, or until each *daikon* softens, and can be easily bent.
2)   Trim the leaves, and set aside for the moment.
3)   Use a dry vegetable brush to clean the *daikon*. Do not wash.
4)   Cut the *daikon* into pieces that fit the container.
5)   Combine the rice bran and salt, mixing thoroughly.
6)   Spread a thin layer of the mixture on the bottom of the crock. Then pack the *daikon* pieces tightly into a layer over the *nuka*.
7)   Alternate with a layer of rice bran-salt mixture then dried *daikon* pieces until all the ingredients are used.
8)   Place the dried *daikon* leaves around the sides and over the top of the last layer.
9)   Cover with a lid the size of the bottom of the container. It should fit inside the crock and rest directly on the ingredients.
10)   Place 2 heavy rocks, each equal to the weight of the *daikon*, on top of the lid.
11)   When the salt has drawn enough liquid from the *daikon* to fill the container, remove one of the rocks.
12)   Store in a cool dark place for at least 8 months before using.
13)   To serve, rinse off the *nuka* under cold running water, then drain *daikon* thoroughly.
14)   If too salty, soak the daikon for a while. It is helpful to change the soaking water occasionally.

15)   Squeeze out excess water, and chop or slice.

   For faster pickling, adjust the proportion of *nuka* and salt. For pickles ready in 3 months, use 1 part salt to 3 parts *nuka*.

Rice Bran (*Nuka*) Pickles (Spring and Summer)

10 cups rice bran (*nuka*)
1½ cups sea salt
3 cups water, approximately
seasonal vegetables (cabbage, carrots, cucumbers, melon rind, etc.)

1)   Toast the *nuka* in a heavy skillet over a low flame for 10 minutes, or until fragrant. Stir constantly.
2)   Remove from heat and allow to cool.
3)   Combine salt and water and boil for 1–2 minutes. Then set aside to cool.
4)   Combine salted water and *nuka* to make a thick paste.
5)   Fill a crock with the paste, pressing it firm.
6)   Insert chopped cabbage leaves, whole or sliced cucumbers, pieces of *kombu*, melon rind or any other seasonal vegetable. If using vegetable slivers, tie them in a small cloth bag.
7)   Store the crock in a cool place. Make sure the *nuka* is pressed firm, and well covered.
8)   Turn and mix the *nuka* every day. If the mixture gets too watery, press out excess liquid through a strainer. Or add bread crumbs or more rice bran.
9)   To serve, rinse off the *nuka* under cold running water, and drain vegetables thoroughly. Then chop or slice.

   Yin vegetables like cucumber can be pickled in 1 day. Turnips and cabbage require 2 days. The hotter the weather, the quicker the vegetables will pickle.

You can keep this *nuka* going for years. The older it is, the better the flavor of the vegetables. When you add fresh vegetables, add more salt. Add more *nuka* as needed.

Chinese Cabbage Pickles

10 lbs Chinese cabbage
1 lb sea salt
1 lemon peel, cut into slivers

1) Quarter the Chinese cabbage heads through the core, but do not separate the leaves.   ·
2) Wash under cold running water.
3) Dry the Chinese cabbage in a cool dark place for 1 day.
4) Spread a layer of salt on the bottom of a crock and add a few slivers of lemon peel.
5) Tightly pack the cabbage in a layer above the salt.
6) Sprinkle the cabbage with salt and a few strips of lemon peel.
7) Add another layer of cabbage so that it crosses the layer below. Then sprinkle with salt and a few slivers of lemon peel.
8) Repeat this process until all ingredients are used.
9) Cover with a lid the size of the bottom of the crock. The lid should fit inside the container and rest directly on the Chinese cabbage.
10) Place a heavy rock on top of the lid.
11) Allow to pickle for at least 10 days (the longer the better).
12) To serve, remove the Chinese cabbage and wash under cold running water.
13) Squeeze to remove excess water, and chop into small pieces.

Quick Pickles (*Asa-Zuke*)

Makes 2–3 Cups

2 turnips or ½ small *daikon* radish, leaves intact
2 Tbsp sea salt
2–3 carrot slivers
1–2 strips of lemon peel

1) Wash the turnip or *daikon* leaves, and chop fine.
2) Sprinkle leaves with a little salt, then squeeze out excess liquid.
3) Cut the turnip into thin half-moons. If using *daikon*, cut into thin rounds, then into quarters.
4) Mix the vegetables together. Then add the salt and lemon peel, and mix well.
5) Place the ingredients in a salad press, and pickle 2–24 hours.

Mixed Pickles (*Achara-Zuke*)

Makes 2–3 Cups

2 turnips, leaves intact
1 heaping Tbsp sea salt
1 small beet, quartered
2 cabbage leaves, cut into 1-inch squares
½ small carrot, cubed

1) Dice the turnips and chop the leaves.
2) Sprinkle the leaves with a little salt, then squeeze out the excess liquid.
3) Place all ingredients in a bowl, and sprinkle with remaining salt.
4) Cover with a plate that fits inside the bowl and rests directly on the vegetables. Then put a stone or heavy weight on top of the plate.
5) Press for 1–3 days.

These pickles are rather yin, so enjoy only a few at a time.

Variation

1) Separate the leaves from a head of cabbage, and rinse well.

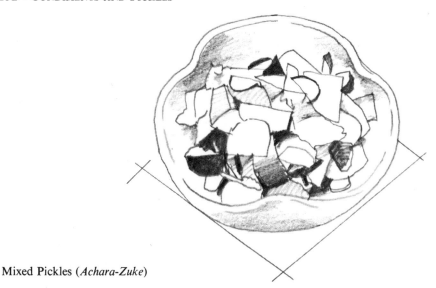

Mixed Pickles (*Achara-Zuke*)

2)   Using a pair of long chopsticks, submerge the stems in a pan of boiling water until they are just tender.

3)   Submerge the upper portions of the leaves for an instant. Then remove, drain, and trim the stems smooth.

4)   Fill each leaf with carrot and cucumber slivers, and roll, tucking in the edges.

5)   Place the cabbage rolls in a bowl, and sprinkle with salt.

6)   Cover with a plate that rests directly on the cabbage. Then put a stone or heavy weight on top of the plate.

7)   Pickle for 2–3 days.

8)   To serve, cut each roll crosswise into 4–5 slices.

5. SAUCES, SPREADS AND SALAD DRESSINGS

Mock Béchamel Sauce (White)   *Makes 1½ Cups*

¼ cup sesame oil
½ cup unbleached white flour
3 cups *kombu dashi* (p. 113) or water
sea salt

1)   Heat the oil in a heavy skillet.
2)   Add the flour and sauté over a medium flame, stirring constantly.
3)   When the lumps have been smoothed out, and while the flour is still pale, remove from heat.
4)   Allow to cool, or dip the bottom of pan into cold water.
5)   Return pan to stove, and gradually add *dashi* or water, stirring until smooth.
6)   Bring to a boil over a medium flame, then reduce flame to low.
7)   Simmer 10–12 minutes. Then season with salt to taste, and simmer 1–2 minutes more.
    To keep the sauce from stiffening, continue to warm over a very low flame, or in a double boiler, until ready to serve.

Variations

A.   For an extra tang, add a pinch of grated nutmeg, ground coriander, ground ginger, or curry powder to the simmering sauce.
B.   For added color and flavor, add ½ cup sautéed or puréed vegetables.
C.   Gravy: After pan-frying any food, add 1–3 parts flour to 1 part oil that remains

in the pan. Then proceed from step 2 of the basic sauce.
D.   Brown Sauce: Substitute whole-wheat flour for white flour. Sauté the flour until it is rich brown and fragrant.
E.   Light Sauce: Substitute whole-wheat pastry flour for the white flour. Sauté until the flour is lightly browned.

Lyonnaise Sauce   *Makes 1½ Cups*

1 cup mock Béchamel sauce
1 tsp sesame oil
1 cup minced onion
¼ tsp sea salt
¼ cup white wine

1)   Prepare the mock Béchamel sauce according to the directions in the preceding recipe.
2)   While allowing the sautéed flour to cool (step 4 of the above mentioned recipe), heat the oil in a heavy skillet.
3)   When oil is hot, add the onion and sauté 4–5 minutes, or until lightly browned. Stir constantly.
4)   Return flour to stove, add water, and bring to a boil.
5)   Stir in the sautéed onion, and simmer 10 minutes.
6)   Season with the salt, pour in the wine, and turn off the heat.
7)   Serve with fish.

Pumpkin-Peanut Sauce   *Makes 1½ Cups*

1 cup puréed pumpkin or squash
2 Tbsp peanut butter
½ cup water
2 pinches sea salt

Blend the ingredients together. Serve at room temperature with vegetable dishes.

Sesame Sauce   *Makes 1 Cup*

1 Tbsp sesame oil
1 small onion, minced
2 Tbsp sesame butter
2 Tbsp water
2 Tbsp soy sauce
1 Tbsp white wine (optional)

1)   Heat a small skillet and coat with the oil.
2)   When oil is hot, sauté the onion over a medium flame for 5 minutes, or until lightly browned.
3)   Add water to cover, place a lid on the pan, and bring to a boil.
4)   Simmer 10–15 minutes, or until tender.
5)   Thin the sesame butter with 2 tablespoons water, then add to the onion.

Sesame Sauce

6)   Stir in the soy sauce, and bring just to a boil.
7)   Add wine (if using) and immediately turn off heat.

This sauce is delicious with rice or boiled vegetables. When serving with fish add 5–6 drops of ginger root juice.

Ginger Soy Sauce

To each tablespoon of soy sauce used, add 1–2 drops of juice from grated ginger root. Delicious with fish.

Lemon Soy Sauce

Into 1 tablespoon soy sauce squeeze 1–2 drops fresh lemon juice. Serve with fish, *tempura*, or *wakame* and cucumber salad (p. 112).

Orange Soy Sauce

To 1 tablespoon soy sauce, add up to 1 teaspoon freshly squeezed orange juice. Good with fish and in summer salads.

Sesame Soy Sauce   *Makes ½ Cup*
(*Goma Joyu*)

1 heaping Tbsp sesame butter
1 Tbsp soy sauce
4 Tbsp water

1)   Combine all ingredients in a small saucepan, and bring to a boil.
2)   Simmer for several minutes. Stir constantly while the sauce thickens.

Kuzu Sauce

Kuzu Sauce

water left over from cooking vegetables
kuzu
soy sauce and / or sea salt to taste (optional)

For a thick sauce use 1 tablespoon *kuzu* for every 1½ cups liquid. For a thin sauce use 1 teaspoon *kuzu* for every 1½ cups liquid.
1) Thin *kuzu* in a little cool water.
2) Add mixture to the leftover vegetable water.
3) Simmer several minutes, stirring while the sauce thickens.

If serving with yang foods the sauce need not be seasoned. If serving with yin foods season sauce with soy sauce and/or salt to taste.

Delicious served with *tofu*, *fu*, or vegetables.

Tsuke-jiru Dipping Sauce *Makes 4 Cups*

4 cups *kombu dashi* (p. 113)
½ tsp sea salt
5 Tbsp soy sauce
1 Tbsp *saké* (optional)
2 Tbsp thin-sliced scallion

1) Bring the *dashi* to a boil.
2) Add the salt and soy sauce, and bring

just to a boil again.
3) Pour in the *saké* (if using), then immediately turn off heat so the alcohol does not evaporate.
4) Serve in individual bowls topped with scallion rounds, and use for dipping.

Leek *Miso* *Makes 1 Cup*

1 Tbsp sesame oil
1 small leek, cut into ¼-in rounds
2½ Tbsp *miso*
2½ Tbsp water

1) Heat a small skillet and coat with the oil.
2) When the oil is hot, sauté the leeks over a medium flame for 1 minute.
3) Add water to half cover, then place a lid on the pan.
4) Simmer over a low flame for about 10 minutes, or until most of the liquid is absorbed.
5) Thin the *miso* in equal parts water, and pour over the leeks. Do not mix yet.
6) Cover pan again, and cook until liquid is absorbed, about 5 minutes.
7) Mix ingredients together for the first time.
8) Remove from heat, and serve as a spread or garnish.

Walnut *Miso* *Makes 1½ Cups*

1 cup shelled walnuts
¼ cup *miso*
¼ cup water

1) In a heavy skillet, roast the walnuts over a medium flame until lightly toasted.
2) Remove from heat and sliver.
3) Place slivers in a *suribachi*, and grind to a paste.
4) Add *miso* and water, and blend to a smooth cream.

Citron *Miso*   *Makes 1 Cup*

5 Tbsp sesame butter
1 Tbsp *miso*
3 tsp *yuzu* (Japanese citron) juice or lemon juice

Blend ingredients together until smooth
and creamy. Delicious with *Chapati* (p. 64).

Sesame (*Goma*) *Miso*   *Makes 1 Cup*

5 Tbsp sesame butter
1 Tbsp *miso*
1 Tbsp water

Mix all ingredients until creamy. Makes a
delicious spread. If desired, add 1–2 teaspoons grated orange rind.

Party Spreads

For accompaniments or hors d'oeuvres at
parties, cut bread into canapé-sized pieces
and spread with any of the following:
   • peanut, sesame or apple butter
   • *azuki* jam (p. 137)
   • pumpkin or sweet potato purée
   • *tekka* or leek *miso*
Arrange attractively on a large platter,
garnish with sprigs of parsley, and serve.

Variations
A.   Deep-fried Canapé
1)   Pour 3 inches oil into a heavy skillet
or deep-fryer and heat to 360°F.
2)   To 1 cup fine-grated carrot or *daikon*
add ½ teaspoon sea salt.
3)   Add 1 tablespoon unbleached white
flour to make a paste.
4)   Spread paste on 20 canapé-sized pieces
of bread, and drop into the hot oil.
5)   Deep-fry until crisp. Then drain on
absorbent paper.
B.   Zakuska (Russian style canapé):
1)   Heat oven to 350°F.

2)   Divide ½ cup salmon roe among 5
slices of bread.
3)   Spread another 5 slices with puréed
sweet potato, and 5 more with sesame
butter.
4)   Put the latter 2 in the oven, and bake
10 minutes.
5)   Arrange on a platter with the salmon
roe slices.

Salad Dressing   *Makes ½ Cup*

4 Tbsp corn or olive oil
1 *umeboshi* plum, shredded or 1 tsp sea salt
1 Tbsp orange juice or 1 tsp lemon juice
1 tsp minced onion, approximately

1)   Pour the oil into a large bowl.
2)   Add the *umeboshi* and juice, and mix
thoroughly.
3)   Gently add the minced onion, and let
stand for 10 minutes.
4)   Add to salad vegetables and toss.

Mayonnaise   *Makes 1 Cup*

1 egg yolk
1 cup corn or olive oil, brought to a boil and
   cooled
1 tsp sea salt or 1 Tbsp *umeboshi* juice (p. 166)
1 tsp lemon juice

1)   Place the egg yolk in a bowl and beat
with a wire whisk.
2)   Add oil drop by drop, to total 1½–2
tablespoons.
3)   Slowly add the remaining oil, beating
constantly.
4)   Add salt and lemon juice, and beat
until thoroughly blended.

Variation
For a delicious tartar sauce, mix 2 tablespoons pickled cucumber, 1 tablespoon
parsley, and 1 hard boiled egg, all minced,
into the mayonnaise, Superb with fish.

6. BEANS

Azuki Beans   *Serves 5–8*

    1 cup *azuki* beans, washed
    1 piece (5 × 3-in) *kombu*, wiped clean
    4 cups water
    pinch of sea salt

1) Place the *kombu* in the bottom of a heavy saucepan.
2) Add the *azuki* beans and 2 cups water, and bring rapidly to a boil.
3) Reduce flame to low, and cover with a tight-fitting lid.
4) Simmer about 30 minutes, or until most of the water is absorbed. Do not stir while the beans simmer.
5) Pour 1 cup cold water down the inside of the pan, and recover.
6) Cook again until most of the water is gone.
7) Add another cup cold water, and again cook until almost dry.
8) Add a pinch of salt and, for the first time, mix gently.

Azuki beans cooked this way should be ready in 50 minutes to 1 hour.

Variation
Azuki Jam:
1) Cook the beans as above, but do not add the salt.
2) Mash the beans in the pot until half have been turned to paste.
3) Season the paste with salt, then mix well.
4) Mash again until all the beans are paste.
5) Place the bean-jam in a large bowl, and

allow to cool.
6) The jam will dry and harden.

Azuki Jam can be used as a spread on bread, as a coating for *mochi* or cut into blocks and eaten cold.

Azuki Bean Potage   *Serves 5*

    3 cups cooked *azuki* beans
    oil for deep-frying
    2 oz *udon* noodles
    1 Tbsp sesame oil
    1 medium onion, cut into thin crescents
    sea salt to taste
    4–5 cups water

1) Pour 2–3 inches oil into a heavy skillet or deep-fryer and heat to 350°F.
2) Break the *udon* into 1-inch lengths, and drop them into the hot oil.
3) Deep-fry 2–3 minutes, or until brown and crisp.
4) Remove and drain on absorbent paper. Then place in a warm oven until ready to use.
5) Heat a heavy saucepan and coat with 1 tablespoon oil.
6) Sauté the onion over a medium flame, stirring gently, for 5 minutes, or until lightly browned.
7) Add the beans, mix well, and sauté for 1 minute.
8) Season lightly with salt and remove from heat.
9) Crush the *azuki*-onion mixture through a strainer, mash in a *suribachi* or purée in an electric blender.
10) Return mixture to the stove, and bring to a boil over a low flame.

11) Add 4–5 cups water, and stir smooth.

12) Serve topped with a sprinkling of deep-fried *udon*.

Azuki Beans with Pumpkin   *Serves 5*

1 cup *azuki* beans, washed
¼–½ lb Hokkaido pumpkin, cubed
4 cups water
pinch of sea salt

1) Cook *azuki* beans as in recipe on page 137, except do not season with salt.

2) Add the cubed pumpkin, and just cover with water.

3) Cook until most of the liquid is absorbed, about 20 minutes. The pumpkin should be very soft by this time.

4) Add a pinch of salt to bring out the natural sweetness of the pumpkin.

Udon Azuki Mold   *Serves 5*

4 oz cooked *udon* noodles
1 cup cooked *azuki* beans (p. 137)
2 Tbsp sesame oil
pinch of sea salt

1) Heat a heavy skillet and coat with the oil.

2) When oil is hot, sauté the noodles over a medium flame for 2–3 minutes.

3) Add the *azuki* beans, and sauté together for 1 minute.

4) Add just enough water to cover the bottom of the pan. Then season with the salt, and simmer until dry.

5) Place the mixture in a rinsed mold, and allow to cool and become firm (refrigerate in summer).

6) Free the edges, invert the mold, and turn out on a serving plate.

7) Serve with sesame sauce (p. 134).

Black Beans   *Serves 5*

1 cup black beans, soaked in 3 cups water for
several hours or overnight
4 cups cold water, approximately
sea salt
soy sauce

1) Drain the beans through a strainer, saving any soaking water.

2) Combine beans and soaking water in a heavy saucepan, adding enough freshwater to equal 4 cups.

3) Bring to a boil over a high flame, then reduce flame to low.

4) Cover, and simmer 1–2 hours, or until tender. Add water during cooking if liquid completely evaporates. Toss pan gently to stir.

5) When done, season with salt and/or soy sauce to taste. Then simmer until dry.

   Always prepare black beans in a saucepan, for their skins fall away easily and could clog the valve of your pressure cooker.

   In Japan this deliciously sweet dish is a must on New Year's Day. The taste grows sweeter after sitting for a day or two. This dish seems simple to make but really requires a delicate hand.

Chick-Peas   *Serves 5*
(*Pressure-Cooked*)

1 cup chick-peas, soaked in 3 cups water overnight
4 cups water, approximately
1 Tbsp sesame oil
2 pinches sea salt

1) Drain the chick-peas through a strainer, saving any soaking water.

2) Combine chick-peas and soaking water. Add enough freshwater to equal 4 cups.

3) Bring rapidly to a boil over a high flame, then reduce flame to low.

4) Cover and simmer 2 hours, or until beans are swollen and tender.

5) Drain beans through a strainer, saving any cooking liquid.

6) Heat a heavy skillet and coat with the oil.

7) When oil is hot, add the beans and sauté over a medium flame for 2–3 minutes.

8) Add the salt and enough of the cooking liquid to cover the bottom of the pan.

9) Simmer until dry. (Use any remaining cooking water in baking.)

■ *To cook under pressure:*

1) Combine the chick-peas with 3 cups water.

2) Bring to pressure over a high flame.

3) Reduce flame to low, and simmer 45 minutes.

4) Turn off heat, and allow pressure to return to normal. Then proceed from step 5 above.

The chick-pea, grown in many parts of the world, has a unique yang quality. In his many travels, George Ohsawa became very fond of it. It is an extremely versatile bean that can be used in over a hundred different ways.

Beignets de Pois Chiche   *Serves 4–5*

2 cups cooked chick-peas (p. 138)
oil for deep-frying
1 cup unbleached white flour
1 cup water
¼ tsp sea salt
1 cup minced onions

Beignets de Pois Chiche

1) Fill a heavy skillet or deep-fryer with 3-inches oil and heat to 360°F.

2) Combine flour with enough water to form a rather thick batter.

3) Add salt, and stir in the chick-peas and minced onions.

4) Drop into the hot oil by the spoonful and deep-fry until golden and crisp.

5) Drain on absorbent paper before serving.

Variation

Substitute 2 cups cooked kidney beans for the chick-peas, and proceed as above.

Chick-Peas with Vegetables   *Serves 5*

3 cups cooked chick-peas (p. 138)
3 large *shiitake* mushrooms
1 piece *koya-dofu*
2 Tbsp sesame oil
2 small onions, minced
1 small carrot, cubed
pinch of sea salt
soy sauce

1) Soak the *shiitake* in cold water for 20–30 minutes. Then remove the hard stems, and slice the caps fine.

2)   Drop the *koya-dofu* into a small pan of boiling water, and cook 2–3 minutes. Then drain.

3)   Press the *koya-dofu* lightly between your palms while rinsing it under cold running water.

4)   When white foam is no longer released, press out excess water, and cut into cubes.

5)   Heat a heavy skillet and coat with the oil.

6)   When oil is hot, sauté the onion over a medium flame for 5 minutes, or until lightly browned.

7)   Add *shiitake*, carrot and *koya-dofu* in that order, sautéing each lightly as added.

8)   Add the chick-peas and enough water to cover.

9)   Bring to a boil, and season with the salt.

10)   Cook 30 minutes, or until all ingredients are tender.

11)   Season with soy sauce to taste, simmer 1–2 minutes longer, and serve.

Chick-Pea Stew   *Serves 5*

4 cups cooked chick-peas (p. 138)
3 Tbsp sesame oil
2 heaping Tbsp unbleached white flour
2 small onions, cut into thin crescents
1 small carrot, diced
1/4 tsp and a pinch of sea salt
4 cups water, approximately
10 medium green beans, rinsed and trimmed
2–3 Tbsp minced parsley or watercress

■ *The flour:*

1)   Heat a heavy skillet and coat with 1 tablespoon oil.

2)   When oil is hot, sauté the flour over a medium flame until brown and fragrant. Stir constantly to heat evenly.

3)   Remove from heat and set aside to cool.

■ *The stew:*

1)   Heat 2 tablespoons oil in a heavy saucepan.

2)   Sauté the onions over a medium flame for 4–5 minutes, or until lightly browned. Stir gently while cooking.

3)   Add the carrot, then the chick-peas, sautéing each lightly as added.

4)   Mix ingredients together, add water to cover and 1/4 teaspoon salt, and bring to a boil over a high flame.

5)   Reduce flame to medium, and gradually stir in the sautéed flour, blending smooth.

6)   Cover pan and cook 40 minutes, or until vegetables are tender and chick-peas fall apart.

■ *The green beans:*

1)   While stew is cooking, bring a small pan of water to a boil and add a pinch of salt.

2)   Drop in the green beans, return to a boil, and cook 5 minutes, or until bright green and just tender.

3)   Drain beans. Then slice fine on a diagonal, and set aside in a colander.

■ *To serve:*

1)   When stew is ready, season with salt to taste.

2)   Serve individual portions garnished with green bean pieces and a sprinkling of minced parsley.

Chick-Pea Croquettes   *Serves 5*

3 cups cooked chick-peas (p. 138), mashed
2 Tbsp sesame oil
1 small onion, minced
1/2 small carrot, minced
1/2 tsp sea salt
3 Tbsp unbleached white flour
oil for deep-frying
1 egg, beaten
2–3 cups bread crumbs or cornmeal

1)   Heat a heavy skillet and coat with the oil.

2)   When oil is hot, sauté the onion over a

Deep-Fried Fava Beans

medium flame for 5 minutes, or until lightly browned. Stir gently while cooking.

3)   Add the carrot, then the chick-peas, and mix the ingredients well. Then add the salt.

4)   Place the mixture in a large bowl, and add enough of the flour to hold it together.

5)   Form into 10 croquettes.

■ *Deep-frying:*

1)   Fill a heavy skillet or deep-fryer with 3 inches oil and heat to 350°F.

2)   Coat the croquettes with remaining flour, and dip into the beaten egg. Then coat thoroughly with bread crumbs.

3)   Drop into the hot oil and deep-fry until golden and crisp. Then drain on absorbent paper.

4)   Serve on a bed of lightly sautéed cabbage.

Deep-Fried Fava Beans

1)   Peel away the bean's outer skin, then score its surface once or twice.

2)   Drop into hot oil and deep-fry until crisp.

3)   Drain on absorbent paper, and sprinkle lightly with sea salt.

Makes a delicious snack with beer.

Kidney Bean Cream   *Serves 5*

½ cup cooked kidney beans
3 Tbsp sesame oil
3 Tbsp whole-wheat flour
1 cup water, approximately
sea salt

1)   Heat a heavy skillet and coat with the oil.

2)   When oil is hot, sauté the flour over a medium flame until lightly browned and fragrant. Stir while cooking.

3)   Remove from heat and allow to cool. Or dip bottom of pan into cold water.

4)   Return pan to stove and add the water, stirring until smooth.

5)   Bring the mixture to a boil, and simmer 10 minutes.

6)   Stir in the beans and simmer 5 minutes more.

7)   Season with salt to taste.

Kidney Bean Purée (*Kinton*)   *Serves 5*

2 cups kidney beans, washed
5 cups water, approximately
¼ tsp sea salt

1)   Combine the beans and water in a heavy saucepan.

2)   Bring to a boil over a high flame, reduce flame to medium, and cover.

3)   Cook 1–2 hours, or until tender. Add more water if necessary.

4)   Place half of the cooked beans in a

separate bowl. Then mash them, and season with salt.

5) Mix whole and mashed beans together, and serve.

Navy Bean Potage
Serves 5

    1 cup navy beans, washed
    1 Tbsp sesame oil
    2 small onions, minced
    8 cups water
    pinch of sea salt
    1 heaping Tbsp *kuzu*
    2–3 Tbsp croutons
    2–3 Tbsp minced parsley

1) Heat the oil in a pressure cooker.
2) Sauté the onions over a medium flame for 5 minutes, or until lightly browned.
3) Add the beans and 3 cups water.
4) Cover and bring rapidly to pressure over a high flame.
5) Reduce flame to low and simmer 50 minutes to 1 hour.
6) Remove from heat and allow pressure to return to normal.

■ *The potage:*
1) Drain bean-onion mixture. Then crush through a strainer, mash well in a *suribachi* or purée in an electric blender.

2) Season with salt to taste.
3) Return to the stove and bring to a boil over a low flame.
4) Add 4–5 cups water and stir smooth.
5) Stir in the *kuzu* thinned in 3 tablespoons cold water, and simmer several minutes more. Stir while the broth thickens.
6) Serve topped with croutons and sprinkled with minced parsley.

We thicken this potage with *kuzu* (yang) because the navy bean is yin. We use mock Béchamel sauce (p. 133) to thicken soups with more yang beans.

Soybeans with Vegetables (*Gomoku-mame*)
Serves 5

    1 cup cooked soybeans
    1 piece *koya-dofu*
    1 Tbsp sesame oil
    2 cups cubed burdock
    ½ cup cubed lotus root
    1 cup cubed carrot
    4–5 cups water
    4 Tbsp sesame butter
    5 Tbsp soy sauce

1) Drop the *koya-dofu* into a small pan of boiling water and cook 2–3 minutes.
2) Press the *koya-dofu* lightly between your

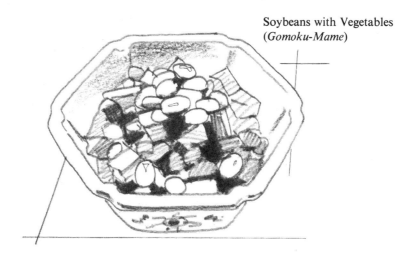

Soybeans with Vegetables
(*Gomoku-Mame*)

palms while rinsing under cold running water.

3) When a white foam is no longer released, press out excess liquid and cube.

■ *The mixture:*

1) Heat the oil in a heavy skillet.

2) Sauté the burdock for several minutes, or until its strong aroma is gone.

3) Add in order, the lotus root, carrot, *koya-dofu*, and soybeans. Then mix the ingredients together.

4) Add enough of the water to cover, and bring to a boil over a high flame.

5) Reduce flame to low, and cover pan.

6) Simmer 30 minutes, or until vegetables are tender.

■ *To serve:*

1) Combine the sesame butter, soy sauce and ½ cup water, and stir until smooth.

2) Spread this sauce evenly over the simmering vegetables when they are done.

3) Simmer until dry before serving.

Cooking with Soy Foods

Okara Stuffed Pouches   *Serves 5*

  3 cups *okara**
  6 pieces *agé*
  10 strips (3-in long) *kampyo*
  2 Tbsp sesame oil
  2 small onions, minced
  1 small carrot, cut into slivers
  ½ cup lotus root, cut into thin rounds, then
      quartered
  ¼ tsp sea salt
  1 piece (3-in square) *kombu*, wiped clean
  5 Tbsp soy sauce

■ *The agé:*

1) Pour boiling water over the *agé* to remove excess oil.

2) Drain, then cut 5 of the pieces into halves, and 1 piece into thin strips.

3) Form pouches by pulling open the centers of the halves.

4) Rinse the *kampyo* in lightly salted water. Then squeeze dry.

■ *The filling:*

1) Heat the oil in a heavy skillet.

2) Sauté the onion over a medium flame for 5 minutes, or until lightly browned. Stir gently while cooking.

3) Add the carrot, then the *agé* strips, and mix the ingredients together.

4) Add the lotus root, salt and water to cover.

5) Bring to a boil, cover pan, and cook 20 minutes.

6) Stir in the *okara*, and cook 5 minutes more. Stir constantly.

■ *The pouches:*

1) Combine the *kombu* with 5 cups water (or enough to cover the pouches) and bring to a boil.

2) Fill the *agé* pouches with the *okara*-vegetable mixture. Then tie each pouch with a *kampyo* strip.

3) Season the *kombu* broth with the soy sauce, and drop in the pouches.

4) Cover the pan, and cook until all the liquid is gone and the pouches are well flavored.

Okara is the dry pulp left over from making *tofu*. It does not keep and should be used immediately.

Tofu Croquettes (*Gammodoki*) *Serves 5*

  2 cakes *tofu*
  oil for deep-frying
  ½ cup minced onion
  ¼ cup minced *shiitake* mushrooms
  ½ cup slivered carrot

¼ tsp sea salt
5 Tbsp fine-grated *daikon* **radish**
5 Tbsp soy sauce

1)   Wrap the *tofu* in a clean cotton cloth, and place between 2 chopping boards set on an angle over the sink. Drain for 30–60 minutes. Or place the *tofu* in a clean cloth and squeeze to remove excess liquid.
2)   Place the drained *tofu* in a *suribachi* and mash.

■ *The croquettes:*
1)   Fill a heavy skillet or deep-fryer with 3 inches oil and heat to 320°–340°F.
2)   Mix onion, *shiitake* and carrot into the *tofu*, and add the salt.
3)   Form the mixture into 4–8 flattened ovals and drop into the hot oil.
4)   Deep-fry 3–5 minutes, or until cooked through and crisp.
5)   Drain on a wire rack or absorbent paper.
6)   Accompany each serving with 1 table-spoon grated *daikon* seasoned lightly with soy sauce for dipping.

Tofu with *Kuzu* Sauce   *Serves 5*

1½ cakes *tofu*, **cut into 2-in cubes**
¼ **tsp sea salt**
2 cups *kombu dashi* **(p. 113)**
2 Tbsp soy sauce
1 Tbsp *kuzu*, **dissolved in 1 Tbsp water**
1 tsp fine-grated ginger root

1)   Bring a small pan of water to a boil, and add the salt.
2)   Drop in the *tofu*, and return to a boil.
3)   Cook just long enough to warm the *tofu* through.
4)   Remove the cubes carefully with a slotted spoon. Then place on prewarmed serving dishes.

■ *To serve:*
1)   Bring the *dashi* to a boil, and add the soy sauce.
2)   Stir in the thinned *kuzu*, and simmer for several minutes. Stir constantly while the *kuzu* sauce thickens.
3)   Serve the *tofu* covered with the *kuzu* sauce and topped with a tiny mound of grated ginger root.

Tofu with *Kuzu* Sauce

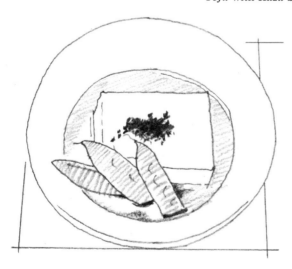

Tofu Roll   *Serves 5*

2 cakes *tofu*, drained and mashed
  (p. 144, *Tofu* Croquettes, steps 1 and 2)
3 pieces *agé*
soy sauce
2 Tbsp sesame oil
1 medium onion, minced
10 fresh mushrooms, rinsed in lightly salted water
  and sliced thin
1 small carrot, thin slivered
¼ tsp sea salt
1 heaping Tbsp powdered *kuzu*

■ *The agé:*
1) Pour boiling water over the *agé* to
remove excess oil.
2) Using scissors, open the *agé* by cutting
along 1 long side and 2 short sides.
3) Place the pieces in a small saucepan
with water to cover, and bring to a boil.
4) Season with 1–2 tablespoons soy sauce
for each cup of water added.
5) Cover the pan, and cook until all the
water is gone, and the *agé* is well flavored.
Then drain.
■ *The mixture:*
1) Heat the oil in a heavy skillet.
2) Sauté the onion over a medium flame
for 5 minutes, or until lightly browned.
Stir gently while cooking.
3) Add mushrooms, then carrot, sautéing
each as added.
4) Add the salt and then the *tofu*, and
sauté the mixture for several minutes.
5) Remove from heat, stir in the powered
kuzu, and allow to cool.
■ *The rolls:*
1) Open the *agé* and spread the surface of
each piece with the sautéed vegetable-*tofu*
mixture.
2) Roll each piece of *agé* into a cylinder,
and steam over a high flame for 20 minutes.
3) Allow to cool before slicing.

Stir-Fried *Tofu*   *Serves 5*

1 cake *tofu*, drained and mashed
  (p. 144, *Tofu* Croquettes, steps 1 and 2)
2 Tbsp sesame oil
1 medium onion, minced
1 small carrot, slivered
1 piece *agé*, cut into thin strips
¼ tsp sea salt
3 Tbsp soy sauce

1) Heat the oil in a heavy skillet.
2) Add the onion and sauté over a medium
flame for 3–4 minutes. Stir gently while
cooking.
3) Add the carrot slivers, then the *agé*
strips.
4) Mix the ingredients together, and sauté
10 minutes.
5) Season with the salt and soy sauce,
and stir in the mashed *tofu*.
6) Reduce flame to low and sauté
10–15 minutes more, stirring constantly.

Tofu Mold   *Serves 5*

1¼ cakes *tofu*, drained
  (p. 144, *Tofu* Croquettes, step 1)
2 pinches sea salt
1 piece *agé*
2 large *shiitake* mushrooms, soaked 20–30
  minutes in cold water
2 Tbsp sesame oil
1–2 medium scallions, cut into thin rounds
1 small carrot, slivered
4 Tbsp soy sauce
¼ cup *kuzu*, thinned in ½ cup cold water
2–3 sprigs parsley

1) Mash the *tofu* in a *suribachi*, and season
with the salt.
2) Pour boiling water over the *agé* to
remove excess oil.
3) Drain and cut the *agé* into thin strips.
4) Trim away the hard stems of the soaked
shiitake, then slice the broad caps fine.
■ *The mixture:*
1) Heat the oil in a heavy skillet.
2) Sauté the scallions over a medium flame

Tofu Mold

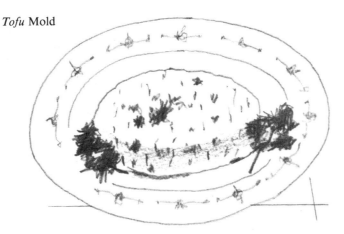

in order of, green stem, white root, then root tendrils.

3)   After 1 minute, add in order, the *shiitake*, carrot and *agé* strips, sautéing each lightly as added.

4)   Add mashed *tofu*, and mix ingredients together.

5)   Sauté 5 minutes more, stirring constantly.

6)   Season with the soy sauce, then stir in the thinned *kuzu*.

7)   Cook 1–2 minutes more, then remove from heat.

8)   Place the mixture in a lightly moistened mold. Allow to cool and become firm.

9)   Invert the mold, and tap out carefully.

10)   Serve individual portions garnished with sprigs of parsley.

Tofu Tempura   *Serves 5*

1½ cakes *tofu*, use dry pack *tofu* if available
oil for deep-frying
1 cup whole-wheat flour
⅔ cup water
¼ tsp sea salt
5 Tbsp fine-grated *daikon* radish
5 tsp soy sauce

If using dry pack *tofu* proceed to step 3.

1)   Wrap *tofu* in a clean cotton cloth and place between 2 cutting boards set at an angle over the sink.

2)   Drain for 30 minutes to 1 hour.

3)   Cut the *tofu* into 1½-in cubes.

■ *Deep-frying:*

1)   Fill a heavy skillet or deep-fryer with 3 inches oil and heat to 350°F.

2)   Combine the flour, water and salt to form a batter.

3)   Dip the *tofu* cubes into the batter, coating thoroughly. Then drop into the hot oil.

4)   Deep-fry 3–5 minutes, or until golden and crisp.

5)   Drain on absorbent paper or a wire rack.

6)   Accompany each serving with a small mound of grated *daikon* lightly seasoned with soy sauce for dipping.

Koya-Dofu Sandwich   *Serves 6*

3 pieces *koya-dofu*
4 cups *kombu dashi* (p. 113)
2 pinches sea salt
4 Tbsp soy sauce
1–2 small carrots, cut into ½–1-in rounds then

cut lengthwise into ¼-in thick slices
oil for deep-frying
1 Tbsp whole-wheat pastry flour
1 Tbsp water
3 sheets *nori*

■ *The koya-dofu:*
1)   Drop the *koya-dofu* into a small pan of boiling water and cook 2–3 minutes. Then drain.
2)   Press the pieces lightly between your palms while rinsing under cold running water.
3)   When white foam is no longer released, squeeze to remove excess liquid.
4)   Bring the *dashi* to a boil, then add the salt and soy sauce.
5)   Drop in the *koya-dofu* and the carrot slices.
6)   Cover and cook 20–30 minutes.
7)   Drain and allow the *koya-dofu* to cool. Save the cooking liquid for use in other dishes.

■ *The sandwiches:*
1)   Fill a heavy skillet or deep-fryer with 3 inches oil and heat to 360°F.
2)   Combine the flour and water to form a thin paste.
3)   Cut each piece of *koya-dofu* vertically then horizontally into halves.
4)   Trim the carrot sticks to the size of the *koya-dofu*, and sandwich between 2 layers of the *koya-dofu*.
5)   Cut the *nori* sheets in half, then trim each half to the length of the *koya-dofu*.
6)   Use the *nori* to wrap each of the 6 sandwiches.
7)   Seal the edges of the *nori* and the exposed ends of the sandwich with the flour paste.
8)   Drop the sandwiches into the hot oil and deep-fry until crisp and golden. Then drain on absorbent paper.

9)   Cut each sandwich diagonally into halves before serving.

Sesame *Tofu* (*Goma-Dofu*)   *Serves 5*

> 1 cup sesame seeds, washed or 3 Tbsp sesame butter
> 1 cup *kuzu*
> 7 cups water
> ½ tsp soy sauce
> ½ cup *kombu dashi* (p. 113)
> few drops juice from grated ginger root
> ½ tsp minced lemon peel

If using sesame butter in place of sesame seeds, proceed to step 3.
1)   Toast the sesame seeds in a heavy skillet over a moderately high flame for 3–4 minutes. Stir constantly and shake pan to heat evenly.
2)   When light brown and fragrant, place the seeds in a *suribachi* and grind to a butter.
3)   Dissolve the *kuzu* in the water and stir into the sesame butter.
4)   Bring to a boil, then simmer over a low flame for 40–50 minutes, or until thick. Stir occasionally.
5)   Pour the mixture into a lightly moistened mold and allow to cool and become firm.
6)   When firm, tap out carefully, and cut into 2-inch cubes.
7)   Serve cubes in small bowls, covered with a sauce made from the soy sauce and *kombu dashi*.
8)   Accent with a few drops of ginger root juice and garnish with the lemon peel.

Deep-Fried *Yuba*   *Serves 4*

> 2 rolls *yuba**, fresh or dried
> 16 snow peas
> oil for deep-frying
> sea salt

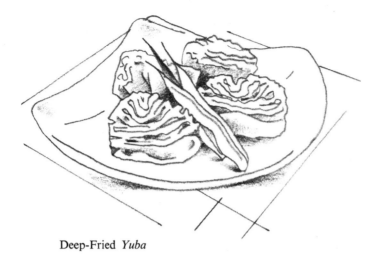

Deep-Fried *Yuba*

1)   Boil the snow peas in lightly salted water until bright green.

2)   Cut the *yuba* into 1¼-inch lengths.

3)   Stick 2 pieces of *yuba* on each of 8 toothpicks.

4)   Pour 3 inches oil in a deep-fryer or heavy skillet.

5)   Drop the sticks of *yuba* in the hot oil and deep-fry until golden and crisp.

6)   Drain on absorbent paper. Then re-move from the toothpicks.

7)   Sprinkle lightly with salt.

8)   Divide the deep-fried *yuba* among 4 serving bowls.

9)   Serve each with 4 of the snow peas as a garnish.

Yuba is made by gently heating soy milk till a film forms on the surface. It is usually sold in dried form.

7. SEAFOOD AND EGGS

Seafood *Tempura*   *Serves 4*

1 lb red snapper, cut into small fillets
pinch of sea salt
oil for deep-frying
4 Tbsp whole-wheat pastry flour
2 eggs, beaten
1 cup bread crumbs or cornmeal

1)   Sprinkle the fillets lightly with salt, and let stand 30–60 minutes.
2)   Fill a heavy skillet or deep-fryer with 3 inches oil and heat to 350°F.
3)   Coat fillets with flour, dip into the beaten egg, then roll in the bread crumbs.
4)   Drop into the hot oil and deep-fry slowly over a medium flame until fish is cooked through, golden and crisp.
5)   Drain on absorbent paper.
6)   Serve with mounds of grated *daikon* lightly seasoned with soy sauce or *tsuke-jiru* dipping sauce (p. 135) accented with a little grated ginger root.

Variations

A.   Small Whole Red Snapper:
1)   Scale and clean the fish. Then sprinkle with salt, and allow to stand 30–60 minutes.
2)   Sprinkle the fish with a few drops water, and coat with powdered *kuzu*.
3)   Drop into hot oil and deep-fry slowly until cooked through, crisp and golden.
B.   Sardines:
1)   Fillet sardines, cutting away the heads.
2)   Dip the fish in *tempura* batter (p. 101), then roll into bread crumbs.
3)   Deep-fry until crisp and golden.
C.   Salmon Fillets:

1)   Sprinkle small fillets with salt and pepper.
2)   Immediately dip fillets into *tempura* batter, then coat with bread crumbs.
3)   Deep-fry until golden, then drain.
4)   Serve with celery strips.
D.   Carp:
1)   Clean but do not scale a 1–1½-pound carp.
2)   Rub fish with salt, and coat thoroughly with powdered *kuzu*.
3)   Drop into hot oil and deep-fry slowly until cooked through and crisp.
4)   Place on a large platter, and serve covered with a *kuzu* sauce of onion, carrot, *shiitake* and green beans (p. 135).

Salmon Burgers   *Serves 5*

1 lb salmon fillets, fine-shredded
2 small onions minced
1 Tbsp fine-grated ginger root
1 cup whole-wheat flour
oil for deep-frying

1)   Combine shredded salmon with minced onions and grated ginger.
2)   Add enough of the flour, and a little water if necessary, to hold the mixture together.
3)   Shape into 5 burgers and pan-fry in ¼ inch oil until crisp and golden.
4)   Use the oil remaining from frying and unused flour to prepare a gravy (p. 133).

Variation

Deep-Frying:
1)   Add 1 cup bread crumbs or cornmeal

to the ingredients listed above.

2)   Shape the mixture into burgers, then roll in bread crumbs.

3)   Drop immediately into 3 inches oil heated to 350°F and deep-fry 2–4 minutes.

4)   When cooked thoroughly, crisp and golden, remove and drain on absorbent paper.

Seafood Dumplings for Soup   *Serves 5*

½ lb cod fillets
½ cup minced onion
½ tsp sea salt
few drops juice from grated ginger root
½ cup whole-wheat flour

1)   Grind the fillets to a paste in a *suribachi*.

2)   Add minced onion, ¼ teaspoon salt, ginger root juice and enough of the flour to hold mixture together.

3)   Form into 8–10 dumplings.

4)   Bring a large pan of water to a boil, and add ¼ teaspoon salt.

5)   Drop in the dumplings, and return to a boil.

6)   Cook until dumplings rise to the surface. Then drain.

7)   Add cooked dumplings to your favorite soup 5 minutes before the soup is ready.

Sea Bream in *Miso*

½ lb sea bream fillets
1 tsp grated ginger root
miso

Rub the raw fillets with the ginger. Then bury in a crock of *miso*. Wait for 1 week.

Carp Soup (*Koi Koku*)   *Serves 5*

1 whole carp, approximately 1 lb in weight
1 Tbsp sesame oil
3 lb burdock root, shaved
1 cup used *bancha* tea twigs and leaves*, tied in a

cheesecloth sack
3 heaping Tbsp *miso*
1 tsp juice from grated ginger root

When purchasing the carp have only the green gallbladder removed at the fish store, leaving the remaining innards intact.

1)   Wash carp well, but do not remove the fins or scales.

2)   Chop into large pieces, and set aside.

3)   Heat a pressure cooker and coat with the oil.

4)   When oil is hot, sauté the burdock until its strong aroma is gone.

5)   Add just enough water to cover and bring to a boil

6)   Add the carp pieces and the *bancha* tea sack.

7)   Cover and bring rapidly to pressure.

8)   Reduce flame to low and simmer 40 minutes.

9)   Turn off heat and allow pressure to return to normal.

10)   Remove *bancha* sack, and add enough water to reach 2 inches above ingredients.

11)   Cover with an ordinary lid and bring to a boil over a high flame.

12)   Thin the *miso* to a cream with 3–4 tablespoons of the cooking broth.

13)   Add the thinned *miso* to the soup, reduce the flame, and simmer 20 minutes.

14)   Stir in the ginger root juice, and turn off heat.

15)   Let stand 3–4 minutes before serving.

Koi koku soup stimulates milk production in nursing mothers, and is very invigorating. It will keep for 1 week if refrigerated.

*The tea twigs and leaves, in combination with the pressure, soften the bones and make them edible. Fresh *bancha* twigs will produce a bitter taste in the soup, so be sure to use *bancha* that has already been used to make tea.

Carp Sashimi (*Koi-no-Arai*)

raw carp fillets
citron *miso* (p. 136)
1 medium cucumber, sliced

1) Cut fresh carp fillets on the diagonal into paper-thin slices.
2) Place in a colander and douse generously with boiling water. Then immediately cool under cold running water.
3) Serve individual portions with citron *miso*.
4) Garnish with cucumber slices that have been rubbed with salt and then squeezed to remove excess liquid.

Shrimp Omelet   *Serves 5*

4 medium shrimp
2 Tbsp snow peas
2 medium scallions, cut into 1-in rounds
4 Tbsp sesame oil
5 fresh mushrooms, rinsed in salted water then quartered
$\frac{1}{4}$ tsp sea salt
1 tsp juice from grated ginger root
4 medium eggs
watercress

1) Drop shrimp into lightly salted boiling water and cook several minutes.
2) While still warm, shell and devein the shrimp, then chop and set aside.
3) Boil the snow peas in lightly salted water until bright green. Then drain.
4) Sauté the scallions in 1 tablespoon oil for several minutes. Stir constantly.
5) Add the mushrooms and shrimp, and sauté lightly.
6) Mix the ingredients together, season with the salt, and sprinkle with the ginger juice.
7) Remove from heat and cool.
■ *The omelet:*
1) In another bowl, beat the eggs well, then add the sautéed shrimp and vegetables.

2) Heat 3 tablespoons oil in a *wok* (a deep round Chinese skillet) and pour in the egg mixture.
3) Cook over a medium-low flame, stirring constantly.
4) Add snow peas just before eggs set.
5) Serve with lightly boiled watercress.

Variation

Substitute $\frac{1}{2}$ cup crab meat for the shrimp and proceed as above.

Fish Condiment   *Makes 1 Cup*
(*Tazukuri*)

1 cup *tazukuri*
1 Tbsp sesame oil
1 Tbsp soy sauce

1) Heat the oil in a heavy skillet.
2) Add the *tazukuri* and sauté 2–3 minutes over a medium flame.
3) Season with soy sauce, and simmer until dry.
4) Serve as a condiment with rice.
   Tazukuri, *chirimen iriko*, and *chuba iriko* (all small dried fish) can be used in place of dried bonito flakes (*katsuo-bushi*) for flavoring soup stocks. They can also be ground and used as a mineral rich condiment with rice. Another delicious way to prepare them is to deep-fry, then simmer in a little soy sauce until dry.

Fish Snack

1$\frac{3}{4}$ cups *tazukuri*
2 Tbsp sesame oil
1 Tbsp soy sauce
poppy seeds or toasted sesame seeds

1) If fish appear dusty, wipe with a dry cloth.
2) Heat the oil in a heavy skillet. Then add the fish and sauté 2–3 minutes.

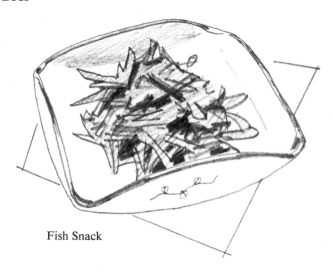

Fish Snack

3) Add the soy sauce and sauté 1 minute more.
4) Place the fish in a bowl and add the seeds. Mix well.
5) Serve in small individual bowls.

Egg *Tofu*   *Serves 5*

5 medium eggs
2 heaping Tbsp whole-wheat pastry flour
3–4 Tbsp water, approximately
¼–½ tsp sea salt

1) Combine the flour and water to form a milky liquid.
2) Beat eggs well and add to the liquid. Then season with the salt.
3) Pour through a strainer to make smooth.
4) Pour the mixture into a rinsed·square mold. Then place mold into a steamer.
5) Cover the steamer with a dry cloth, then with a lid.
6) Steam over a high flame for 20 minutes. Then remove mold and allow to cool.
7) Tap out carefully onto a serving plate, and cut mixture into 5 blocks.
8) Serve with *tsuke-jiru* dipping sauce

(p. 135), and top with toasted and chopped sesame seeds.

Egg Custard (*Chawan-Mushi*)   *Serves 4*

2 medium eggs
8 small shrimp
8 small fillets sea bream, cut into ½-in cubes
soy sauce
4–5 spinach leaves
4 fresh mushrooms, cut in half
¼ tsp sea salt
4 cups *kombu dashi* (p. 113)

■ *The preparation:*
1) Boil the shrimp in salted water for several minutes. Then shell and devein.
2) Cook the sea bream until tender in equal parts soy sauce and water.
3) Boil the spinach in lightly salted water until bright green. Then drain and set aside. When cool, cut into 1-inch lengths.
■ *The custard:*
1) Divide the shrimp, fish and mushrooms among 4 custard cups.
2) Beat the eggs well, and add the salt. Then stir in the *dashi*.
3) Use the egg-*dashi* mixture to fill each cup four-fifths full.

4) Place tops on cups and steam 15–20 minutes over a high flame.

■ *To pressure cook:*

1) Pour an inch of water in the pot. Then place the cups on a rack over the water.

2) Bring rapidly to pressure, reduce flame to low, and cook 5 minutes.

3) Remove from heat, and allow pressure to return to normal.

■ *To serve:*

1) Uncover the custard cups, place several pieces of spinach on top of each, then quickly recover.

2) Serve hot in place of soup or as a side dish.

3) Let each person season with soy sauce to taste.

Rolled Omelet (*Datemaki*)   *Serves 5*

6 medium eggs
½ tsp sea salt
2 Tbsp whole-wheat pastry flour
3 Tbsp minced watercress or parsley
1 Tbsp sesame oil

■ *The mixture:*

1) Beat the eggs well while adding the salt.

2) Slowly sprinkle in the sifted flour, and beat well. Then add the watercress.

■ *The omelet:*

1) Heat the oil in a small skillet.

2) Pour in the eggs, cover, and cook over a medium flame. When set, turn carefully and cook 1–2 minutes more. Omelet should be ½ inch thick.

3) Place omelet on a plate and allow to cool. Then trim into a square or rectangle.

4) Place trimmed omelet on a *sudare* or bamboo mat. Then roll into a cylinder, gently pressing firm.

5) Tie *sudare* closed with a thin string or use rubber bands. Then set aside to cool thoroughly.

6) When cool, remove mat, slice and serve.

Variation

1) Set the trimmed omelet on a *sudare* or bamboo mat.

2) Place a row of lightly boiled watercress along the near edge of the omelet, and a row of lightly sautéed carrot slivers along the far edge.

3) Roll omelet from both edges until they meet. Then wrap in the mat and tie closed with string or use rubber bands.

4) Allow to cool thoroughly. Then remove mat, slice roll, and serve.

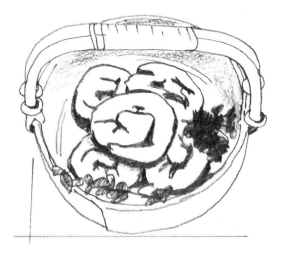

Rolled Omelet (*Datemaki*)

8. PASTRIES AND DESSERTS

Tarte aux Pommes *Makes a 9-inch Pie*

3 medium apples
1 tsp cinnamon
2 heaping Tbsp *kuzu*
3 cups water
Dough:
1 cup whole-wheat pastry flour
$\frac{1}{4}$ tsp sea salt
3 Tbsp sesame oil
$\frac{1}{4}$–$\frac{1}{2}$ cup water

■ *The dough:*
1) Combine the flour and salt, mixing well.
2) Add the oil, and rub mixture gently between your palms to blend evenly.
3) Add water to gradually form an elastic dough. Then knead 8–10 minutes, until smooth.
4) Shape into a ball, and cover with a damp cloth. Then let stand in a cool place for 30 minutes.
5) Roll out on a floured board. Then use dough to line a 9-inch pie plate. Flute the edges.
■ *The filling:*
1) Peel the apples, and slice into very thin crescents.
2) Dip slices into salted water.
■ *The pie:*
1) Preheat oven to 400°F.
2) Fill pastry-lined pan with the apple slices, and sprinkle with cinnamon. Then cover with foil.
3) Bake 30 minutes. Then remove foil and continue to bake until apples are nicely browned.
■ *Serving:*
1) While pie is baking, dissolve the *kuzu*

in 3 cups water. Then bring to a boil, and simmer 30 minutes. Stir occasionally.
2) After removing pie from oven, cover top with *kuzu* sauce. Then set aside.
3) When pie has cooled and *kuzu* has thickened, slice and serve.

Chestnut-Apple Pie *Makes a 9-inch Pie*

1 cup shelled chestnuts
2$\frac{1}{2}$ cups and 2 Tbsp water
pinch of sea salt
2 Tbsp whole-wheat pastry flour
1 Tbsp ground cinnamon
2 medium apples, peeled, dipped into lightly salted water, chopped
1 egg yolk, beaten
Dough:
1$\frac{1}{2}$ cups whole-wheat pastry flour
$\frac{1}{2}$ tsp sea salt
3 Tbsp sesame oil
$\frac{1}{4}$–$\frac{1}{2}$ cup water

■ *Filling:*
1) Pressure cook the chestnuts 40–45 minutes in 2$\frac{1}{2}$ cups water. Then remove pressure regulator and allow steam to escape.
2) Season chestnuts with a pinch of salt, then grind through a food mill or purée in a *suribachi.*
3) Combine 2 tablespoons flour, 2 tablespoons water and $\frac{1}{2}$ tablespoon cinnamon. Add chopped apples and mix thoroughly.
■ *Dough:*
1) Combine 1$\frac{1}{2}$ cups flour with $\frac{1}{2}$ teaspoon salt, and mix well.
2) Add the oil and rub mixture gently between your palms to blend evenly.
3) Add the water gradually to form an

elastic dough. Then knead 8–10 minutes, until smooth.

4) Shape dough into a ball, and wrap in a damp cloth. Then set aside in a cool place for 30 minutes.

■ *Baking:*

1) Preheat oven to 450°F.

2) Set aside ½ cup of dough. Roll out remaining dough on a floured board, and use to line a 9-inch pie plate.

3) Roll reserved dough into a thin sheet and set aside.

4) Spread the chestnut purée over the bottom of the dough-lined pan. Then cover with the chopped apple mixture.

5) Sprinkle with remaining cinnamon, and top with the reserved round of dough. Then brush top of pastry with beaten egg yolk.

6) Bake 30–40 minutes, or until nicely browned.

Variation

For a pie that is more yang, use 2–3 cups cooked *kokoh* (p. 56) or *azuki* jam (p. 137) for the filling.

Pumpkin-Apple Strudel *Makes 9-inch Pie*

½ lb pumpkin, peeled
1 medium sweet potato, peeled
2 pinches sea salt
2 medium apples, peeled then chopped
1 egg yolk, beaten

Dough:
3 cups whole-wheat pastry flour
1 tsp cinnamon
½ tsp sea salt
6 Tbsp sesame oil
1 cup water, approximately

■ *Filling:*

1) Steam the pumpkin and sweet potato over a high flame until tender.

2) Purée together in a *suribachi* or grind through a food mill. Then season with a pinch of salt.

3) Simmer the apples in a small saucepan for 5–10 minutes. Stir occasionally.

4) Season with a pinch of salt. Then blend the apples into the pumpkin purée.

■ *Dough:*

1) Combine the flour, cinnamon and ½ teaspoon salt, mixing well.

2) Add the oil, and rub the mixture through your palms to blend evenly.

3) Gradually add enough water to form an elastic dough. Then knead 8–10 minutes, until smooth.

Pumpkin-Apple Strudel

4) Form dough into a ball, and wrap in a damp cloth. Then set in a cool place for 30 minutes.

■ *The strudel:*

1) Separate the dough into 2 portions, 1 slightly larger than the other.

2) On a floured board, roll out the smaller piece into a rectangular sheet approximately $2\frac{1}{2}$ inches wide. Then arrange the purée mixture down the center of the sheet.

3) Roll out the larger piece into a rectangular sheet a little larger than the first. Then fold the sheet lengthwise into halves, and score it crosswise at $\frac{1}{2}$-inch intervals.

4) Place larger sheet of dough on top of the smaller, covering the filling. Then attach the edges of the upper pastry to the edges of the lower to form a cylinder. Pinch the edges of each sheet together to seal.

5) Place the cylinder on a lightly oiled cookie sheet, and brush the top with beaten egg yolk.

6) Bake in a preheated 350°F oven for 30–40 minutes, or until well browned. Allow to cool before serving.

Apple Pie   *Makes 9-inch Pie*

4 medium apples, peeled, cored, and diced
1 Tbsp raisins
pinch of sea salt
1 tsp cinnamon
Dough:
1$\frac{1}{2}$ cup whole-wheat pastry flour
$\frac{1}{2}$ tsp sea salt
3 Tbsp sesame oil
$\frac{1}{4}$–$\frac{1}{2}$ cup water, approximately

■ *Filling:*

1) Place the apples and raisins in a saucepan with enough water to prevent burning.

2) Bring to a boil and simmer 15–20 minutes, or until turned to a sauce.

3) Season with a pinch of salt and remove from heat.

■ *Dough:*

1) Combine the flour and $\frac{1}{2}$ teaspoon salt, mixing well.

2) Add the oil, and rub mixture gently between your palms to blend evenly.

3) Gradually add water to form an elastic dough. Then knead 8–10 minutes, until smooth.

4) Shape into a ball, and wrap in a damp cloth. Then set in a cool place for 30 minutes.

■ *The pie:*

1) Set aside $\frac{1}{2}$ cup dough.

2) On a floured board, roll out remaining dough, and use it to line a 9-inch pie pan.

3) Roll reserved dough into a thin round sheet, and set aside.

■ *Baking:*

1) Fill dough-lined pan with apple-raisin mixture, and sprinkle with cinnamon.

2) Top with the reserved round of dough, and seal edges with a fork. Prick a few holes in the dough to allow moisture to escape during baking.

3) Bake in a preheated 450°F oven for 30 minutes or until nicely browned.

Apple Dumplings   *Makes 5 or 6*

3 medium apples, peeled
1 medium egg yolk, beaten
Dough:
2 cups whole-wheat pastry flour
$\frac{1}{2}$ tsp sea salt
1 tsp cinnamon
2$\frac{1}{2}$ Tbsp sesame oil
$\frac{3}{4}$ cup water, approximately

■ *Filling:*

Cut the apples into halves, and core the centers. Then dip in salted water and set aside.

■ *Dough:*

1) Combine the flour, salt and cinnamon, mixing well.

2)   Add the oil and rub mixture between your palms to blend evenly.

3)   Add water gradually to form an elastic dough. Then knead 8–10 minutes, until smooth.

4)   Shape dough into a ball, and wrap in a damp cloth. Then set in a cool place for 30 minutes.

■ *The dumplings:*

1)   Divide the dough into 5–6 parts. Then on a floured board, roll each piece into a thin 5–6 inch round.

2)   Place 1 piece of apple at the center of each round. Then fold over the dough, and pinch edges closed with a fork.

3)   Arrange dumplings on a lightly oiled cookie sheet, and brush with egg yolk.

4)   Bake in a preheated 400°F oven for 20–30 minutes.

Pumpkin Cookies   *Makes 15–20*

1½ cups whole-wheat pastry flour
½ tsp sea salt
1 tsp cinnamon
1 cup pumpkin or squash purée
2 Tbsp peanut butter
1 medium egg yolk, beaten

1)   Preheat oven to 350°F.

2)   Combine flour, salt, and cinnamon, mixing well.

3)   Blend in pumpkin purée and peanut butter to form a dough. Add a little water if necessary.

4)   Knead lightly for 3–4 minutes, or until smooth and elastic.

5)   On a floured board, roll into a ⅓-inch thick sheet. Then cut into small rounds.

6)   Place rounds on a lightly oiled cookie sheet. Then brush tops with beaten egg yolk.

7)   Bake 25 minutes, or until nicely browned.

Sandwich Cookies   *Makes 20*

1 cup buckwheat flour
1 cup whole-wheat pastry flour
½ tsp sea salt
2 Tbsp sesame oil
½ cup water, approximately
1 tsp cinnamon
½ cup crushed peanuts
2 Tbsp raisins
1 egg yolk, beaten

1)   Preheat oven to 350°F.

2)   Combine the flours and salt, mixing well.

3)   Add the oil, rubbing mixture between palms to blend evenly.

4)   Gradually add water to form a dough. Then knead lightly for 3–4 minutes, until smooth and elastic.

5)   On a floured board, roll into a ¼-inch thick sheet. Then cut into halves.

6)   Place 1 piece on a lightly oiled cookie sheet and sprinkle with cinnamon. Then cover with peanuts and raisins.

7)   Top with second sheet, and press lightly together.

8)   Score horizontally and vertically with a cookie cutter or heavy knife. Then brush tops of cookies with beaten egg yolk.

9)   Bake 20–25 minutes, or until nicely browned.

Chestnut and *Azuki* Pudding   *Serves 5*

1 cup chestnut purée
1 cup *azuki* jam (p. 137)

1)   Fill a rinsed shallow mold with the chestnut purée, and top with the *azuki* jam. Press firm.

2)   Allow to cool and firm before slicing.

Sweet Millet with *Azuki* Sauce   *Serves 5*

1 cup glutinous millet, washed
2½ cups water

pinch of sea salt
1½ cups *azuki* jam (p. 137)

1) Combine the millet, 1½ cups water and the salt in a pressure cooker. Cook 20 minutes.
2) Remove from heat and allow pressure to return to normal.
3) Thin the *azuki* jam with 1 cup water.
4) Just before serving, bring the thinned *azuki* jam just to a boil.
5) Serve the sweet millet topped with the *azuki* sauce.

Azuki-Chestnut Rolls *Serves 6–8*

½ cup *azuki* beans, washed
3 cups water
½ cup shelled chestnuts
pinch of sea salt
Dough:
2 cups whole-wheat pastry flour
½ tsp sea salt
2–3 Tbsp sesame oil
¼–½ cup water

■ *Filling:*
1) Boil the *azuki* beans in 1½ cups water for 20–30 minutes, or until wrinkled.
2) In another pan, cook the chestnuts in 1½ cups water.
3) Combine beans and chestnuts, and simmer 40–60 minutes, or until pasty.
4) Season with a pinch of salt, then purée the mixture in a *suribachi* or an electric blender.
■ *Dough:*
1) Combine the flour and ½ teaspoon salt, mixing well.
2) Add the oil and rub the mixture between your palms to blend evenly.
3) Gradually add enough water to form an elastic dough. Then knead 8–10 minutes, until smooth.
4) Shape dough into a ball and wrap in a damp cloth. Then set aside in a cool place for 30 minutes.

■ *The rolls:*
1) Divide dough into 6–8 parts. On a floured board, roll out each part into a thin rectangular sheet about ¼ inch thick.
2) Spread some purée over each sheet, and roll into a cylinder. Seal the edges with a few drops of water.
3) Place rolls on a damp cloth in a steamer and cook over a high flame for 20 minutes.
4) Cut into ¼-inch rounds and serve.

Camellia Sweet Rice *Serves 5*

1½ cups sweet brown rice, washed
1½ cups water
2 pinches sea salt
½ cup pumpkin, *azuki* or chestnut purée
5 camellia leaves*

1) Combine the rice, water and salt in a pressure cooker, and cook 25 minutes.
2) Remove from heat and allow pressure to return to normal.
3) Place half the rice in a *suribachi*. Then pound to a paste with a moistened pestle.
4) Mix the paste with the whole rice. Then divide the mixture into 10 parts.
5) Flatten each part into a 2-inch flat round.
6) Place 1 tablespoon of purée at the center of each round. Then shape into ovals.
7) Serve sandwiched between 2 camellia leaves.

*In place of camellia leaves, you may substitute another variety of edible leaves found in your neighborhood.

Sweet Rice Dumplings *Makes 10*
(*Kashiwa Mochi*)

2 cups sweet brown rice flour
½ tsp sea salt
1½ cups boiling water, approximately
½–¾ cups *azuki* jam (p. 137) or pumpkin purée
10 beech or oak leaves

Sweet Rice Dumplings
(*Kashiwa Mochi*)

■ *Dough:*
1)   Combine the flour and salt, mixing well.
2)   Gradually add the water while stirring vigorously. To stir, use 4 long chopsticks held in one fist. Or use a wooden fork with four tines.
3)   When well mixed and cool enough to touch, knead dough 10 minutes, or until smooth.
4)   Lay a damp cloth in a steamer and place dough on top. Steam 20 minutes over a high flame.
■ *The dumplings:*
1)   Place steamed dough in a *suribachi*. Then pound 5–10 minutes with a moistened pestle.
2)   Divide into 10 parts. Then, on a floured board, press each into a flat round ¼ inch thick and 4 inches in diameter.
3)   Place 1 tablespoon jam at the center of each round. Then fold over one side of the dough to form a half-moon. Seal edges by pinching with your fingers.
4)   Wrap each dumpling with a leaf, shinny surface facing the dough.
5)   Replace on the damp cloth in the steamer and cook 10 minutes before serving.

Sweet Rice Cakes with Sauce (*Gozen Shiruko*)   *Serves 5*

> 10 pieces *mochi*
> 1 cup *azuki* jam (p. 137)
> ½ cup chestnut purée
> 1 cup water, approximately
> 1 Tbsp sesame oil
> 1½–½ Tbsp minced *miso* pickles (p. 129), optional

1)   Combine the *azuki* jam and chestnut purée. Then thin to a cream with the water.
2)   Bring just to a boil, then turn down heat. Keep warm over a very low flame.
3)   Heat a heavy skillet and coat with the oil.
4)   When oil is hot, brown the *mochi* over a medium-low flame until they are puffed and golden. Turn once.
5)   Divide the freshly toasted *mochi* among 5 serving bowls.
6)   Pour the warm cream over the *mochi*, and garnish with chopped *miso* pickles, if using.

Three-Colored Dumplings (*Dango*)   *Makes 2 Dozen*

> 1 lb sweet brown rice flour
> ½ tsp sea salt

2 cups boiling water
Topping:
    1 cup sesame seeds
    1 Tbsp water
    ½ Tbsp soy sauce
    1 cup pumpkin purée or *azuki* jam (p. 137)
    1 cup soybean flour

■ *Sesame topping:*

1)   Roast the sesame seeds in a heavy skillet over a medium-high flame for 2–3 minutes, or until fragrant. Stir constantly.

2)   Grind the seeds in a *suribachi* until their oil is expelled, about 20 minutes. Add the water and soy sauce to form a paste.

■ *Dumplings:*

1)   Combine the flour and salt, mixing well.

2)   Gradually add the boiling water while stirring vigorously. To stir, use 4 long chopsticks held in one fist. Or use a wooden fork with four tines.

3)   When well mixed and cool enough to touch, knead 10–20 minutes, until dough is smooth and elastic.

4)   Divide the dough into 24 pieces, and roll into small balls.

5)   Place the balls on a damp cloth in a steamer. Cook for 20 minutes. Or boil in a large pan of water for the same time.

6)   Remove the dough and allow to cool.

■ *Serving:*

1)   Coat 8 dumplings with pumpkin purée or *azuki* jam, 8 with the sesame paste and 8 with soybean flour.

2)   Place 1 of each type on a skewer in the order of pumpkin, sesame and soybean flour, and serve.

Variations

A.   Use equal parts sweet brown rice flour and millet flour, and proceed as above.

B.   Green Dumplings:

1)   Drop ¼ pound mugwort, dandelion or watercress into a small pan of salted water and cook 1–2 minutes, or until just tender.

2)   Drain and squeeze gently to remove excess water. Then tear into small pieces.

3)   Place the steamed or boiled dumplings in a *suribachi*, and work the mugwort in with your fingers. Then reroll into small balls.

4)   Coat dumplings with soy sauce and grill until lightly browned. Then skewer and serve.

C.   Sautéed or Deep-Fried:

After steaming or boiling the dumplings, place them in a lightly oiled skillet. Sauté 10 minutes over a medium flame, stirring constantly and shaking the pan. Or deep-fry in *tempura* oil until crisp and golden. Drain before serving.

D.   Spiral Dumplings:

1)   On a floured board, roll out the dough into 3 rectangular sheets. Then roll into long cylinders about 1 inch in diameter.

2)   Steam on a damp cloth for 20 minutes. Then allow to cool.

3)   Roll 2 threads together in a double-helix, and wrap around the cylinders. Pull the thread through the cooked cylinders to slice.

4)   Serve coated with *azuki* jam.

Pumpkin-*Azuki* Balls with *Kuzu* Sauce   *Serves 5*

    ½ lb pumpkin purée
    ½ pound *azuki* jam (p. 137)
    1 cup *kuzu*
    2½ cups water
    pinch of sea salt

1)   Form the pumpkin purée and *azuki* jam separately into 1 inch balls. Then arrange on a rinsed platter.

2)   Dissolve the *kuzu* in 1 cup water and add the salt. Pour through a strainer to make smooth.

3)   Add 1½ cups water and bring to a boil.

4)   Simmer 20–30 minutes, until almost translucent. Stir constantly.

5)   Pour *kuzu* sauce over the balls to cover completely. There should be a thin *kuzu* coating on each ball.

6)   Allow to cool and become firm. Or refrigerate and serve chilled.

Apple Gelatin   *Serves 5*

    1 stick *kanten*
    2 cups water
    ¼ tsp sea salt
    1 medium apple, cooked and puréed
    1 egg, yolk and white beaten separately
    ¼ tsp grated lemon rind

1)   Combine the *kanten* and water in a saucepan, and bring to a boil. Stirring constanty, simmer 20–25 minutes, or until stringy.

2)   Season the *kanten* with the salt, and divide between 2 small saucepans.

3)   Add the apple purée to 1 pan, and quickly fold in the beaten egg yolk.

4)   Bring just to a boil and pour immediately into a rinsed mold. Place in the refrigerator to chill.

5)   Beat the egg white until stiff. Then fold into the *kanten* in the other pan, adding the lemon rind.

6)   Pour this egg white *kanten* over the chilled apple *kanten*. Then cool again.

7)   When firm, tap out and include both types in each serving.

Sesame Gelatin   *Serves 5*

    1½ sticks *kanten*
    2 cups water
    1 cup sesame seeds, washed
    ¼ tsp sea salt
    mint leaves
    soy sance

1)   Dissolve the *kanten* in the water and bring to a boil.

2)   Simmer uncovered for 20–25 minutes,

or until stringy. Stir occasionally.

3)   Roast the sesame seeds in a heavy skillet over a medium flame for 4–5 minutes, or until browned and fragrant. Stir constantly.

4)   In a *suribachi*, grind the seeds to a butter, seasoning with the salt.

5)   Blend the fresh sesame butter into the simmering *kanten*. Then pour into a rinsed mold.

6)   Allow to cool and harden. Then cut into 5 blocks.

7)   Serve on mint leaves, and season to taste with soy sauce.

Fruit Gelatin   *Serves 5*

    2 sticks *kanten*
    3 cups water
    2 cups diced fresh fruit
    1¾–1½ tsp sea salt

1)   Combine the *kanten* and water in a saucepan, and bring to a boil.

2)   Simmer 20–25 minutes, or until stringy. Stir occasionally.

3)   Add the diced fruit and simmer 15 minutes more. Then season with the salt.

4)   Pour into a rinsed shallow mold and chill.

Pumpkin and Chestnut Gelatin   *Serves 5*

    2½ sticks *kanten*
    4 cups water
    ½ tsp sea salt
    ¾ lb pumpkin purée
    ½ lb chestnut purée

1)   Combine the *kanten* and water in a saucepan and bring to a boil.

2)   Simmer 20–25 minutes, stirring occasionally.

3)   Season with the salt and divide between 2 small saucepans.

4)   Add the pumpkin purée to 1 pan and bring just to a boil. Pour immediately into

a rinsed mold, and chill.

5) Add the chestnut purée to the other pan and bring just to a boil. Pour into a separate rinsed mold, and chill.

6) When firm, tap out and include both types in each serving.

For added color, serve on maple or chrysanthemum leaves.

Azuki-Chestnut Gelatin   *Serves 5*

1 stick *kanten*
1½ cups water
pinch of sea salt
3 cups *azuki*-chestnut paste (p. 159)

1) Combine the *kanten* and water in a saucepan and bring to a boil.

2) Simmer 20–25 minutes, stirring occasionally.

3) Add the salt and stir in the *azuki*-chestnut mixture.

4) Bring just to a boil, pour immediately into a rinsed mold, and chill.

5) When firm, tap out, cut into desired shapes, and serve.

Watermelon Soft Gelatin   *Serves 4*
(*Awayuki*)

4 cups watermelon juice
1 egg white
sweetener of your choice

1) Boil the juice in a heavy pot until reduced to half the volume.

2) Beat the egg white until stiff.

3) Mix concentrated juice into the egg white, and add the sweetener.

4) Divide among 4 serving dishes.

Baked Apples   *Serves 4*

4 medium apples, washed
½–1 cup sesame butter (*tahini*)
2–3 Tbsp soy sauce
sea salt

1) Core apples but leave bottoms intact.

2) Fill each apple with 1–2 tablespoons sesame butter seasoned lightly with soy sauce.

3) Sprinkle apples lightly with salt, then arrange in a baking pan containing ½-inch water.

4) Bake 20–25 minutes in a preheated 350°F oven.

Variation

1) Peel and quarter 2 apples.

2) Place 1 tablespoon pumpkin purée at the center of 8 pieces of aluminum foil. Each piece should be 4-inch square.

3) Embed 1 tender chestnut, several peanuts and 1 apple quarter in the pumpkin purée.

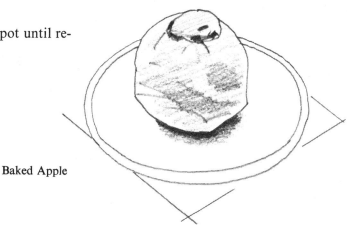

Baked Apple

4)   Gather corners of foil together and twist up to close.

5)   Bake 20 minutes in a preheated 350°F oven.

Fresh Fruit Delight (*Mitsumame*)

Serves 5

    1 stick *kanten*
    2 cup water
    2 cups diced fresh fruit (apples, melon, etc.)
    ½ tsp sea salt*, or sweetener of your choice

1)   Combine *kanten* and water in a saucepan and bring to a boil.

2)   Simmer uncovered 20–25 minutes, or until stringy. Stir occasionally.

3)   Pour *kanten* into a rinsed shallow mold, and chill.

4)   When firm, dice. Then arrange on glass dishes with diced fruit.

5)   Serve sprinkled with salt or, for special occasions, with a little sweetener.

*Salt brings out the natural sweetness of fruits and vegetables.

Applesauce

Serves 5

    5 medium apples, peeled, cored and quartered
    pinch of sea salt

1)   Place the apple quarters in a pressure cooker, and add just enough water to prevent burning.

2)   Add the salt, bring to pressure and simmer 5 minutes. Then allow pressure to return to normal.

■ *To boil:*

Grate the apples and simmer in a saucepan for 20–30 minutes. Season with salt while cooking.

Variations

A.   Add tender whole chestnuts and/or ½ cup chestnut purée to the applesauce. Simmer together 5–10 minutes.

B.   Apple Butter:

Place the applesauce in a heavy pot and simmer uncovered 3–4 hours, or until thick and deep brown. Season with salt to taste.

Strawberry Cream

Serves 5

    1 pint fresh strawberries
    1 cup mock Béchamel sauce (p. 133)

1)   Rinse the strawberries in lightly salted water. Then remove their small green leaves.

2)   Mash with a fork and serve individual portions covered with a lightly salted mock Béchamel sauce.

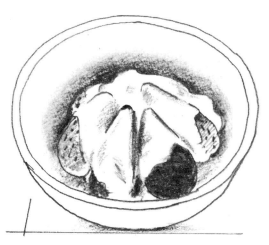

Strawberry Cream

9. BEVERAGES

Bancha Tea

Bancha is made from the three year old growth of twigs and leaves from a variety of tea bush grown in Japan. It is a nutritious, soothing drink enjoyed by children and adults alike.

1) Dry-roast the tea in a heavy skillet over a medium flame until browned. Shake the pan and stir constantly to prevent scorching.
2) Remove from pan and cool. Then store in an airtight jar.
3) Add 1–2 tablespoons to 1½ quarts boiling water. Simmer 10–20 minutes.
■ *For a milder taste:*
1) Place the *bancha* in a teapot and add boiling water.
2) Steep several minutes. Then strain and serve.

To reuse the leaves, boil for 10 minutes, adding a pinch of fresh *bancha*. When a 1-inch layer has formed on the bottom of the pot, discard (or save for use in *Koi Koku*, p. 150).

Variation
Sho-Ban:
Fill a cup with 1 teaspoon soy sauce and add hot *bancha*. This yangizing drink is a remedy for fatigue.

Barley Tea (*Mugicha*)

1) Dry-roast unhulled barley over a medium-high flame until almost black. Stir constantly. Or oven-roast by spreading the barley on a cookie sheet and cooking in a 225°F oven for several hours.
2) Simmer 2 heaping tablespoons of the roasted barley in 1 quart water for 5 minutes. Strain before serving.

This is a cooling drink served chilled during hot weather.

Dandelion Root Coffee

1) Wash dandelion root and dry thoroughly. Then mince.
2) Dry-roast in a heavy skillet over a low flame.
3) Allow to cool. Then grind in a food mill or coffee grinder.
4) Simmer 2 tablespoons in 1 quart water for 10 minutes or more. Add a dash of salt during brewing.

Grain Tea

1) Dry-roast brown rice (or any other grain) over a medium flame for 10–20 minutes, or until a rich brown color. Shake the pan and stir constantly to prevent. burning.
2) Add 2 tablespoons of the grain to 1 quart boiling water. Simmer 10 minutes. Add a pinch of salt while brewing.
3) Strain and serve.

Variation
Brown Rice-Bancha Tea (Genmai Cha):
1) Combine equal parts roasted rice and roasted *bancha*.

2) Place in a teapot and add boiling water.
3) Steep for 10 minutes and serve.

Mu Tea

Mu tea is made from 16 herbs long used in Chinese medicine. In *Mu* tea these herbs are especially combined according to the principles of yin and yang. This tea has a particularly strong action upon the stomach and should be brewed weak if served immediately after a meal. Very yang, it may be taken chilled during hot weather. Available prepackaged at macrobiotic outlets.

Simmer 1 package of *Mu* tea in 1 quart water for 10–15 minutes. The ingredients may be used a second time.

For a stronger brew, simmer 1 packet in 3 cups water for 30 minutes.

Soba Tea

1) Season liquid left over from cooking noodles with soy sauce to taste.
2) To thicken, add buckwheat flour and heat for several minutes.

Grain Coffee (*Yannoh*)

Yannoh is a nutritious coffee made from 5 different grains. Enjoyed at breakfast, it is an excellent source of energy. It is available prepackaged at macrobiotic outlets and natural food stores.

1) Add 1 tablespoon *yannoh* to each cup water used.
2) Add a pinch of salt and simmer 15–20 minutes.
3) Strain through a cheesecloth to serve. May be served chilled.

Grain Milk (*Kokoh*)

1) Add 2 heaping tablespoons *kokoh* to 1 quart water.
2) Bring to a boil, stirring constantly.
3) Simmer 20–30 minutes, seasoning with a pinch of salt if desired.

Apple Juice

1) Chop apples and cook in 1½–2 parts water.
2) When tender, mash and strain. Then add a pinch of salt.
3) Serve chilled.

Umeboshi Juice

1) Shred 1–2 *umeboshi* and bring to a boil in 1 quart water.
2) Simmer 1 hour. Then strain, saving the liquid.

Serve chilled during the summer for a thirst quenching drink.

This juice may also be used as a salad dressing or seasoning in place of salt.

GLOSSARY

Agar—a gelatin made from a type of sea
  vegetable
Agé—fried bean curd (*tofu*)
Aonori—green *nori*
Arai—chilled raw fish
Azuki—tiny, hard red bean; the most yang
  bean

Bancha—green tea made from three-year-
  old leaves and twigs of tea bush
Biifun—rice flour noodles
Burdock—a wild root vegetable valued for
  its strengthening qualities

Chirimen iriko—small dried fish

Daikon—Japanese white radish from six
  inches to several feet long
Dango—dumplings
Dashi—basic soup stock, also used in
  cooking vegetables
Datemaki—rolled omelet

Fu—dried wheat gluten

Ginger—a pungent root with medicinal
  properties
Gomashio—sesame seeds and salt table
  condiment
Gammodoki—a deep-fried cake made of a
  mixture of *tofu* and vegetables
Genmai cha—tea made by boiling brown
  rice
Goma—sesame seeds
Goma joyu—a mixture of sesame seed paste
  and soy sauce
Goma miso—a mixture of sesame seed
  paste and *miso*

Hatcho miso—a *miso* made from soybeans,

salt and water, aged for three years
Harusame—literally "spring rain;" soybean
  gelatin noodles
Hijiki—a black stringy sea vegetable

Jinenjo—a wild potato native to Japan

Kampyo—dried gourd strips
Kanten—agar, a sea gelatin
Karinto—a snack made by deep-frying
  dough
Katsuobushi—dried bonito used primarily
  in *dashi*
Kimpira—a sautéed vegetable dish
Kinton—a bean purée combined with
  seasonal fruits and nuts for dessert
Kofu—a wheat-gluten product
Koi koku—whole carp cooked with burdock
  and *miso*
Kokoh—a mixture of roasted and finely
  ground rice, sweet rice, oatmeal, soybeans
  and sesame seeds
Kombu—dried kelp; comes in hard sheets
Kome miso—a light *miso* made from rice,
  soybeans, salt and water
Konnyaku—translucent cake made from
  starch of the devil's-tongue plant
Koya-dofu—dried *tofu*
Kurumabu—wheel-shaped cake of steamed
  wheat gluten
Kuzu—a vegetable root gelatin

Lotus root—root of a type of water lilly;
  good for respiratory organs

Maki-yuba—strips of soybean-gluten wound
  into a little cake
Miso—bean paste made with soybeans, salt
  and grain, fermented by a special enzyme

Miso-zuke—vegetables pickled in *miso*

Mitsumame—a *kanten* and fruit dessert

Mochi—a dumpling or rice cake made from pounded sweet rice

Mugicha—barley tea

Mugi-miso—a mild *miso* made with barley, soybeans, salt and water

Musubi—rice balls

Mu tea—tea made from 16 herbs long used in Chinese medicine

Ninjin—carrot

Nori—dried laver, a sea vegetable

Nuka—rice bran

Oden—traditional Japanese stew

Ohagi—small balls of partially pounded sweet brown rice

Okara—the dry pulp left over from making *tofu*

Okonomi yaki—pancakes

Renkon—lotus root

Sea salt—salt produced from salt water; rich in trace minerals

Seitan—pieces of wheat gluten cooked in soy sauce

Shiitake—Japanese mushroom

Shirataki—shredded form of *konnyaku*

Soba—buckwheat noodles

Soboro—a traditional Japanese method of grating and certain foods

Sudare—bamboo mat used for rolling foods

Suiton—soup with dumplings

Suribachi—earthenware mortar with serrated interior

Surikogi—wooden pestle

Tahini—sesame butter

Takuwan—*daikon* pickles in rice bran and salt

Taro potato—a hairy skinned potato valued for its medicinal and food value sometimes called albi

Tazukuri—dried fish approximately 3 inches long

Tekka—a mixture of minced vegetables and *miso*, sautéed for several hours; used as a condiment

Tempura—batter-fried foods

Tofu—bean curd

Tsukemono—generic term for pickles

Udon—wheat-flour noodles

Umeboshi—small pickled plums

Wakame—long strands of sea vegetable

Yannoh—coffee made from 5 different grains

Yuba—film that forms when soy milk is heated

Yuzu—citron

Zenibu—a small round cake of wheat gluten with a hole at the center

Zoni—*mochi* soup

BIBLIOGRAPHY

Abehsera, Michel. *Cooking for Life*. Binghamton, N. Y.: Swan House.

Aihara, Cornellia. *Macrobiotic Kitchen*. Tokyo: Japan Publications, Inc.

Aihara, Cornellia. *The Dō of Cooking*. Oroville, Calif.: George Ohsawa Macrobiotic Foundation.

Carrel, Alexis. *Man the Unknown*. New York: Harper and Row.

Chishima, Kikuo. *Revolution of Biology and Medicine*. Gifu, Japan: Neo-Haematological Society Press.

Colbin, Annemarie. *The Book of Whole Meals*. Brookline, Mass.: Autumn Press.

Dufty, William. *Sugar Blues*. New York: Warner Publications.

East West Foundation. *A Dietary Approach to Cancer According to the Principles of Macrobiotics*. Brookline, Mass: East West Publications.

East West Foundation. *A Nutritional Approach to Cancer*. Ibid.

East West Foundation. *Cancer and Diet*. Ibid.

East West Foundation. *Macrobiotic Case Histories*. Vols. I through VI. Ibid.

East West Foundation. *Report on the First North American Congress of Macrobiotics*. Ibid.

East West Foundation. *Standard Recommendations for Diet and Way of Life*. Ibid.

Esko, Edward and Wendy. *Macrobiotic Cooking for Everyone*. Tokyo: Japan Publications, Inc.

Esko, Wendy. *Introducing Macrobiotic Cooking*. Tokyo: Japan Publications, Inc.

Estella, Mary. *Natural Foods Cookbook*. Tokyo: Japan Publications, Inc.

Fukuoka, Masanobu. *The One-Straw Revolution: An Introduction to Natural Farming*. Emmaus, Pa: Rodale Press.

Gilbert, Margaret Shea. *Biography of the Unborn*. New York: Hafner.

Jacobsen and Brewster. *The Changing American Diet*. Washington, D. C.: Center for Science in the Public Interest.

Kohler, Jean and Mary Alice. *Healing Miracles from Macrobiotics*. West Nyack, N. Y.: Parker Publishing Co.

Kushi, Michio. *Acupuncture: Ancient and Future Worlds*. Brookline, Mass.: East West Foundation.

Kushi, Michio. *Oriental Diagnosis*. London: Sunwheel, Ltd.

Kushi, Michio. *How to See Your Health: The Book of Diagnosis*. Tokyo: Japan Publications, Inc.

Kushi, Michio. *Natural Healing Through Macrobiotics*. Ibid.

Kushi, Michio. *The Teachings of Michio Kushi*, Vols. I and II. Ibid.

Kushi, Michio. *The Book of Macrobiotics: The Universal Way of Health and Happiness*. Tokyo: Japan Publications, Inc.

Kushi, Michio. *The Book of Dō-In: Exercise for Physical and Spiritual Development.* Ibid.

Kushi, Aveline. *How to Cook with Miso.* Ibid.

Kushi, Michio and Jack, Alex. *Cancer Prevention Diet.* New York: St. Martins Press.

Mendelsohn, Robert S., M. D. *Confessions of a Medical Heretic.* Chicago, Ill.: Contemporary Books.

Muramoto, Noboru. *Healing Ourselves.* New York: Avon; London: Michael Dempsey/Cassell.

Ohsawa, George. *Acupuncture and the Philosophy of the Far East.* Boston, Mass.: Tao Books.

Ohsawa, George. *The Book of Judgment.* Los Angeles: Ohsawa Foundation.

Ohsawa, George. *Cancer and the Philosophy of the Far East.* Binghamton, N. Y.: Swan House.

Ohsawa, George. *Guidebook for Living.* Los Angeles: Ohsawa Foundation.

Ohsawa, George. *Practical Guide to Far-Eastern Macrobiotic Medicine.* Oroville, Calif.: George Ohsawa Macrobiotic Foundation.

Ohsawa, George. *The Unique Principle.* Ibid.

Ohsawa, George. *Zen Macrobiotics.* Los Angeles: Ohsawa Foundation.

Sacks, Castelli, Donner, and Kass. "Plasma Lipids and Lipoproteins in Vegetarians and Controls." Boston: *New England Journal of Medicine.* May 29, 1975.

Sacks, Rosner, and Kass. "Blood Pressure in Vegetarians." *American Journal of Epidemiology*, Vol. 100, No. 5, Baltimore: Johns Hopkins University.

Sakurazawa, Nyoiti (George Ohsawa), edited by Dufty, William. *Macrobiotics.* London: Tandem Books. Published in the U.S.A. under the title *You Are All Sanpaku.* New York: University Books.

Select Committee on Nutrition and Human Needs, U.S. Senate. *Dietary Goals for the United States.* February 1977.

Surgeon General's Report on Health Promotion and Disease Prevention. *Healthy People.* Washington, D. C. September, 1979.

Wilhelm and Baynes. *I Ching.* Princeton: Princeton University Press.

Yamamoto, Shizuko. *Barefoot Shiatsu.* Tokyo: Japan Publications, Inc.

Periodicals

East West Journal. Brookline, Mass.

Kushi Institute Study Guide, Kushi Institute Newsletter, Brookline, Mass.

The Order of the Universe. Brookline, Mass. East West Foundation.

Nutrition Action, Washington D. C.: Center for Science in the Public Interest.

The Macrobiotic Review. Baltimore, Md.: East West Foundation.

Spiral. Community Health Foundation, London.

Le Compas. Paris.

INDEX